AF904407

# *The Chinese Economy, 1870-1949*

**Albert Feuerwerker**
*The University of Michigan*

CENTER FOR CHINESE STUDIES
THE UNIVERSITY OF MICHIGAN
ANN ARBOR

MICHIGAN MONOGRAPHS IN CHINESE STUDIES
ISSN 1081-9053
SERIES ESTABLISHED 1968
VOLUME 71

Published by
Center for Chinese Studies
The University of Michigan
Ann Arbor, Michigan 48109-1290

Originally published in Volumes 11 and 12 of
*The Cambridge History of China*
© 1980, 1983 Cambridge University Press
Reprinted with the permission of Cambridge University Press

New matter in this edition
© 1995 Center for Chinese Studies, The University of Michigan
All rights reserved

Printed and made in the United States of America

♾ The paper used in this publication meets the minimum requirements
of the American National Standard for Information Sciences—
Permanence of Paper for Publications and Documents
in Libraries and Archives ANSI/NISO/Z39.48—1992.

**Library of Congress Cataloging-in-Publication Data**

Feuerwerker, Albert.

The Chinese economy, 1870-1949 / Albert Feuerwerker.
p. cm.—
(Michigan monographs in Chinese studies, ISSN 1081-9053 ; 71)
Includes bibliographical references and index.
ISBN 0-89264-118-5 (alk. paper)
1. China—Economic conditions—1644–1912.
2. China—Economic conditions—1912–1949.
I. University of Michigan. Center for Chinese Studies.
II. Title. III. Series.
HC427.F47 1995
330.951—dc20 95–42914
CIP

For

Alison and Paul

# Contents

# Maps

# Tables

# Preface

The two chapters reprinted here from *The Cambridge History of China,* Vol. 11 (Late Ch'ing 1800-1911, Part 2) and Volume 12 (Republican China 1912-1949, Part 1) were published in 1980 and 1983 respectively. Apart from renumbering the tables in one series and correcting a number of minor errors, the original texts have not been changed for this edition. They were written during the late 1970s, and reflect the state of the published literature on late imperial China and the republican era before the time that research in Ch'ing and republican archives in the People's Republic of China was possible for foreign (and most Chinese) scholars. That access (to the First Historical Archives in Beijing for the Ch'ing dynasty, to the Second Historical Archives in Nanjing for the republic, and to other provincial and local collections in such locales as Shanghai and Sichuan) has slowly become available in the post-1979 "open door" era. (Of course, many of us benefited greatly from a much earlier access to the archival materials held by the Palace Museum and by Academia Sinica in Taiwan). The research now underway will surely enormously enrich our understanding of China's last imperial dynasty and of the first half of the twentieth century in all areas, including the history of China's economy which my chapters attempt to summarize. I believe that I offer here a reasonable—and therefore still useful—wrap-up of what we knew on the eve of the opportunities that the most recent era presents both for research in depth and detail and for the reconceptualization that will also inevitably emerge. The late John King Fairbank pressed me to get these pieces out of my desk drawer and into print in *CHOC.* For this and much else I remain grateful to his memory.

A.F.
Ann Arbor, Michigan
October 2, 1995

# I.
# Economic Trends in the Late Ch'ing Empire, 1870–1911

There was little of the Chinese economy prior to the twentieth century that was not included within the agricultural sector or quite intimately connected with it.[1] The bulk of the following essay ought properly to be devoted to an analysis of the structure and development of Chinese agriculture in the nineteenth century and its implications for the rest of the economy. I have, however, while discussing agriculture first, given roughly equal attention to handicrafts, modern industry, trade and commerce, and the fiscal system. If these divisions are so obviously the customary ones, I can only plead my own limitations and the possible extenuation that—with honorable and increasing exceptions—the studies of China's modern economic history upon which I have had to rely for this survey are themselves conventionally descriptive works.

The treatment of material in all of the following sections is unavoidably selective. I have in each case focused on what was new or changing in the last five decades of the Manchu dynasty against a background which, until 1911 and long afterwards, remained a basically unaltered mix of the factors of production operating within a largely constant social context. This is not to imply that nothing of importance changed in the last century of imperial China. On the contrary, ideological and political storms uprooted the Confucian empire. Fundamental economic change and modern economic growth, however, did not come of their own momentum out of the late-Ch'ing economic system. They were pre-eminently the by-products of a new and possibly still tenuous political integration which itself was achieved only after decades of political strife, foreign invasion and civil war.

One must begin by reluctantly accepting that precise quantitative information of a global kind—as opposed to a fair amount of suggestive local and partial data—is not available and probably cannot be satisfactorily derived for pre-republican China. Nowhere is this more apparent than in the case of so fundamental a measure as national income. Table 1 reproduces, with modifications, the only attempt, of which I am aware, to estimate China's gross national product in the nineteenth century. The individual components were often arbitrarily arrived at, but it is doubtful whether substantial amounts of more reliable information can be assembled. These estimates roughly indicate the relative sizes in the 1880s of the several sectors of the economy.

TABLE 1
ESTIMATED GROSS NATIONAL PRODUCT OF CHINA IN THE 1880s

| Sector | Amount (1,000 taels) | | | % |
|---|---|---|---|---|
| Agriculture | | 2,229,941 | | 66.79 |
| Nonagriculture | | 1,108,816 | | 33.21 |
| mining | 47,800 | | 1.43 | |
| manufacturing* | 128,000 | | 3.77 | |
| construction | 30,000 | | 0.90 | |
| transportation | 30,000 | | 0.90 | |
| trade | 220,000 | | 6.59 | |
| finance | 74,645 | | 2.24 | |
| residential housing | 164,000 | | 4.91 | |
| government services | 164,000 | | 4.91 | |
| professional, gentry and other services | 241,313 | | 7.23 | |
| net income from abroad | 11,258 | | 0.34 | |
| Total | | 3,338,757 | | 100.00 |

* almost entirely handicraft.

*Source:* Chung-li Chang, *The income of the Chinese gentry* (1962), p. 296. The principal shortcomings of this estimate, apart from the admittedly critical data question, are Chang's probable overstatement of the share of gentry services, and the much more serious reliance on 1887 official data for the area of cultivated land. As I suggest in the next section, these data and thus the share of agriculture should be adjusted upward by at least one-third. This I have done and, leaving Chang's other components unchanged, I have accordingly recalculated the percentages.

## 1. Agriculture

While there were changes in detail and alterations in the size or quality of certain components, the technology and organization of Chinese agriculture differed little in 1911 from what it had been in 1870. (Even into the 1930s it remained largely unchanged.) The principal changes were: a slow but perceptible population increase unaccompanied by an equivalent extension of cultivated land; a resulting decrease—particularly in North China—in the size of the average farm; changes in the pattern of crops grown, partly in response to the increasingly adverse man-land ratio and partly in response to new external market opportunities; the absolute and relative decline of cotton spinning as a peasant handicraft and a partial restructuring of the sources of rural non-agricultural income in response to this decline; some differentiation of land-holding patterns in the immediate hinterlands of the growing treaty ports from those of the bulk of the rural interior of China; and a completion of the process already long under way by which the distinction between various legal forms of land tenure was dissipated.

No useful demographic data for the last half of the nineteenth century are of course available. The official estimates for the 1840s put China's population at a little more than 400 million persons; these, it has been argued, while not accurate in detail are relatively good data.[2] The Taiping Rebellion and the other great mid-century uprisings not only resulted in substantial population losses, especially in central China, but also produced a breakdown of the refurbished *pao-chia* system which had collected the reasonably reliable population data for the period 1776–1850. The century between 1851 and 1949, despite the availability of various figures, is practically a demographer's vacuum.[3]

There are, nevertheless, sufficient qualitative indications from which to assert, if not to measure, a slowly increasing population from the 1870s until the end of the dynasty. Migrations of population from provinces to the west and north which had not been so severely afflicted gradually repopulated the Yangtze valley provinces that the civil wars had ravaged. The last four decades of the Manchu dynasty were internally relatively peaceful and, compared to mid-century, prosperous. While the wars with France in 1884–85 and with Japan in 1894–95 were politically and diplomatically of great significance, they had no major demographic effect. The great famine of 1877–78 in North-West China and lesser but still serious famines in 1892–94 and 1900 unquestionably resulted in temporary population losses. Such crises, caused by drought and floods, had been endemic in the past and were experienced again in the twentieth century, for example in 1901, 1928, 1931, and 1935. They are inherent components of the demographic pattern characteristic of many "underdeveloped" countries which combines a high but widely fluctuating death-rate and a high but relatively stable birth-rate to produce slow but substantial population increments.

But, how large an increment? C. M. Chiao and J. L. Buck have estimated from birth- and death-rates observed in 4,216 farm families from four provinces in 1924–25 that the rural population of China might possi-

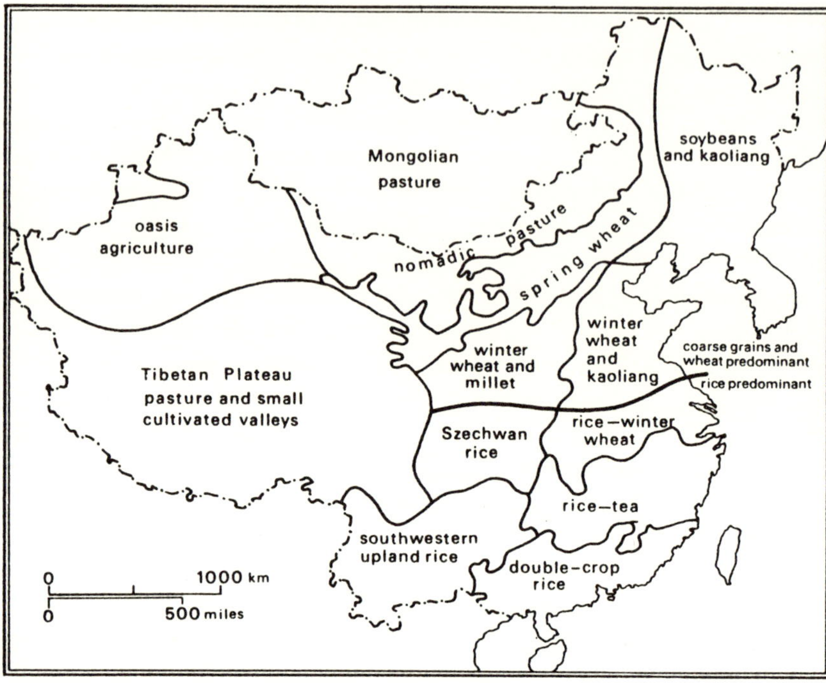


Map 1. Major crop areas

bly have grown at an average rate of 1.4 per cent per annum between the 1860s and the 1920s.[4] Such a rate of increase, if uninterrupted, would have resulted in a doubling of the population during these seven decades, and on the face of it appears too high as an actual long-term average although it might have been valid in some areas for shorter periods. In 1934, the National Agricultural Research Bureau of the Ministry of Industry produced, from retrospective and thus tenuous data assembled by its crop reporters, an estimate of changes in the rural population and the area of farm land between 1873 and 1933 which I reproduce in table 2. A population increase of 17 per cent for the forty years 1873–1913, or an annual average of slightly less than 0.5 per cent, is suggested. Assuming a total population of between 350 and 400 million in 1873, by 1913 this total would have increased to between 410 and 468 million. Bearing in mind that the mid-century population was somewhat more than 400 million, that the Taiping and other civil wars resulted in severe population losses, and that the population of China in 1953, after many years of war and civil war, was enumerated at 583 million in the closest thing to a real census that China has ever experienced, these estimates for 1873 and 1913 are at least not unreasonable.

TABLE 2
INDEX NUMBERS OF CHANGES IN CHINA'S RURAL POPULATION AND AREA OF FARM LAND, 1873–1933
(1873 = 100)

| | Population | Farm land |
|---|---|---|
| 1873 | 100 | 100 |
| 1893 | 108 | 101 |
| 1913 | 117 | 101 |
| 1933 | 131 | 101 |

*Source:* Department of Agricultural Economics, National Agricultural Research Bureau, Ministry of Industries, *Crop reporting in China*, 1934, pp. 48-53.

TABLE 3
CHANGES IN THE SIZE OF FARMS, 1870–1930

| Regions, areas, and locations | Number of locations reporting | Average crop area per farm (hectares) | | | |
|---|---|---|---|---|---|
| | | *1870* | *1890* | *1910* | *1930* |
| China | 55 | 1.37 | 1.35 | 1.06 | 0.92 |
| wheat region | 29 | 1.75 | 1.77 | 1.32 | 1.10 |
| rice region | 26 | 0.67 | 0.81 | 0.77 | 0.72 |
| Wheat Region Areas | | | | | |
| spring wheat (Kansu, Tsinghai) | 2 | 0.48 | 0.51 | 0.66 | 0.71 |
| winter wheat-millet (Honan, Shansi, Shensi) | 8 | 1.14 | 1.28 | 0.97 | 0.81 |
| winter wheat-kaoling (Anhwei, Honan, Hopei*, Kiangsu, Shantung) | 19 | | | | |
| Rice region areas | | 2.19 | 2.18 | 1.53 | 1.26 |
| Yangtze rice-wheat (Anhwei, Chekiang, Honan, Hupei, Kiangsi, Kiangsu) | 15 | 0.77 | 0.99 | 0.84 | 0.79 |
| rice-tea (Hunan, Kiangsi) | 6 | 0.42 | 0.42 | 0.76 | 0.74 |
| Szechwan rice (Shensi, Szechwan) | 2 | 0.82 | 0.76 | 0.64 | 0.55 |
| double-crop rice (Fukien) | 1 | 0.58 | 0.54 | 0.55 | 0.53 |
| south-western rice (Kweichow) | 2 | — | 0.52 | 0.48 | 0.36 |

* Hopei province was, of course, called Chihli in the late Ch'ing period.
*Source:* John Lossing Buck, *Land utilization in China. Statistics*, p. 288.

The National Agricultural Research Bureau's respondents, as table 2 indicates, reported that the farm area in their several localities showed no increase comparable to the slow but continuing population growth which occurred. The resultant worsening of the man-land ratio is reflected in the historical data on average farm size shown in table 3, collected by J. L. Buck's field investigators for his monumental land utilization study. Buck's respondents overwhelmingly attributed the reported decreases in average farm size to increases in the population of their areas. In North China (Buck's winter wheat-kaoliang areas) the decline in average farm size was more striking than in Central China (the rice-wheat and rice-tea areas).

TABLE 4
PERCENTAGE OF CHOU AND HSIEN IN NINE PROVINCES REPORTING ABOVE NORMAL, NORMAL, AND BELOW NORMAL HARVESTS, 1821–1910

| | Number of reports* | Above normal | Normal | Below normal |
|---|---|---|---|---|
| 1821 | 1,114 | 42.99 | 54.30 | 2.69 |
| 1825 | 1,192 | 46.47 | 51.67 | 1.84 |
| 1830 | 1,321 | 39.64 | 61.54 | 1.51 |
| 1835 | 1,229 | 20.17 | 65.58 | 14.23 |
| 1840 | 1,304 | 25.07 | 67.02 | 7.89 |
| 1845 | 1,306 | 29.24 | 63.93 | 6.81 |
| 1850 | 1,019 | 22.27 | 72.32 | 5.39 |
| 1855 | 979 | 14.09 | 65.67 | 20.22 |
| 1860 | 752 | 20.21 | 59.04 | 24.73 |
| 1865 | 1,087 | 5.79 | 53.81 | 40.38 |
| 1870 | 1,255 | 4.86 | 45.01 | 50.11 |
| 1875 | 1,308 | 6.19 | 53.66 | 40.13 |
| 1880 | 1,309 | 7.79 | 52.94 | 39.26 |
| 1885 | 1,246 | 6.26 | 49.51 | 44.22 |
| 1890 | 1,309 | 5.27 | 45.37 | 49.35 |
| 1895 | 1,243 | 3.94 | 45.29 | 50.76 |
| 1900 | 1,190 | 4.28 | 42.85 | 52.85 |
| 1905 | 1,198 | 4.00 | 43.24 | 52.75 |
| 1910 | 1,126 | 4.61 | 37.74 | 57.63 |

* For eight of the nine provinces both summer and autumn reports are included; the number of *chou* and *hsien* reporting is thus about half the number of annual reports

*Source:* Calculated from data in Li Wen-chih, comp., *Chung-kuo chin-tai nung-yeh shih tzu-liao ti-i-chi, 1840–1911* (Source materials on the history of agriculture in modern China, 1st collection, 1840–1911), pp. 761-69, which are based on reports submitted in response to the following edict: "An edict to the Hu-pu. Hereafter, in reporting the harvest results of the several provinces, use the following categories; eight *fen* [i.e., 80 per cent of a theoretical maximum] is to be taken as a rich harvest, six to seven *fen* as a normal harvest, and five *fen* or less as a poor harvest." *Ta-Ch'ing Kao-tsung shun-huang-ti shih-lu* (Veritable records of the Ch'ien-lung Emperor of the Ch'ing dynasty), 339. 41a-b, 14 June 1749 (vol. 22, p. 5151 of Taipei reprint, 1964).

The difference is attributable to the much greater demographic losses from the Taiping Rebellion in the provinces south of the Yangtze River and the consequent temporary fall in the man-land ratio in Central and South China. As population migrated to these then relatively less-crowded provinces from more crowded areas, the man-land ratio rose and average farm size after 1900 slowly declined.

While it is certain that rural living standards between 1870 and 1911 did not improve, there is no conclusive evidence that population growth and declining average farm size were accompanied by a drastic secular fall in the peasant standard of living. The semi-annual official reports from the provinces to Peking on the quality of the summer and autumn harvests do indicate a definite downward trend in the course of the nineteenth century. It is reasonable to expect that some deterioration occurred during the catastrophic rebellions of the 1850s and 1860s as table 4 suggests. A continued decline after 1870, however, is not convincingly confirmed by the numerous reports of local crop conditions which appear annually in the *Reports and returns on trade* by the Imperial Maritime Customs. My suspicion is that the higher proportion of poorer harvests reported in the last decade of the dynasty in part reflects the efforts of the provinces to resist Peking's importunate demands for increased tax remittances, which are described below in the discussion of government and the economy. The depopulation attributable to the rebellions, moreover, could be called a Malthusian safety valve which temporarily reduced the inexorable pressure of population on land.

Conditions of individual farmers and of spatially separate localities of course differed widely, with the difference between survival and misery often depending upon uncertain weather, the rapacity of the local officials and the presence or absence of civil war and banditry in the locality. Overall, however, total crop production between 1870 and 1900 probably increased adequately to support the larger population. This increment was not due to any major changes in farm technology or organization. No important new crops or seed varieties (like corn and early-ripening rice earlier in the dynasty) were introduced in the second half of the nineteenth century. The middle decades of civil war, moreover, had seen a substantial destruction of capital stock which was only gradually replaced. Irrigation, water storage and control, and grain storage facilities were not extended or improved beyond their eighteenth-century levels. The increase in crop production was apparently the result mainly of a shift by farmers to crops which yielded a larger amount of food or income per unit of land and at the same time required more labor for their cultivation. Crop shifts of this kind in the early twentieth century, as the man-land ratio continued to worsen, are shown in the data on trends in crop acreage between 1904–09 and 1924–29 collected by J. L. Buck's investigators and summarized in table 5. These indicate a progressive substitution of corn, sweet potatoes, and sesame for barley, kaoliang, and millet as food crops, and also an increase in such cash crops as cotton to supply the expanding mills of Shanghai and Tientsin. For the period 1870–1911, unfortunately, not even such imperfect although suggestive data are available; but if changes of this kind could occur amidst the political instability and civil war of the early Republic, they are not implausible in the relative stability of the late Ch'ing decades. Some partial clues are provided by an examination of trends in the exportation of agricultural products between 1870 and 1911.

TABLE 5
TRENDS IN CROP ACREAGES BETWEEN 1904–09 AND 1930–33

| | Number of localities reporting | Estimated percentage of total crop area* | | | |
|---|---|---|---|---|---|
| | | 1904–09 | 1914–19 | 1924–29 | 1930–33 |
| *Crops whose average increased or was unchanged* | | | | | |
| broad beans | 7 | 9 | 9 | 9 | 8 |
| corn | 22 | 11 | 14 | 16 | 17 |
| cotton | 29 | 11 | 14 | 18 | 20 |
| opium | 13 | 14 | 3 | 11 | 20 |
| peanuts | 18 | 9 | 8 | 11 | 11 |
| rapeseed | 5 | 15 | 21 | 27 | 28 |
| rice | 17 | 40 | 41 | 37 | 40 |
| sesame | 7 | 4 | 8 | 10 | 9 |
| soy-beans | 7 | 8 | 9 | 10 | 8 |
| sweet potatoes | 18 | 10 | 11 | 12 | 13 |
| wheat | 29 | 26 | 27 | 27 | 27 |
| *Crops whose acreage decreased* | | | | | |
| barley | 10 | 24 | 23 | 20 | 19 |
| indigo | 12 | 10 | 7 | 2 | — |
| kaoliang | 14 | 26 | 23 | 20 | 16 |
| millet | 15 | 22 | 18 | 17 | 17 |
| sugar cane | 10 | 7 | 6 | 5 | 6 |

* in the reporting localities
*Source:* Buck, *Land utilization*, p. 217

In value terms, tea was China's most important single export until 1887 when it was overtaken by silk. The proportion of tea to total exports fell steadily from 54 per cent in 1871 to 18 per cent in 1898 and 11 per cent in 1906. While the decline in the absolute quantity of tea exported was far less precipitous, it does suggest that tea acreage did not increase during the four decades under consideration. The exportation of raw and manufactured silk as measured by both quantities and values increased throughout the four decades. This suggests the likelihood that additional land was devoted to growing mulberry and oak trees. In North China and Manchuria the leaves of oak trees fed the worms from whose silk "pongee," an increasingly important export fabric, was woven.

From 1888 to 1919, with the single exception of 1899, China exported more raw cotton than it imported. This completely reversed the import surplus shown between 1870 and 1887 (except 1874). At first glance it might appear that the growing exportation of raw cotton is a strong indication that the total cotton crop increased significantly in the last two decades of the Ch'ing. But matters were not in fact so simple. The increase in cotton exports was accompanied by a steady rise in raw cotton prices and by a simultaneous growing inflow of relatively inexpensive machine-spun yarn from India and Japan. The conjunction of these three trends suggests that cotton production did not expand or did not expand sufficiently to meet both domestic and export demand, that the resulting higher domestic prices of cotton and yarn induced weavers to purchase the cheaper imported commodity, and that in turn a reduced domestic demand diminished the inducement to increase raw cotton production.

One crop which definitely expanded in acreage during the last decades of the nineteenth century was opium. In value terms opium was China's largest single import until the mid-1880s. Opium and cotton goods together made up about two-thirds of China's imports in the 1870s and early 1880s; by 1898 the share of the two had fallen to about 50 per cent. This decline was entirely due to a decrease in the quantity (although not the value, which continued to rise) of opium imported, while cotton goods imports increased rapidly. The principal reason for the fall in the quantity of opium imports was the steady spread of domestic opium cultivation. Unfortunately no data are available with which to measure even roughly the area of land newly planted with poppy to replace the imported article. The significant price rises per unit at the very end of the Ch'ing and in the first years of the Republic were caused by market speculation in a reduced quantity of the drug as the first step towards its *de jure* if not *de facto* suppression. The legal import trade was abolished at the end of 1917, while efforts to suppress domestic cultivation subsequently varied in success with the morals and financial needs of the local warlords in whose territories the poppy was grown.

Again, judging from data on the quantity and value of exports between 1879 and 1915, it appears possible that there was a substantial increase in crop acreage of soy-beans, rapeseed, sesame and peanuts. Before the 1890s the trade in these commodities was negligible. From the turn of the century, the value of bean products and vegetable oils exported shot quickly upward, the oils going largely to Europe where they were used chiefly in soap manufacture, and the beans and bean cake as well as oil to Japan. The chief producing and exporting area was Manchuria; the flow of population from North China to Manchuria after the Russo-Japanese War was possibly related to an important expansion of soy-bean cultivation. Moreover, efforts to suppress the opium crop in North China led farmers to increase their planting of beans, sesame and peanuts as a substitute cash crop. On the other hand, important changes in domestic consumption patterns were taking place simultaneously, which may suggest that the new bean and oil exports represented not so much an increased crop as a diversion to export of products hitherto consumed at home. From the 1890s there was a rapid increase in imports of kerosene, which replaced the more expensive vegetable oils used to make candles for illumination and other purposes. The remarkable growth in bean and oil exports, then, probably overstates the extent to which cultivation patterns were altered before 1900, although Buck's data give a strong indication, as we have seen, that the acreage of these and other cash crops did increase from the early twentieth century.

Only a very crude estimate of the production of major crops in a typical year at the end of the nineteenth century is possible. Data in the Kuang-hsu edition (1899) of the *Collected statutes* (*Ta-Ch'ing hui-tien*) on the area of land under cultivation—with some adjustments the official figure for 1887 is 847,760,554 *mou*—are imperfect in detail and in any case represent a substantial understatement of the actual cultivated area. The underlying unit of measurement in many localities was a "fiscal" *mou* used to convert different grades of land to a single standard; some land reclaimed after 1712 had remained unregistered; and the property of the more powerful local elite was not always fully reflected in the tax rolls. The precise degree of under-registration is not known, but judging from J. L. Buck's 1929–33 agricultural survey findings, an upward adjustment by one-third would be quite conservative. Cultivated land (which I take as equivalent to the crop area) in the late-nineteenth century was then perhaps 1,130,344,579 *mou*. No comprehensive nineteenth-century data are available for the proportions of the total crop area planted in individual crops. If, however, the averages of Buck's 1929–33 percentages and those for 1931–37 by the National Agricultural Research Bureau are adjusted for the changes between 1904–09 and 1930–33 shown in table 5, an approximation of the situation in the last decades of the dynasty is possible. Based on these estimates, table 6 presents at least a plausible guess as to the output of major crops in the late-nineteenth century.

TABLE 6
ESTIMATED ANNUAL PRODUCTION OF MAJOR CROPS, c. 1900

| | Percentage of crop area | Crop acreage (*mou*) | Typical yield per *mou* (piculs) | Output (piculs) |
|---|---|---|---|---|
| Rice, unhusked | 30.2 | 341,364,190 | 3.89 | 1,327,906,699 |
| Wheat | 26.3 | 297,280,735 | 1.39 | 413,220,222 |
| Kaoliang | 12.5 | 141,293,125 | 1.73 | 244,437,106 |
| Millet | 11.6 | 131,120,020 | 1.64 | 215,036,833 |
| Barley | 10.2 | 115,295,190 | 1.47 | 169,483,929 |
| Soy-bean | 6.7 | 75,733,115 | 1.39 | 105,269,030 |
| Corn | 4.2 | 47,474,490 | 1.87 | 88,777,296 |
| Cotton, lint | 2.4 | 27,127,500 | 0.27 | 7,324,441 |

*Sources:* Buck, *Land Utilization*, p. 217; Ta-chung Liu and Kung-chia Yeh, *The economy of the Chinese mainland: national income and economic development, 1933–1959*, table 30, p. 130, table A-9, p. 300.

The fate of cotton spinning, the most important single rural handicraft in the nineteenth century, is discussed in the following section. In the relatively "developed" lower Yangtze area (and possibly in Kwangtung as well), where commerce and manufacture were most advanced and where the impact of foreign trade was most substantial, the post-Taiping decades saw an increase in absentee land ownership, representing the investment of commercial profits by successful merchants, brokers, and compradors. Absenteeism in this sense is to be distinguished from the fact that the great majority of the rural elite did not of course reside in the peasant villages in which they owned land; their normal habitat was the rural town, at the level of the hsien city or lower. One form which this development took was the growth of the landlord bursary (*tsu-chan*) by means of which individual owners, primarily urban businessmen, entrusted their lands and tenants to the management of the bursary owner and received a proportionate share of the profits after taxes and other expenses were met. It is impossible to estimate the extent of this phenomenon, but enough cases have been found by Muramatsu Yūji to suggest that in Kiangsu at least it was more than incidental.[5] The bursary owners tended to be well-placed members of the rural elite (gentry) who were able to call upon official assistance (even to the extent of the arrest and imprisonment of delinquents) to collect tenant rents. While rural class relations were never the proper subject for a pastoral idyll even under the best Confucian landlord, absenteeism in the late nineteenth century introduced an increasing element of harshness which became intolerable in the twentieth.

The official Ch'ing land records of 1887 still record the existence, in addition to private land (*min-t'ien*), of substantial acreage especially in North China and Manchuria of banner land (*ch'i-ti*), military land (*t'un-t'ien*), imperial manors (*chuang*) and the like. These reflect the intention of the early Manchu rulers to superimpose a land system corresponding to the Manchu political and social structure upon that of conquered China. In reality, by the late nineteenth century little remained, apart from differential rates of land tax, of these earlier distinctions. The combined effects of population growth, inadequate official stipends, and the preponderant influence of the underlying Chinese system of private land ownership had in practice almost entirely homogenized the various legal forms of land tenure. Banner land as well as private land was farmed by Chinese tenants in small, scattered plots which by one or another subterfuge were freely rented, mortgaged, bought or sold.

The land held under some form of official tenure, bursary land and private land in general were not normally farmed as contiguous estates with hired agricultural labor. The continued rarity of "capitalist" commercial farming is the first of several aspects of late-Ch'ing agriculture which remained constant alongside the several changes that I have recounted. Examples can be cited of large landholdings by officials, wealthy gentry and monopoly merchants in excess of 10,000 *mou* throughout the nineteenth century; holdings of this size, however, were quite unusual. Ownership of land in late-Ch'ing China was skewed, but there were few large agricultural holdings comparable to the great estates of Europe and other parts of Asia or the giant ranches and commercial farms of the United States. The landowner normally ranged from the owner-farmer cultivating perhaps 20-30 *mou* in North China and 12-15 *mou* in the south, to some two million local elite families whose median holdings were perhaps 100-50 *mou,* most of which was normally rented to tenants.[6] Tenancy, as in the twentieth century, was much more common in the south (the "rice region") than in the north (the "wheat region"); perhaps, again as in later decades, 50 per cent of farming families could be classified as tenants or part-owners. Some signs of increasing numbers of tenancies can be observed in districts which had suffered prolonged famine and in areas near the major commercial centers, but there is little evidence that land tenure patterns changed radically in the last four decades of the dynasty.

Rents were paid either in money or in kind; if the latter, they were commonly 50 per cent of the major crop. Reported cash rents in the 1880s vary from 0.6 taels to 2.66 taels per *mou,* approximately 5 to 10 per cent of the value of land in these localities. (Compare the National Agricultural Research Bureau's estimate of average cash rents as 11 per cent of land values in the 1930s.) This suggests that, after deductions for taxes and other costs, the return on investments in land, while relatively secure so long as political stability was maintained, was only one-half as large as the 10 to 20 per cent which could be realized from commerce or moneylending. The comparatively low rate of return probably limited any tendency to increasing concentration of land ownership. The real burden of tenancy depended upon other stipulations of the landlord-tenant contract in addition to rent. Individual examples of better and worse terms are available for the nineteenth century—labor service, short-term leases, rent deposits and the like—but we lack systematic evidence from which to conclude that the late-nineteenth-century situation was a progressively worsening one, rather than a perpetuation of the same wretched existence, for the numberless poor.

One piece of evidence—Professor Muramatsu's discovery that landlord bursary income from rents increased sharply between 1905 and 1917—does suggest that the local elite were able to pass on to their tenants much of the burden of the increased taxation of the dynasty's last decade. These additional levies, which are discussed later in this essay, were assessed on the provinces in order to obtain funds for the Boxer indemnity payments. Given the historical ability of influential landowners to evade their proportionate shares of the ordinary tax burden (most commonly by paying none or only part of the "extras" which had over time become attached to nominal land tax quotas), it is not unlikely that owner-farmers as well as the tenants of larger landlords ultimately paid a disproportionate part of the added taxation.

It is the overall stability of the agricultural system rather than any significant departures up or down from the traditional norms that is most remarkable. The equilibrium was satisfied at a very low level of subsistence for the great majority of the millions of farming families who constituted 80 per cent of China's population. The hazards of flood, famine and epidemic were compounded by the absence of inexpensive means of bulk transportation and of an effective central government which could channel funds and food from surplus to deficit areas. Few peasants could realistically expect ever to be better off than their fathers or grandfathers had been. Yet after the great Taiping and Nien uprisings no major peasant revolts threatened the Ch'ing government or the elite-dominated rural society. One might suggest that the absence of a substantial peasant-based revolutionary movement (the role of the omnipresent secret society was ambiguous—as often as not it was controlled by or in cooperation with the local elite) may be taken as an indication that "restoration" and "self-strengthening" were remarkably effective in suppressing traditional forms of domestic discontent—if not anti-dynastic nationalism and foreign political and economic incursions. The stability, in a narrower sense, of patterns of agricultural organization and land utilization was the consequence less of political conservatism than of the constraints of the available technology and of the social values which motivated the population.

Very large estates, as I have noted, were not common. Moreover, the average land actually cultivated by an individual farming family, owner or tenant, was very small; beyond a certain point larger owners found it preferable to let their excess land rather than farm it with hired labor. Twentieth-century data show a high correlation between the size of the farm household and farm size, an indication that the unit of cultivation was close to the minimum subsistence level. Miniature cultivation was aggravated by the fact that farms tended to be broken up into several nonadjacent parcels usually of different qualities or types of land. Considerable land was wasted in boundary strips, excessive labor time was used to travel from parcel to parcel, and rational irrigation practices were impeded. The rarity of latifundia, the tiny family farm, and parcelization of the typical holding, were all in part the consequence of traditional inheritance practices—in particular of the absence of primogeniture. For elite and peasant alike, the death of the head of the family was usually followed by the equal division of its holdings among all surviving sons who commonly established themselves as separate households. *Fen-chia* ("dividing the family"), as the process was called, might be resisted for a generation or more, but the elite ideal of the large extended family did not often survive the inevitable tensions. Hence, as in the forest primeval, individual oaks sprang up, matured, aged and decayed while the forest itself continued magnificently to dominate the countryside. Parcelization was obviously the outcome of successive efforts to provide each heir with roughly equivalent amounts of the several types of land (paddy, upland, orchard and so on) which had constituted the patrimonial farm.

Ownership of a substantial acreage, before or after *fen-chia,* did not imply management of that land as a unit. Local elite families would farm with hired labor only a portion of their holdings. In addition to the inadequacies of rural credit facilities, to the poverty of management techniques themselves, and to the unstable market for cash crops, there were limits on the quantity of land which would yield greater profits from direct cultivation than from tenant rents. These limits were set by the immense but uneven labor requirements of the existing farm technology. The potential employer of large quantities of farm labor was faced with high supervisory costs and diminishing returns from non-family labor which was used intensively but only at peak seasonal periods. Only improved seeds, more and better fertilizers and expanded irrigation—that is, significant technological changes which did not occur—would have fully justified large-scale farming to supply a distant market.

The agricultural sector of the Chinese economy in the last decades of the Ch'ing dynasty was thus characterized by a factor mix in which land and capital were in short supply and the superabundance of labor was subject to some diminishing returns. It was, however, if not for the long run at least for the purposes of any middle-term prediction, in a stable equilibrium with no endogenous economic reason why it should not continue to reproduce itself. It is a tribute to the traditional technology that so vast a population and so high a culture in its upper strata could be supported even if for the majority the level of subsistence was low indeed. The many centuries of basic investment of immense quantities of human labor in altering the land—by terracing, irrigation, flood control and drainage—had made possible perhaps from as early as the seventeenth century an output of 2.3 metric tons of rice per crop hectare. This is an important benchmark which represents the theoretical maximum yield of pre-modern agricultural technology (that is, without major current inputs of improved seeds, fertilizers, pesticides and so on). China's average rice yield per crop hectare reached only 2.47 metric tons in the 1930s and 2.54 metric tons in the years 1955/56–1960/61. In the latter period India's yield was no more than 1.36 metric tons.[7] But the gap between stability and stagnation is narrow. The equilibrium of traditional agriculture had been reached at a very low level of per capita output of which a very high proportion was consumed by the agricultural producers. Only a small quantity of marketable surplus was available either as industrial raw material or to feed the non-farm sector. Conversely, the effective demand for urban manufactured products was limited. Thus the immediate possibilities either of extensive industrialization or of agricultural development were narrowly constrained by the disabilities of the agricultural sector.

## 2. Handicraft Industry

The simplistic indictment of "foreign capitalism" by some contemporary Chinese historians for having progressively "crushed" and "exploited" domestic handicraft industry from the mid-nineteenth century onward is belied by the actual state of the Chinese economy as late as the 1930s. In the middle of that decade, even in the cotton textile industry which allegedly suffered most severely from the "incursion of foreign capitalism," 61 per cent of the cotton cloth produced in China (in square yards; if the unit of measurement were yards the proportion would be 73 per cent) was woven by handicraft methods.[8] Anyone who would claim that the Hunan or Szechwan peasant in the 1930s dressed in Naigaiwata cottons, smoked BAT cigarettes, and used Meiji sugar has a big case to prove. In 1933, the output of handicrafts accounted for an estimated 68 per cent of the total value of industrial output. Of course the relative share of handicrafts was greater in 1870 or 1911, prior to or in the early stages of the development of the small modern industrial sector which began in the 1890s, than it was in the 1930s. And in some important handicraft industries, notably cotton spinning, a sharp decline occurred from the nineteenth century to the twentieth. On both theoretical and empirical grounds, however, there is reason to believe that the total domestic and export demand for handicrafts did not decline in the twentieth century, and *a fortiori* that handicraft industry as a whole was not seriously undermined between 1870 and 1911.

But to reject the crudest formulations is not to deny either that significant structural changes in the handicraft industrial sector took place in these four decades or that the strain and dislocation occasioned by these developments adversely affected substantial parts of the population.

Handicraft industry in mid-nineteenth-century China was carried on either in handicraft workshops, predominantly urban in location but present also in rural areas, or in individual households both in urban and rural locations. The distinction between these two forms of handicraft is sometimes quite arbitrary as peasant weavers, for example, in addition to the weaving performed by household labor, might accumulate sufficient funds to purchase several looms which were operated with hired labor; urban craftsmen might similarly employ non-kin workers to supplement the labor of family members in milling rice or ginning cotton, "Handicraft workshops" or "manufactories" *(shou-kung-yeh kung-ch'ang)* were relatively large-scale shops as yet unequipped with power machinery. These enterprises, essentially removed from the household nexus and using the labor of several households, included such undertakings as salt wells and refineries in Szechwan, copper mines in Yunnan, pottery kilns like that at Ching-te-chen in Kiangsi, rice and wheat milling in cities throughout China, and the calendering and dyeing of cotton cloth in Kiangsu. No measure is or ever will be possible of the absolute extent of this extra-household manufacturing.[9] There can be no doubt, however, that it was vastly overshadowed both in employment and in output by the handicraft production of individual households, either ancillary to farming in rural China or performed by full-time urban and semi-urban craftsmen.

The most important household handicraft in rural China was the spinning and weaving of cotton. Because of its significance in the economy of the late-Ch'ing period, I shall first discuss developments in the handicraft cotton textile industry in some detail. The history of handicraft production in general during this period can then be assessed in the light of the fate of cotton textiles. From the Yuan dynasty onward cotton culture and manufacture had spread rapidly, cotton cloth becoming the principal daily article of clothing for all except the very wealthy. While cotton cultivation was fairly widely distributed, the principal producing areas were in the Yangtze valley provinces. It was in this region that cotton handicrafts were most concentrated and highly developed. Large areas in the Yangtze delta were better suited to growing cotton than food crops, and in the relatively humid climate of Kiangsu yarn of greater tensile strength and evenness could be spun. From Kiangnan (the area south of the lower reaches of the Yangtze River) and the districts around Shasi in Hupei, for example, large quantities of baled raw cotton and woven piece goods were carried by water and on the backs of porters to Manchuria and North China, to Szechwan via the Yangtze, to Yunnan and Kweichow in the south-west, and to the southern coastal provinces. It was more profitable for Kiangnan peasants to concentrate their productive resources on growing cotton and on weaving (and on spinning only what was required by that weaving) rather than to spin themselves all the cotton that they grew. Thus spinning by rural households for their own consumption with supplies from the Yangtze valley provinces and with local raw cotton was carried on to varying degrees throughout China. And locally woven cloth supplemented that which came from Hupei and Kiangnan.

But only in the leading cotton-producing areas had the handicraft production of cotton textiles developed into a major industry serving other than an immediate local market. From the weaving districts in southern Hupei, for example, cloth was brought by peasant weavers or petty merchants to the daily piece-goods market in Shasi. The wholesale merchants who purchased in this market graded the cloth by quality and stamped each grade with a well-known "chop" (trademark) which was accepted as a guarantee of quality in the markets of Yunnan and Kweichow to which the goods were sent. Cloth from Hupei reached northern Yunnan via Szechwan, first by water on the Yangtze and its tributaries, then on the backs of porters who carried loads as large as 117 pieces of cloth weighing 220 pounds, and then by pack animal on the Yunnan mountain roads. Kweichow was reached mainly via Hunan employing the Tungting Lake and the Yuan River which flows into it. This was not, by contemporary standards, a petty trade either in size or in the distances traversed. As late as 1895, by which time there had already been radical changes in the structure of the handicraft cotton industry, more than 200,000 bales of raw cotton and 300,000 bales of piece goods were being imported annually into Szechwan largely from Hupei. And some 3,200,000 pieces of cloth were reaching northern Yunnan each year from Shasi. Similarly, China south of Amoy, North China, and Manchuria were supplied mainly from Kiangnan. Moreover, substantial quantities of hand-woven cotton cloth were exported from Canton to England and the United States. Until 1831 England purchased more "nankeens" (cloth manufactured in Nanking and other places in the lower Yangtze region) each year than she sold British-manufactured cloth to China.

Spinning and weaving in the cotton regions for the most part were carried on by individual rural households, to a small extent on a nearly full-time basis but more often in addition to the production of food crops upon which the family was chiefly dependent. Yarn was either spun in the household, or obtained in exchange from the merchants who purchased the cloth which the peasants wove. The income from textile handicrafts formed a larger part of the total income of poorer farmers with the smallest farms than it did of the more affluent. Preparation of the warp prior to weaving, for example, was commonly undertaken in small peasant households to supplement meager agricultural incomes. For the cotton regions as a whole, however, maintenance of the minimum living standards of the dense rural population was critically dependent upon the market for raw cotton and cloth. The calendering and dyeing of cotton cloth tended to be concentrated in market towns and cities which also were the distributing centers for the finished product. These finishing processes were often controlled by the larger cloth merchants and carried out by hired labor, usually paid on a piece-work basis, in "handicraft workshops" owned by these merchants or, as in Soochow, by intermediary "contracting agents" (*pao-t'ou*) to whom the workers paid a monthly fee from their piece-work earnings for the use of the plant and equipment. In general, before the last quarter of the nineteenth century the cloth merchants exercised no similar direct control over the weaving of the cloth which was, as I have stated, usually executed on their own account by peasant households. In the urban areas handicraft manufacture was still under relatively strict guild supervision; the individual master craftsman and not the handicraft workshop was the dominant form of industrial organization.

The unusually perceptive comprador Cheng Kuan-ying offered one version of the changes which occurred in the cotton textile handicraft industry in the second half of the nineteenth century:

> Cotton is grown in the coastal regions, and spun into yarn and woven into cloth. In addition to supplying local needs, the cloth and yarn were shipped in considerable quantities to the western and northern provinces. But when foreign yarn and cloth began to be imported, the population responded to their lower price and high quality and one after another bought and used them. Thus half of the profits of spinning and weaving in the southern provinces was usurped. Now, in the treaty ports and the cities and towns of the interior,

TABLE 7
QUANTITY AND VALUE OF COTTON YARN AND CLOTH IMPORTS, 1871–1910

| | Yarn | | | Cloth | | |
|---|---|---|---|---|---|---|
| | 1,000 piculs* | 1,000 haikwan taels† | Average value per picul (haikwan taels) | 1,000 pieces‡ | 1,000 haikwan taels | Average value per piece (haikwan taels) |
| 1871 | 70 | 1,877 | 26.81 | 14,439 | 24,877 | 1.72 |
| 2 | 50 | 1,372 | 27.44 | 12,241 | 21,435 | 1.75 |
| 3 | 68 | 3,130 ? | 46.03 ? | 8.989 | 16,202 | 1.80 |
| 4 | 69 | 1,969 | 28.54 | 9,763 | 16,301 | 1.67 |
| 5 | 91 | 2,747 | 30.19 | 10,720 | 17,315 | 1.62 |
| 6 | 113 | 2,839 | 25.12 | 11,870 | 17,377 | 1.46 |
| 7 | 116 | 2,841 | 24.49 | 11,117 | 15,959 | 1.44 |
| 8 | 108 | 2,521 | 23.34 | 9,158 | 13,509 | 1.48 |
| 9 | 138 | 3,191 | 23.12 | 12,772 | 19,409 | 1.52 |
| 1880 | 152 | 3,648 | 24.00 | 13,561 | 19,735 | 1.46 |
| 1 | 172 | 4,228 | 24.58 | 14,931 | 21,818 | 1.46 |
| 2 | 185 | 4,505 | 24.35 | 12,159 | 18,201 | 1.50 |
| 3 | 228 | 5,242 | 22.99 | 11,500 | 16,805 | 1.46 |
| 4 | 261 | 5,584 | 21.39 | 11,229 | 16,557 | 1.47 |
| 5 | 388 | 7,871 | 20.20 | 15,706 | 23,623 | 1.50 |
| 6 | 383 | 7,869 | 20.55 | 14,041 | 21,181 | 1.51 |
| 7 | 593 | 12,591 | 21.23 | 15,267 | 24,457 | 1.60 |
| 8 | 683 | 13,496 | 19.76 | 18,664 | 30,942 | 1.66 |
| 9 | 679 | 13,019 | 19.17 | 14,275 | 23,116 | 1.62 |
| 1890 | 1,081 | 19,392 | 17.94 | 16,561 | 25,629 | 1.55 |
| 1 | 1,211 | 20,984 | 17.25 | 17,601 | 32,307 | 1.84 |
| 2 | 1,304 | 22,153 | 16.99 | 16,359 | 30,555 | 1.87 |
| 3 | 982 | 17,863 | 18.19 | 12,498 | 27,275 | 2.18 |
| 4 | 1,160 | 21,397 | 18.45 | 13,343 | 30,708 | 2.30 |
| 5 | 1,132 | 21,209 | 18.74 | 13,437 | 31,865 | 2.37 |
| 6 | 1,621 | 32,010 | 19.75 | 18,919 | 47,233 | 2.50 |
| 7 | 1,571 | 34,430 | 21.92 | 16,914 | 44,233 | 2.62 |
| 8 | 1,959 | 39,295 | 20.06 | 15,524 | 38,324 | 2.47 |
| 9 | 2,745 | 54,941 | 20.01 | 19,419 | 48,524 | 2.50 |
| 1900 | 1,488 | 30,187 | 20.29 | 15,964 | 45,419 | 2.85 |
| 1 | 2,273 | 49,012 | 21.56 | 16,688 | 50,640 | 3.03 |
| 2 | 2,448 | 54,794 | 22.38 | 22,958 | 72,752 | 3.17 |
| 3 | 2,738 | 67,736 | 24.74 | 19,272 | 60,884 | 3.16 |
| 4 | 2,281 | 59,516 | 26.09 | 18,704 | 64,568 | 3.45 |
| 5 | 2,554 | 67,209 | 26.32 | 35,760 | 114,244 | 3.19 |
| 6 | 2,541 | 65,141 | 25.64 | 28,734 | 87,587 | 3.05 |
| 7 | 2,273 | 57,515 | 25.30 | 18,193 | 61,401 | 3.37 |
| 8 | 1,823 | 46,173 | 25.33 | 16,906 | 64,725 | 3.83 |
| 9 | 2,406 | 62,464 | 25.96 | 21,196 | 74,827 | 3.53 |
| 1910 | 2,282 | 62,831 | 27.53 | 17,013 | 67,852 | 3.99 |

* piculs or *tan* of 133.33 lbs.

† the haikwan tael was first used in 1874; 1871–73 values are the estimated equivalents in haikwan taels of values given in local taels in the customs returns.

‡ of varying sizes, but commonly 40 yards long and 36 inches wide; cotton items measured in dozens or yards—perhaps 1 or 2 per cent of the total in square yards—rather than pieces are not included here.

*Source:* Yang Tuan-liu and Hou Hou-pei, *Liu-shih-wu-nien lai Chung-kuo kuo-chi mao-i t'ung-chi* (Statistics of China's foreign trade during the last sixty-five years), tables 4, 9; China. Inspectorate-General of Customs, *Decennial reports ..., 1922–1931*, 1.113, 182.

> only twenty or thirty per cent of the people wear native cloth while seventy or eighty per cent wear foreign cloth.[10]

Foreign merchants and consular officials in late nineteenth-century China would have been amused to read Cheng's warnings to his countrymen; their reports in contrast were full of repeated complaints about the difficulty of penetrating the Chinese market, especially in the interior provinces. The mercantile community pointed particularly to restrictions on foreign residence in the interior and to the burden of the likin (*li-chin*) transit tax. The more perceptive of the consuls, however, recognized that the strength of the handicraft weaving industry was the principal obstacle to clothing every Chinese in Lancashire cottons.

Cheng Kuan-ying and the foreigners in the treaty ports, in fact, shared the truth between them. Foreign imports of cotton yarn and cloth began to increase significantly after the 1858–60 treaties opened additional treaty ports, including three on the Yangtze. This growth was facilitated by the newly gained right to inland steam navigation in China, by the transit pass system which permitted an additional one-half of the import duty to be paid on foreign goods in lieu of likin, and by the opening of the Suez Canal in 1869 which lowered shipping costs from Europe. Table 7 shows the annual quantity and value of cotton goods imports for the period 1871–1910. Cotton yarn and piece goods in 1871 made up about one-third of China's imports by value. While in succeeding years they fluctuated around that proportion of total imports, from the 1880s until 1920 (the peak year) imported cotton manufactures grew by leaps and bounds. The quantity of yarn imports increased twenty-four times—from 97,451 to 2,363,000 piculs (*tan*)—if the average annual amounts for the two decades 1871–80 and 1901–10 are compared. After 1913 a decline began as domestic machine-spun yarn progressively replaced imported yarn. While the imports of cotton piece goods exceeded yarn in value in every year except 1898, 1899, and 1903, their growth—a twofold increase between 1871–80 and 1901–10, from 11,463,010 to 21,442,000 pieces—was not nearly so spectacular. The importation of piece goods did, however, continue to grow until the 1920s and was cut sharply only when the Nanking government regained tariff autonomy. Paradoxically, the very success of yarn imports in the last four decades of the Manchu dynasty indirectly came to be the major obstacle to the equally rapid development of cloth imports. Yarn imports had a critical effect upon the structure of China's cotton textile handicrafts.

The average values per picul of imported yarn and per piece of imported cloth given in table 7 indicate a falling trend in yarn prices from the mid 1870s until almost the end of the century. Cloth prices also declined in the 1870s but began to rise again in the late 1880s and more sharply than the later increase in yarn prices. The major factor behind the appearance of cheaper yarn was the entry into the Chinese market on a large scale of the products of Bombay spinning mills which replaced the more expensive English yarn. From the 1890s Indian yarn was supplemented by increasing inflows of machine-spun yarn from Japan. The decline in the price of yarn was gradual; it extended over some two decades. It is all the more significant in that over the whole period 1871–1910 the gold value of the haikwan tael was itself steadily falling.

While imported machine-spun yarn was becoming cheaper, the price of Chinese raw cotton was rising. This price increase was a consequence of large exports of raw cotton to Japanese mills from the early 1890s onward, while the cotton crop increased little if at all before the spectacular growth of the modern textile industry in China during and after World War I. Together with the limited capacity of a fragmented and technologically backward agricultural sector to respond quickly to export demand, the importation of cheaper foreign yarn itself, which weakened the demand for native handspun, reduced the farmer's incentive to increase his raw cotton acreage. "The most curious feature in connection with the native cotton industry," reported an English mission to China from Blackburn, Lancashire, in 1896–97, "is the high price of the raw material in comparison with other agricultural produce."[11] Increasingly the handicraft weaver turned to imported machine-spun yarn, at least for his warp and sometimes for the weft as well.

In the 1870s and 1880s South China, Kwangtung in particular, was the main market for imported yarn, absorbing over half of the total. This proportion, however, fell steadily to about a fifth of total yarn imports. By the 1890s two regions, (1) North China and Manchuria and (2) the middle and upper Yangtze valley provinces of Anhwei, Kiangsi, Hupei, Hunan, and Szechwan, together with Yunnan and Kweichow, were each receiving about 30 per cent of the total and thus constituted the major markets for imported yarn. The Kiangnan area, where cotton handicrafts were concentrated, absorbed annually about 10 per cent of yarn imports with large fluctuations from year to year. It is evident that the principal markets for imported machine-spun yarn were those regions where cotton growing and handicrafts were least developed. Cheap imported yarn made possible the economical development of handicraft weaving in districts which previously had purchased cloth or relatively expensive raw cotton from Kiangnan or Hupei. Marginal handicraft spinning declined and cloth woven locally with warps of imported yarn and wefts of domestic handspun, competed with pure handspun cloth and foreign piece goods in such areas as Szechwan, for example, where it was reported that "Indian cotton yarn is killing what little local cultivation of cotton there was, and, when woven, is encroaching on homespun cloths and to a much less degree on imported grey shirtings."[12]

TABLE 8
CAPITAL, LOOMS, AND WORKERS IN 142 HANDICRAFT WEAVING WORKSHOPS, ESTABLISHED 1899–1913

| | Number of workshops for which data given | Total | Average | Largest | Smallest |
|---|---|---|---|---|---|
| Capital (Ch. $) | 67 | 660,220 | 9,854 | 70,000 | 200 |
| Number of looms | 37 | 3,307 | 89 | 360 | 12 |
| Number of workers | 96 | 14,972 | 156 | 1,264 | 5 |

*Source:* P'eng Tse-i, comp., *Chung-kuo chin-tai shou-kung-yeh shih tzu-liao, 1840–1949* (Source materials on the history of handicraft industry in modern China, 1840–1949), 2. 369-76.

The most obvious consequences of the increasing inflow of foreign yarn was thus a geographical dispersion of the handicraft weaving industry which in the first half of the nineteenth century had been concentrated in the major cotton-growing provinces. While the older weaving centers were hurt at first, in order to compete in their former markets they too had to adopt machine-made yarn. From the late 1890s Japanese yarn began to be used in large quantities for warp threads in the Shasi and Hankow areas. Although imported yarn did not win a large market there, Kiangnan handicraft weavers in the early twentieth century became the major purchasers of the output of the growing cotton mills of Shanghai. The adoption of machine-made yarn, moreover, strengthened the handicraft weaving industry as a whole. Cloth produced with a mixture of imported and handspun yarn was particularly suited in price and durability to the contemporary Chinese market. Spinning and weaving for household consumption with domestic raw cotton continued to be important in many areas of rural China, but a significant part of spinning for the market was displaced first by imported yarn and then by machine-made yarn from Chinese- and foreign-owned mills in the treaty ports.

While weaving continued to be primarily an individual household handicraft, in some areas by the turn of the century other forms of industrial organization had appeared. These changes were facilitated by the supply of cheaper machine-made yarn and also by improved foot-treadle wood looms and iron-gear looms introduced from Japan which increased the weaver's daily output. One estimate records the establishment of 142 handicraft weaving workshops in the period 1899–1913, 69 of these in Kiangsu where they were supplied with Shanghai-made yarn, 15 in Shantung, 14 in Chihli (Hopei), 9 in Szechwan, 7 each in Shansi, Fukien and Kwangtung, 6 in Hupei, 4 in Manchuria, 3 in Chekiang and 1 in Kweichow. Table 8 indicates the size and equipment of these establishments.

*A verlag* type of weaving, in which cloth merchants put-out yarn to rural weavers some of whom had abandoned their farming and wove for a piece-work wage the patterns stipulated by their merchant employer, also developed in a number of places alongside rural weavers who wove on their own account. No data are available to indicate the actual extent of this putting-out system, some notable examples of which were in Kao-yang and Pao-ti in Chihli (Hopei), Wei-hsien in Shantung, and Hsia-shih in Chekiang. In the first three of these four examples, putting-out developed fairly rapidly from the first decade of the twentieth century until the mid-1920s. It flourished especially during and immediately after World War I, but declined sharply thereafter. For those people who could no longer rely on agricultural income as a cushion against fluctuating demand, rural weaving of this type was an inherently precarious occupation. It was an industry which produced for a non-local market but lacked the modern organization and financial facilities to respond to inevitable change.

The main reason for the much slower growth of cloth than of yarn imports was the extent and strength of the handicraft weaving industry which, as I have stated, was increased by the adoption of machine-made yarn. Relatively little imported cloth was used in rural areas; its principal sale was to the wealthier craftsmen and merchants in the cities and towns. The British consul in Amoy reported in 1886:

> It is well known already that the many millions of lower-class Chinese toiling and moiling throughout the 18 provinces, and in huge territories beyond them, do not wear foreign-made cloths, but homespun. Ask a Chinaman why this is, and he tells you that the poor wear suits of native cotton, because such

> clothing lasts three, four, or five times as long as foreign cloth, because it wears less easily, and because it is much warmer in winter. Why is it warmer? Because, he says, the yarn of which the native fabric is made is quite different from the foreign, and warmer by nature. While, therefore, the well-to-do merchant is wearing out three or four suits of handsomely finished *yang-pu,* the mechanic, the field-hand, the porter, and the boatman are and must be content with one suit of coarser but, in fact, better material.[13]

And the combination of a machine-made warp with a handspun weft made an even better cloth to compete with foreign piece goods. "No doubt the common shirtings are being superseded by native cloth woven by hand from imported yarn," the Blackburn mission acknowledged, "and for this there seems no help."[14]

TABLE 9

SOURCES OF ESTIMATED YARN AND CLOTH CONSUMPTION, 1871–80 AND 1901–10

| | | | | |
|---|---|---|---|---|
| | 1. Cotton yarn | | | |
| | 1871–80 | | 1901–10 | |
| | *tan* | % | *tan* | % |
| Domestic mills | — | — | 1,055,040 | 17.98 |
| Imports | 97,451 | 1.96 | 2,363,000 | 40.27 |
| Handicraft | 4,882,381 | 98.04 | 2,449,715 | 41.75 |
| Total | 4,979,832 | 100.00 | 5,867,755 | 100.00 |
| | 2. Cotton cloth | | | |
| | 1871–80 | | | |
| | yds | % | sq. yds | % |
| Domestic mills | 414,805,000 | 11.40 | — | — |
| Imports | 3,224,960,440 | 88.60 | 376,165,000 | 18.92 |
| Handicraft | 3,639,765,440 | 100.00 | 1,612,480,220 | 81.08 |
| Total | | | 1,988,645,220 | 100.00 |
| | 1901–10 | | | |
| | yds | % | sq. yds | % |
| Domestic mills | 25,200,000 | 0.57 | 24,494,400 | 0.97 |
| Imports | 721,400,000 | 16.23 | 654,200,000 | 25.87 |
| Handicraft | 3,699,890,434 | 83.20 | 1,849,945,217 | 73.16 |
| Total | 4,446,490,434 | 100.00 | 2,528,639,617 | 100.00 |

*Source:* Albert Feuerwerker, "Handicraft and manufactured cotton textiles in China, 1871–1911," *Journal of Economic History,* 30.2 (June 1970): 338-78.

On the assumption that the average annual raw cotton crop in the decade 1871–80 was 7 million piculs and that it was approximately the same size in 1901–10, I have attempted to estimate the sources of the yarn and cloth consumed in an average year in these two decades. Table 9 summarizes this estimate. It will be seen immediately that the total consumption of cotton yarn increased with the population growth from the first period to the second. The handicraft spinning of yarn, however, which had a near monopoly in the first period, declined drastically both in absolute terms and as a proportion of the total yarn supply. Output fell by 2.4 million piculs, so that only half as much handspun yarn was produced in an average year in 1901–10 as in 1871–80. From 98 per cent of the total yarn consumed, handspun fell to 42 per cent. Handspun yarn was replaced by both domestic and imported machine-spun products. While in the first period there were as yet no modern spinning mills established in China, by 1901–10 Chinese- and foreign-owned mills in and near the treaty ports produced nearly 18 per cent of the total yarn consumed, in absolute terms an output approximately equal to the entire increase in total yarn consumption from 1871–80 to 1901–10. But far more important was the growth of imported yarn which by 1901–10 was nearly equal in quantity to the handicraft output. From 2 per cent of the total in 1871–80 it had increased to 40 per cent in 1901–10; in absolute terms, it was twenty-four times larger in the later period than in the earlier.

Total consumption of cloth, whether measured in yards or in square yards, also increased as the population grew. The output of domestic weaving mills, nonexistent in 1871–80, was still barely noticeable in 1901–10; the great expansion was to come only from the early 1920s. Imported cotton piece goods, while they increased from the first period to the second, did so only to a moderate degree as compared with imported yarn. From 11 per cent (yards) and 19 per cent (square yards) of the total consumption in an average year in 1871–80 cloth imports grew to 16 and 26 per cent in an average year in 1901–10. The contrast with the quite remarkable increase in yarn imports is entirely due to the fact that the handicraft weaving industry held its own very well in the face of foreign competition from the earlier decade to the later.

The relative position of handicraft cloth declined slightly, but the absolute amount of cloth woven increased from 3.2 US billion yards in an average year in 1871–80 to 3.7 US billion yards in an average year in 1901–10. This was a creditable growth which shows the strength of this sector but which would certainly have been larger in the absence of foreign cloth imports. Some of those many peasants who had once engaged in spinning as an ancillary occupation undoubtedly turned to weaving as a replacement for their lost employment, but the most generous comparison of the labor lost by the 2.4 million picul decline in handspun yarn with that which could be absorbed by the increment of 600 or 700 million yards of handwoven cloth indicates that only 10 to 20 per cent of the total could have been accommodated. One cannot but conclude that among the peasant households in the regions where cotton spinning had been important, many were unable either to find urban employment for some of their family members or to increase their production and marketing of cash crops. For them the always precarious equilibrium between income and necessary expenditure was profoundly shaken.

This certainly is one source of the indictment of the "incursion of foreign capitalism" to which I referred at the beginning of this section. No other handicraft industry was as important a supplement to rural incomes as cotton spinning and weaving. Although many other handicrafts maintained themselves or expanded in the last half of the nineteenth century, from the undoubted disruption of handicraft spinning the broader and unjustified claim has been advanced that the whole of the traditional handicraft sector was undermined by foreign imports and domestic factory products. There is also a second source which helps to account for the sometimes vitriolic tone of the indictment. Foreign capitalism, it is argued, not only crushed and exploited native handicrafts; it was even more culpable because it short-circuited the normative progression that should have taken place, according to the Chinese reading of Marx on European capitalism, from commodity production by individual households through handicraft workshops to modern factory industry. In China, handicraft workshops and the putting-out system were prevented by foreign capitalism from playing the role they had allegedly played in Europe as the critical intermediary stage to the full-scale development of capitalism. In China the evidence supports the fact although not necessarily the interpretation—handicraft workshops appeared in substantial numbers only after modern industries had been brought forth directly or indirectly by foreign investment, and then only as ancillaries to the mechanized factories. Thus both handicraft and modern industry in late nineteenth- and early twentieth-century China were subservient to foreign capitalism.[15]

Certain handicraft industries unable to compete with imported products, for example native iron and steel production in Hunan and Kiangsi, had nearly disappeared by the end of the nineteenth century. Others expanded in response to export demand during all or part of the four decades from 1870 to 1911. Raw silk from 1887, when it replaced tea, was China's most important single export. While the proportion of silk to total exports declined, the actual quantity of silk exported increased throughout the period. Some of the raw silk was reeled in steam filatures, accounting for 40 per cent of the total exported in 1899. This was a relatively late development which became dominant only in the twentieth century, and in any case the steam filatures were hardly one step removed from handicraft workshops. The Commissioner of Customs at Chefoo, Shantung, reported in 1912:

> The reeling of wild silk for export from the Manchurian cocoon is a comparatively modern industry, introduced in the seventies, since when it has developed considerably. Steam filatures, of which there are now three in existence, have, so far, not proved a success; but the foot-reel of foreign pattern has long been generally adopted, in place of the native hand-reel, with excellent results. There were 40 filatures at work during 1911; they employ over 14,000 hands, and their annual output is 14,000 piculs. No improvement in processes can be recorded.[16]

A preliminary reconnaissance of the contemporary literature records at least 415 handicraft reeling filatures, mainly in Kwangtung, Szechwan, and Shantung, in the period 1892–1913.[17] Silk weaving was performed entirely on handlooms and was a major industry in South and Central China. The exportation of silk piece goods increased fairly steadily from the 1870s until the early 1920s when the competition of rayon fabrics began to be felt.

Handicraft tea processing, on the other hand, probably reached its maximum in the mid-1880s, after which Chinese exports of tea which had increased steadily from the opening of the treaty ports declined sharply. This fall resulted largely from the competition of Indian and Ceylon teas produced in colonial circumstances in which, in contrast to China, the exporters had sufficient control over production to maintain quality standards. In the case of tea, and of silk as well, the only overall data available are for exports. There is, however, no indication in contemporary writings that domestic demand declined in the late Ch'ing period, and with the population growth already postulated earlier in this chapter this is unlikely to have been the case. Thus the relative export success of silk and the growth and then decline of tea exports taken together, while they do not suggest a new flourishing of handicraft industry, contradict with equal force any assumption that handicraft was in mortal crisis at the end of the Manchu dynasty.

Oil pressing, rice milling, mining by native methods, together with silk weaving among the larger handicrafts, were little affected by imported or domestic manufactured goods in the nineteenth century. Oil pressing in handicraft workshops in fact expanded rapidly from the 1890s in response to the demand for soy-bean oil by European soap manufacturers and for bean, bean cake, and oil in Japan. The use of vegetable oils for lighting was, however, steadily supplanted by kerosene imports from the 1890s. Such minor handicrafts as the production of firecrackers, fans, bamboo furniture, Chinese medicines and agricultural tools—commodities for which there were no import substitutes—were not affected at all. The ginning of cotton for export in handicraft workshops with imported Japanese foot-treadle gins expanded in the port cities. Moreover, several new industries developed, for example, cotton knitting and the production of matches in handicraft workshops. Much of this growth of handicraft at the turn of the century occurred in the form of handicraft workshops established in urban areas. There were apparently no comparable new developments in the rural areas apart from the putting-out organization of weaving already discussed. A slowly growing rural population, deprived in the course of the nineteenth century of a significant part of its income from cotton spinning, thus, perhaps increasingly, saw the departure of one or more family members for temporary or permanent employment in workshops, factories, and shops of the cities and towns. In 1911, however, this was still a minor trend.

## 3. Modern Industry

Even for the small modern industrial sector which gradually appeared in the last part of the nineteenth century, the quantitative data that can be assembled are at best only gross approximations; information on output before 1912 is, for example, almost completely lacking. This is surprising since these enterprises were located primarily in the treaty ports, were recorded in the English-language press either because of their foreign sponsorship or because of their novelty if the entrepreneurs were Chinese and are reflected in the documents of the Ch'ing officials who promoted many of them. The most recent and probably the best estimates that have been made suggest that prior to 1895 approximately 103 foreign-owned industrial enterprises, most of them small firms, were inaugurated in China. They and the Chinese-owned firms to be discussed below were often differentiated from handicraft industries only by the fact that they employed some power-driven machinery. In a strict sense manufacturing by foreigners was illegal under the treaties; but it existed nevertheless, for the most part in the Shanghai foreign concessions with a smaller number at other treaty ports. Prior to the 1890s the Chinese government did not interfere with the establishment of these petty foreign factories. When, however, Li Hung-chang and other officials began to promote their own manufacturing enterprises, they were able until 1895 to secure Peking's support to prevent foreigners from undertaking such major ventures as cotton textile mills. The estimated number and capital in 1894 of these foreign industrial firms are shown in table 10.[18]

TABLE 10
ESTIMATED NUMBER AND CAPITALIZATION OF FOREIGN-OWNED INDUSTRIES IN CHINA IN 1894*

| Type of firm | Number | Capital (Ch. $) |
|---|---|---|
| Shipyards: construction and repairs | 12 | 4,943,000 |
| Tea processing | 7 | 4,000,000 |
| Machine silk reeling | 7 | 3,972,222 |
| Processing of exports and imports (other than tea and machine silk) | 19 | 1,493,000 |
| Other light manufacturing | 39 | 3,793,000 |
| Electric power and waterworks | 4 | 1,523,000 |
| Total | 88 | 19,724,000 |

* Includes a small number of firms based in Hong Kong.

*Source:* Sun Yü-t'ang, comp., *Chung-kuo chin-tai kung-yeh shih tzu-liao, ti-i-chi, 1840–1895 nien* (Source materials on the history of modern industry in China, 1st collection, 1840–1895), 1. 242-47. Admittedly based on incomplete data.

From 1895 to 1913, following the legalization of foreign industry in the treaty ports by the Treaty of Shimonoseki, at least 136 additional foreign-owned manufacturing and mining enterprises were set up, with initial capital investments in excess of Ch.$100,000. These included 40 joint Sino-foreign firms which for all practical purposes were under foreign control. (All foreign-owned mines regardless of the size of their capitalization have been included in the above figure.) The total initial capitalization of these firms was Ch.$103,153,000, and some of their characteristics are shown in table 11.

While the establishment of the English, French, German, and Russian firms was fairly evenly distributed over the two decades, all but two of the

Japanese enterprises were begun in 1904 and later—evidence of Japan's increasing economic penetration of Manchuria after the Russo-Japanese War. Coal mining was the biggest field of investment, and Britain the largest investor. The high proportion of Sino-foreign mining enterprises reflects the influence of the Ch'ing government's mining regulations which, prior to 1902, required 30 to 50 per cent of the capital in any mining venture to be provided by Chinese investors. Of the 32 mining enterprises, 9 were British, representing a capital of Ch.$37,930,000 out of a total in this sector of Ch.$49,969,000 and representing a similar proportion of the total direct British investment in industry. Britain and Japan accounted for all of the firms under "engineering and shipyards," and for a very high proportion under each of the other categories, giving them together 86 out of 136 firms and Ch. $76,000,000 out of the Ch. $103,000,000 total initial capital. These foreign and Sino-foreign firms were, apart from the coal mines which were located primarily in Chihli and Manchuria, concentrated in Shanghai, the northern treaty ports and Manchuria. From 1906 to 1913, 53 firms including mines were inaugurated in Manchuria, largely by Japanese investors. The average size of the initial capital of the 136 enterprises was Ch.$758,000.

The data are even less satisfactory about Chinese-owned manufacturing and mining enterprises at the end of the Ch'ing dynasty (other than the joint Sino-foreign firms included above). There were, first, about 19 government-owned arsenals and shipyards, the largest of which were located in Shanghai (established by Tseng Kuo-fan and Li Hung-chang in 1865), Nanking (Li Hung-chang, 1865) and Hanyang (Chang Chih-tung, 1890). In addition to manufacturing munitions and a small number of steamships, the government arsenals were generally equipped with machine shops for the production and repair of tools and parts. A number of them operated training programs for technicians and, as at the translation bureau of the Shanghai Arsenal, produced compilations and translations which served as textbooks for late-nineteenth-century Chinese students of science and engineering.

Secondly, a number of official and semi-official mining, smelting and textile enterprises had been undertaken from as early as 1872. Of these pioneering ventures, the largest and best-known, such as the Kaiping Coal Mines, the Hanyang Ironworks and its coal and iron mines (Hanyehping), Chang Chih-tung's Hupei Textile Mill and Li Hung-chang's Shanghai Cotton Cloth Mill, gradually passed out of the purview of the officials who

TABLE 11
NATIONALITY, INDUSTRY, LOCATION, SIZE OF INITIAL CAPITALIZATION OF FOREIGN AND SINO-FOREIGN MANUFACTURING AND MINING FIRMS ESTABLISHED IN CHINA, 1895-1913

| | Number of firms | | | | Initial capitalization (Ch. $1,000) | | | |
|---|---|---|---|---|---|---|---|---|
| | 1 Foreign | 2 Sino-foreign | 1 + 2 | Percentage of total | 1 Foreign | 2 Sino-foreign | 1 + 2 | Percentage of total |
| Nationality | | | | | | | | |
| England | 28 | 9 | 37 | 27.21 | 25,465 | 24,216 | 49,681 | 48.16 |
| France | 4 | 2 | 6 | 4.41 | 2,986 | 1,609 | 4,515 | 4.38 |
| Germany | 9 | 3 | 12 | 8.82 | 6,534 | 1,147 | 7,681 | 7.45 |
| Japan | 35 | 14 | 49 | 36.03 | 19,829 | 6,501 | 26,330 | 25.53 |
| Russia | 9 | 8 | 17 | 12.50 | 3,866 | 2,782 | 6,648 | 6.44 |
| United States | 6 | 2 | 8 | 5.88 | 2,551 | 689 | 3,240 | 3.14 |
| other | 5 | 2 | 7 | 5.15 | 3,028 | 1,950 | 4,978 | 4.83 |
| Total | 96 | 40 | 136 | 100.00 | 64,259 | 38,894 | 103,153 | 100.00 |
| Industry | | | | | | | | |
| mining | 10 | 22 | 32 | 23.53 | 18,533 | 31,436 | 49,969 | 48.44 |
| engineering and shipyards | 7 | 0 | 7 | 5.15 | 2,895 | 0 | 2,895 | 2.81 |
| electric power and water works | 16 | 3 | 19 | 13.97 | 10,772 | 742 | 11,514 | 11.16 |
| spinning and weaving | 12 | 4 | 16 | 11.76 | 10,325 | 2,190 | 12,515 | 12.13 |
| foodstuffs | 34 | 5 | 39 | 28.68 | 15,126 | 2,022 | 17,148 | 16.62 |
| other | 17 | 6 | 23 | 16.91 | 6,608 | 2,504 | 9,112 | 8.83 |
| Total | 96 | 40 | 136 | 100.00 | 64,259 | 38,894 | 103,153 | 100.00 |

| | | | | | | | | | |
|---|---|---|---|---|---|---|---|---|---|
| Location | | | | | | | | | |
| Kiangsu | 33 | 11 | 44 | 32.35 | 18,501 | 5,121 | 23,622 | 22.90 | |
| Chihli | 7 | 6 | 13 | 9.56 | 4,645 | 24,309 | 28,954 | 28.07 | |
| Hupei | 8 | 2 | 10 | 7.35 | 3,576 | 1,609 | 5,185 | 5.03 | |
| Shantung | 5 | 1 | 6 | 4.41 | 3,503 | 92 | 3,595 | 3.49 | |
| Manchuria | 37 | 16 | 53 | 38.97 | 18,680 | 5,332 | 24,012 | 23.28 | |
| other | 6 | 4 | 10 | 7.35 | 15,354 | 2,431 | 17,785 | 17.24 | |
| Total | 96 | 40 | 136 | 100.00 | 64,259 | 38,894 | 103,153 | 100.00 | |
| Size of initial capitalization | | | | | | | | | Average capital (Ch. $1,000) |
| less than 100,000 | 2 | 5 | 7 | 5.15 | 120 | 288 | 408 | 0.40 | 58 |
| 100,000-249,999 | 32 | 15 | 47 | 34.56 | 5,021 | 2,213 | 7,234 | 7.01 | 154 |
| 250,000-499,999 | 30 | 7 | 37 | 27.21 | 11,623 | 3,132 | 14,755 | 14.30 | 399 |
| 500,000-999,999 | 17 | 6 | 23 | 16.91 | 12,887 | 4,088 | 16,975 | 16.46 | 738 |
| 1,000,000-4,999,999 | 14 | 5 | 19 | 13.97 | 20,622 | 7,541 | 28,163 | 27.30 | 1,482 |
| more than 5,000,000 | 1 | 2 | 3 | 2.21 | 13,986 | 21,632 | 35,618 | 34.53 | 11,873 |
| Total | 96 | 40 | 136 | 100.00 | 64,259 | 38,894 | 103,153 | 100.00 | 758 |

*Source:* Calculated from Wang Ching-yü, comp., *Chung-kuo chin-tai kung-yeh shih tzu-liao, ti-erh-chi, 1895-1914 nien* (Source materials on the history of modern industry in China, 2nd collection, 1895-1914), 1.2-13.

had sponsored them and into the hands of private Chinese investors, or under foreign control in the case of Kaiping. No satisfactory estimate has been made of the size of the investment represented by the arsenals; and the data concerning the *kuan-pan* (official-managed), *kuan-tu shang-pan* (official-supervised and merchant-managed) and *kuan-shang ho-pan* (official and merchant jointly managed) varieties of official and semi-official firms are not always clearly distinguished from those purporting to describe manufacturing and mining enterprises established by private Chinese entrepreneurs *(shang-pan,* merchant-managed). The distinctions between semi-official and private undertakings of this type were in any case largely formal ones and perhaps of secondary significance as I shall indicate below. A recent search of the contemporary literature has yielded information about 75 manufacturing firms other than the arsenals referred to above (for example, silk reeling, cotton ginning, cotton spinning, flour milling, matches, paper mills) and 33 coal and metal mines established between 1872 and 1894 in which private investment played a greater or lesser role. Many of these were short-lived and often they were small, being distinguished from handicraft workshops only by their employment of some steam or electric power.[19]

From 1895 Chinese-owned manufacturing enterprises, like the foreign-owned, increased in number. But the total growth of the industrial sector in this period of China's early industrialization was minute in absolute terms and modest when compared to the relatively large spurt of new enterprises which began production in the period 1918–22. Ch'ing government efforts, after the disasters of the Sino-Japanese War and the Boxer Uprising, to promote industry by such measures as the creation of a Ministry of Commerce (later reorganized as Agriculture, Industry, and Commerce) in 1903 and the promulgation of a "Company Law" in 1904 may have contributed to this limited expansion. Certainly the burgeoning anti-imperialist nationalism of provincial merchants and gentry was a factor. The principal force behind the establishment of new firms, however, was the manifest profitability of the first few enterprises undertaken in most industrial sectors and especially in the manufacture of consumers' goods to be marketed in the treaty-port areas. Successful foreign- and Chinese-owned firms were earning annual returns on the initial market value of their capital investments of 10 per cent or more in the first decade of the twentieth century. The total market, however, was severely limited by the low level of effective demand in the bulk of rural China. Consequently successive firms entering any particular industry, after the first few pioneers, faced a situation of increasing risk and uncertainty. This risk was reinforced by the fact that many of the pioneer firms had been established on the initiative of important provincial officials, or with the aid of official funds, or with official support in such forms as partial tax exemptions or the monopoly of certain markets. Thus the Shanghai Cotton Cloth Mill (began production 1890, reorganized 1894) and the Hanyehping Coal and Iron Co. (began production 1894, reorganized 1896) were under Sheng Hsuan-huai's direction as *kuan-tu shang-pan* enterprises and were dependent on the backing of the provincial leaders, Li Hung-chang and Chang Chih-tung respectively. But even such nominally private (*shang-pan*) enterprises Chang Chien's Tasheng Cotton Mill (began production 1899) and the Chou Hsüeh-hsi's premier Chee Hsin Cement Co. (began production 1907) owed their initial success to the official support which their sponsors because of their own official ties, were able to obtain—from Chang Chih-tung and Liu K'un-i in the former case and from Yuan Shih-k'ai for Chee Hsin. Given a limited market, the lack of a modern banking system which could systematically channel savings into industrial investment, a central government whose financial resources were severely limited, and competition from imported goods and foreign-owned factories in China, it is perhaps not surprising that some regional officials and the entrepreneurs who were associated with them attempted to establish limited but protected industrial empires for their mutual profit. Few purely private ventures could expect success.

The link between economic success and political power, which had characterized such monopolies as that of the Cohong or the salt merchant of an earlier period and was manifest again in Kuomintang China in the 1930s and 1940s, was not broken during the era of China's early industrialization.

Between 1895 and 1913, according to a recent estimate, at least 549 Chinese-owned private and semi-official manufacturing and mining enterprises using mechanical power were inaugurated. Their total initial capitalization was Ch.$120,288,000. This estimate excludes arsenals, mints, and also apparently a relatively small number of purely official undertakings. Some of the characteristics of these 549 firms, which include all with a initial capital of Ch.$10,000 or more for which data could be found and about which there is more information than for the enterprises started before 1895, are given in tables 12-14.

The peak years for the establishment of modern industry during the two decades surveyed were 1905–08. In this four-year period, 238 firms

TABLE 12
NUMBER AND INITIAL CAPITAL OF CHINESE-OWNED MANUFACTURING AND MINING ENTERPRISES INAUGURATED 1895–1913, BY INDUSTRY

| Industry | Number of enterprises | Percentage of total | Initial capital (Ch. $1,000) | Percentage of total | Average capital (Ch. $1,000) |
|---|---|---|---|---|---|
| Coal mining | 42 | 7.65 | 14,508 | 12.06 | 345 |
| Metal mining and smelting | 39 | 7.10 | 7,565 | 6.29 | 194 |
| Metal working | 15 | 2.73 | 2,787 | 2.32 | 186 |
| Public utilities (water and electricity) | 46 | 8.38 | 21,600 | 17.96 | 470 |
| Cement | 3 | 0.55 | 2,620 | 2.18 | 873 |
| Bricks, tiles | 12 | 2.19 | 651 | 0.54 | 543 |
| Pottery | 7 | 1.28 | 772 | 0.64 | 110 |
| Glass | 10 | 1.82 | 3,429 | 2.85 | 343 |
| Matches | 26 | 4.74 | 3,444 | 2.86 | 132 |
| Candles, soap | 18 | 3.28 | 805 | 0.67 | 45 |
| Cotton ginning | 3 | 0.55 | 280 | 0.23 | 93 |
| Cotton spinning | 19 | 3.46 | 10,454 | 8.69 | 550 |
| Cotton weaving and dyeing | 27 | 4.92 | 1,261 | 1.05 | 47 |
| Silk reeling | 97 | 17.67 | 11,584 | 9.63 | 119 |
| Wool weaving | 7 | 1.28 | 5,215 | 4.34 | 745 |
| Hemp weaving | 4 | 0.73 | 1,000 | 0.83 | 250 |
| Other weaving | 6 | 1.09 | 732 | 0.61 | 122 |
| Rice milling | 9 | 1.64 | 1,012 | 0.84 | 113 |
| Flour milling | 53 | 9.65 | 8,622 | 7.17 | 163 |
| Oil pressing | 28 | 5.10 | 4,752 | 3.95 | 170 |
| Cigarettes, tobacco | 20 | 3.64 | 1,378 | 1.15 | 69 |
| Other foodstuffs | 15 | 2.73 | 3,111 | 2.59 | 207 |
| Paper | 14 | 2.55 | 5,929 | 4.93 | 424 |
| Printing | 6 | 1.09 | 1,160 | 0.97 | 193 |
| Leather tanning | 11 | 2.00 | 4,608 | 3.83 | 419 |
| Other | 12 | 2.19 | 1,009 | 0.84 | 84 |
| Total | 549 | 100.00 | 120,288 | 100.00 | 219 |

*Source:* Calculated from Wang Ching-yü, *Chung-kuo chin-tai kung-yeh shih tzu-liao*, 2. 869-920.

with total initial capitalization of Ch. $61,219,000 began operation. Much of the machinery installed came from abroad, which is reflected in the fact that annual imports of tools and machinery in 1905–08 were more than double the annual value in 1895–1904. Machinery imports continued to grow after 1908, but the number of new enterprises opened fell sharply until the much larger industrialization spurt of 1918–22. These trends perhaps suggest increased capital investment in the privileged established firms combined with an increasing difficulty in entering the limited market for new firms. They may also reflect a shift of venture capital to provincial

TABLE 13
NUMBER AND INITIAL CAPITAL OF CHINESE-OWNED MANUFACTURING AND MINING ENTERPRISES INAUGURATED 1895–1913, BY LOCATION

| Location | Number of enterprises | Percentage of total | Initial capital (Ch. $1,000) | Percentage of total |
|---|---|---|---|---|
| Anhwei | 18 | 3.28 | 1,868 | 1.55 |
| Chekiang | 29 | 5.28 | 4,346 | 3.61 |
| Chihli (other than Tientsin) | 34 | 6.19 | 11,951 | 9.94 |
| Tientsin | 17 | 3.10 | 4,219 | 3.51 |
| Fukien | 19 | 3.46 | 1,461 | 1.21 |
| Honan | 12 | 2.19 | 1,890 | 1.57 |
| Hunan | 24 | 4.37 | 3,968 | 3.31 |
| Hupei (other than Wuhan) | 9 | 1.64 | 1,937 | 1.61 |
| Wuhan | 28 | 5.10 | 17,240 | 14.33 |
| Kiangsi | 13 | 2.37 | 2,383 | 1.98 |
| Kiangsu (other than Shanghai) | 70 | 12.75 | 13,510 | 11.23 |
| Shanghai | 83 | 15.12 | 23,879 | 19.85 |
| Kwangsi | 5 | 0.91 | 1,424 | 1.18 |
| Kwangtung (other than Canton) | 68 | 12.39 | 5,038 | 4.19 |
| Canton | 16 | 2.91 | 5,791 | 4.81 |
| Kweichow | 1 | 0.18 | 79 | 0.07 |
| Manchuria | 44 | 8.01 | 4,922 | 4.09 |
| Shansi | 10 | 1.82 | 3,038 | 2.53 |
| Shantung | 20 | 3.64 | 4,614 | 3.84 |
| Shensi | 1 | 0.18 | 405 | 0.34 |
| Szechwan | 19 | 3.46 | 2,248 | 1.87 |
| Yunnan | 5 | 0.91 | 1,671 | 1.39 |
| Other | 4 | 0.73 | 2,406 | 2.00 |
| Total | 549 | 100.00 | 120,288 | 100.00 |

*Source:* Same as table 12

railway projects inspired by the nationalist "rights recovery" activities of the last years of the dynasty.

In both numbers and initial capital the bulk of these new industries was concentrated in such light manufacturing fields as textiles (260 firms or 29.14 per cent of the total, with a capitalization of Ch.$30,246,000 or 25.14 per cent of the total) and the processing of foodstuffs (125 firms or 22.76 per cent; Ch.$18,875,000 or 25.69 per cent). Mines accounted for 14.75 per cent of the firms and 18.35 per cent of the initial capitalization. Their relative importance reflects again the considerable success of the late Ch'ing "rights recovery movement" which accomplished the cancellation of a substantial number of foreign mining concessions during the first decade of the twentieth century, although sometimes at the price of clearly excessive compensation payments. The 46 electric power plants or waterworks were established in the larger cities in all the provinces of China proper with the exception of Shensi, Kwangsi, and Kweichow. They varied greatly in size and were most often to be found in the treaty port cities of the Yangtze valley and south-east coastal provinces.

With the exceptions of silk reeling, which after 1900 was increasingly performed in steam filatures, iron mining at Ta-yeh for export to Japan, and to a lesser extent oil pressing, these Chinese-owned modern industries were not engaged in processing raw materials for export. Only three modern cotton ginning plants, for example, are recorded. Much export processing continued to be primarily a handicraft industry, although supplemented by the output of foreign-owned processing plants. Cotton weaving and dyeing, even in the urban areas, remained also at the handicraft stage or were performed in small plants with minimal power machinery in the vicinity of the new cotton spinning mills.

Many of these new manufacturing enterprises were, in fact, small. Of the 160 firms in the textile line, 97 were steam silk filatures of which 54 were very small plants located in Kwangtung. The 21 filatures located in Shanghai were each several times larger than those in the south, but the average initial investment for all 97 was only Ch. $119,000. Of the 549 enterprises, 303 had initial capitals of less than Ch.$100,000. The average capitalization of the remaining 246 Chinese-owned firms (capitalized at Ch.$100,000 and over) was Ch.$432,000 compared with an average investment of Ch.$758,000 for the 136 foreign and Sino-foreign enterprises in table 11.

TABLE 14
INITIAL CAPITALIZATION OF CHINESE-OWNED MANUFACTURING AND MINING ENTERPRISES, INAUGURATED 1895–1913

| Size of initial capitalization (Ch. $) | Number of enterprises | Percentage of total | Initial capital (Ch. $1,000) | Percentage of total | Average capital (Ch. $1,000) |
|---|---|---|---|---|---|
| 10,000- 49,999 | 214 | 38.98 | 5,899 | 4.90 | 28 |
| 50,000- 99,999 | 89 | 16.21 | 7,052 | 5.86 | 79 |
| 100,000-249,999 | 104 | 18.94 | 17,731 | 14.74 | 170 |
| 250,000-499,999 | 85 | 15.48 | 29,901 | 24.86 | 352 |
| 500,000-999,999 | 40 | 7.29 | 27,980 | 23.26 | 700 |
| 1,000,000 and over | 17 | 3.10 | 31,725 | 26.37 | 1,866 |
| Total | 549 | 100.00 | 120,288 | 100.00 | 219 |

*Source:* Wang Ching-yü, *Modern industry,* 2. 1041.

Chinese-owned enterprises could of course locate in the interior, if they wished, as well as in Shanghai and other treaty ports. Of 468 non-mining enterprises, 239 were located in treaty-port cities and 229 in places other than treaty ports. As the foreign-owned non-mining firms were all located in the treaty ports, and marketed their products primarily in these places, the existence of Chinese firms in inland locations suggests that there was some degree of complementarity as well as competition between the markets served by foreign industries in China and Chinese-owned enterprises. However, Chinese-owned modern manufacturing firms in the treaty ports had much larger initial capitalization and average size than the inland firms, as table 15 indicates. The four cities of Shanghai, Wuhan, Tientsin, and Canton, as may be seen from tables 13 and 15, were the most important manufacturing centers. Shanghai, for example, led in at least the following industries: metal working, cotton textiles, silk reeling, flour milling, oil pressing, printing, candles and soap.

TABLE 15
NUMBER AND INITIAL CAPITALIZATION OF TREATY-PORT AND INLAND CHINESE-OWNED MANUFACTURING FIRMS, 1895–1913

| | Number | Percentage of total | Initial capital (Ch.$1,000) | Percentage of total | Average capital (Ch.$1,000) |
|---|---|---|---|---|---|
| Inland enterprises | 229 | 48.93 | 33,158 | 33.76 | 145 |
| Treaty-port enterprises | 239 | 51.07 | 65,057 | 66.24 | 272 |
| Shanghai, Wuhan, Tientsin, Canton | 144 | 30.77 | 51,129 | 52.06 | 355 |
| Other treaty ports | 95 | 20.30 | 13,928 | 14.18 | 147 |
| Total | 468 | 100.00 | 98,215 | 100.00 | 210 |

*Source:* Same as table 12.

The foregoing data are of value only in suggesting gross trends. It is likely that some firms were either omitted or counted more than once, that a proportion of those undertaken failed during the period under consideration, and that the initial capital may have been overestimated in some cases (or quickly increased in others). It would therefore be misleading to take a simple sum of the number of firms and the magnitude of their capitals under the several categories discussed above as the absolute magnitude of China's nineteenth-century industrialization. The best that can be said is that by the end of the Ch'ing dynasty there were perhaps 500-600 foreign and Chinese mining and manufacturing enterprises employing mechanical power, and that the total capitalization of these firms was in the vicinity of Ch.$200,000,000.

Among these firms, it is estimated that 116 Chinese-owned enterprises and 40 foreign-owned employed 500 or more workers each, with a total of 130,985 in the former and 109,410 in the latter. The 500 employee cut-off point is arbitrary, of course, but if it is adopted these 240,395 workers may be considered the extent of the "modern" labor force in China in the period 1900–10.

Some part of the investment in the nineteenth-century foreign factories was held by Chinese shareholders resident in the treaty ports, principally compradors of foreign trading firms or merchants dealing in silk, tea and imported yarn and cloth. This was especially true of the foreign-owned coastal and riverine steamship lines and of banks, insurance companies and goods warehouses which are not included in the data on manufacturing firms in table 10. But it was also the case in silk reeling, electric light and power utilities and, after 1895, in the newly established cotton textile mills. One recent study has identified 130 large Chinese shareholders who had invested in 44 foreign firms between 1860 and 1900.[20] Another sample, for 1896–1910, lists 78 Chinese investors, individuals and firms, in 17 foreign-owned factories mainly in Shanghai. Of these firms, 6 were cotton mills and 2 flour mills.[21] The total size of the investment by Chinese in foreign enterprises reflected in these two samples cannot be estimated. But such investment does testify to the availability of funds (often the profits of participation in foreign trade) in the treaty ports if there were prospects of substantial profits. The special status of foreigners and their concessions in the treaty ports provided the needed assurance. When Chinese entrepreneurs could give similar guarantees of potential profit, some of those who had invested in foreign firms also put their "comprador capital" into Chinese-owned ventures. The special privileges of the *kuan-tu shang-pan* enterprises, and of others formally in the private sector but dependent in varying degrees on official favors, were intended to provide precisely this assurance.

But, as I have already stated, the overall prospects for modern manufacturing industry in late-Ch'ing China were limited. The institutions—a modern banking system in particular—for channeling non-treaty-port savings into industry did not exist. The central government was ideologically and politically incapable of establishing and guaranteeing the framework of legal, commercial and educational institutions without which modern enterprise could not thrive. Nor was it able, in the absence of tariff autonomy and in view of the special privileges foreigners had exacted, to provide protection for "infant" Chinese-owned firms against competition from imports and the products of foreign firms in China. And, above all, it would have required a basic reorganization of the agricultural sector to provide the raw materials for industrial growth, food for an expanded urban population, and a sufficient market for increased output. The late-nineteenth-century Chinese economy was admittedly poor: the technology of Europe's industrial revolution was just beginning to appear in the coastal cities, and the rural population lived with an increasingly adverse man-land ratio and an agricultural technology which over the centuries had been exploited to the limits of its potential. But it was not an absolute shortage of capital which constrained China's early industrial development.

As of 1912, manufacturing firms registered with the Ministry of Agriculture and Commerce reported a total capitalization of Ch.$54,804,000. In the same year, traditional banks (*ch'ien-chuang*, "money shops") and pawnshops registered with the ministry were capitalized at a total of Ch. $164,854,000.[22] The resources of the economy, limited as they were, remained sterilized in traditional vessels which only fundamental political change could shatter.

## 4. Domestic and Foreign Commerce

The economy of late-Ch'ing China was, at its given level of technology, characterized by a high degree of commercial development. Goods and traders moved extensively throughout the country and, to a limited extent, the domestic economy had developed links with the world market. At the most basic level, the peasants of every rural area bought and sold regularly at the periodic markets of the standard market towns which served their groups of villages. Here such agricultural surplus as they produced and the products of handicraft manufacture were exchanged for other local commodities or for goods manufactured in the treaty-port cities or imported from abroad which, in small quantities, had flowed down through successive levels of the marketing system to the final consumer. These thousands of basic markets, of which Skinner estimates there were 63,000 early in the twentieth century,[23] were linked in turn to two higher level markets—

intermediate and central—and ultimately to the great trading cities of the coast such as Tientsin, Shanghai, and Canton.

At each level the markets were populated by itinerant peddlers, local merchants and agents of firms from all markets except the basic ones. At its upper levels—the central markets and above—the marketing system interpenetrated with the administrative hierarchy of the Ch'ing government. The rural central markets and the urban city and regional markets were the loci of the officially regulated merchant middlemen and the merchant *guilds* (*ya-hang*) through whom the bureaucratic elite regulated and taxed the commerce of the empire. Also in these upper markets were found the exchange banks (often operated by families from Shansi province and hence known as "Shansi banks") through whose drafts large sums were transferred from one upper level market to another. Other types of "native banks," such as the money shops (*ch'ien-chuang*) which advanced funds to local merchants—usually on personal security and occasionally on the security of designated goods—and also changed money from one local currency standard to another, were also located in the upper level markets. In the basic markets, barter was not unknown and the financial institutions were limited to the local moneylender and the petty "shroff" or moneychanger.

The discreteness of the 63,000 rural basic markets and the structure of the marketing hierarchy as a whole were closely related to the degree of development of the means of transportation. The upper level markets were located on or at the termini of the principal water and, in North China, overland routes by which goods and persons were transported, while the basic markets were situated on the progressively less accessible feeder trails and waterways. The intricate and highly developed periodic marketing structure continued to flourish not only in late nineteenth-century China but well into the twentieth century as well, as a result of the relative absence of two critical changes: (1) improved transportation at the local level, which would make intermediate and higher level markets as easily available to the peasant as his traditional basic market; and (2) a linking of the higher level markets to industrial centers within and outside China by superior steamship and railway communications with a consequent increase in the inflow and outflow of commodities, which in turn would decrease the self-sufficiency of the households which traded at the basic markets.

Certainly the bulk, perhaps as much as three-quarters, of all the trade in nineteenth-century China consisted of small-scale local trade. This was confined to the basic and intermediate market levels by high transport costs, by the profits of multitudinous middlemen at each successive level of the marketing system, and to some extent too by the relative self-sufficiency in basic grains of much of rural China.

"For the most part, trade takes to the water when it can," the Commissioner of Customs at Lungchow noted in 1892.[24] This observation was applicable both to short-haul grain shipments within major producing regions (for example, from the Hunan districts bordering the Tungting Lake to the major markets of Hsiang-t'an or Changsha) and to the thousand-mile trip from the rice surplus province of Hunan to the deficit regions in the Yangtze Delta. Nevertheless the total amount of long-distance shipping of such a bulky, low-priced commodity as grain was very small. Even in the early twentieth century, the total freight and marketing cost of bringing rice by junk from Anhwei to Shanghai was almost double the original price of the rice in the Anhwei village where it was produced.[25] The long-distance trade—between higher level markets, but of course originating or terminating ultimately at the basic level—consisted for the most part of commodities with a relatively high value per ton whose production was favored by the resources or climate of a particular region: raw cotton and cotton textiles from Kiangnan; salt from the brine wells of Szechwan or the coastal evaporating pans of Kiangsu; opium from Yunnan, Kweichow, and Szechwan; sugar from Kwangtung and Fukien; copper and lead from Yunnan; teas from the middle and lower Yangtze valley; and silk from Chekiang, Kiangsu, Kwangtung and Szechwan. These products could bear the high freight and handling markup because of their higher values in relation to weight—in the case of tea for example, which was worth perhaps ten times as much per picul as an equivalent weight of rice, this might be 15 or 20 per cent between Anhwei and Shanghai. There were no alternative sources of supply, And they were consumed in disproportionate amounts by the wealthier residents (the gentry) of the towns and cities for whom the question of price was relatively less important.

In Central and South China in particular the major rivers and their branches and tributaries were the arteries and capillaries of commerce. A twentieth-century estimate, which appears applicable to the late Ch'ing as well, suggests that there were at least 4,000 miles of waterways suitable to steamer traffic, 15,000 miles more which could be navigated by steam launches, and an additional 27,000 miles open to "native craft" of all kinds. Perhaps 25,000 miles of Yangtze waterways were ultimately navigable from Shanghai—by ocean steamer to Hankow, then by light-draft steamer to

Ichang where goods were repacked and loaded on to junks, thence through the Yangtze rapids with the aid of trackers to Chungking;[26] from Chungking on progressively smaller junks via the upper Yangtze and its tributaries to northern Szechwan and to Kweichow, and by stream and porter into Yunnan. In the smallest streams the vessels may have been no more than bamboo rafts turned up at the bows; or maybe they were flat-bottomed skiffs, drawing perhaps nine inches of water fully loaded, whose crewmen were often in the water lifting and shoving. While the West River from Canton was navigable by steamer only to Wuchow on the Kwangsi border, thousands of junks on that stream and its tributaries carried goods further into and out of Kwangsi, Kweichow and Yunnan. A third major trade route (by which teas and silks were brought to Canton before the opening of Shanghai) proceeded via the North River from Canton, by porter over the Cheling or Meiling passes in the Nan-ling Mountains to the headwaters of the Hsiang and Kan rivers in Hunan and Kiangsi respectively, and then through the Tungting and Poyang lakes to the Yangtze. The necessity for overland porterage over the Nan-ling Mountains and the limited hinterlands of Ningpo, Foochow, and Amoy favored the development of Shanghai as the major foreign trade port, and the Yangtze as the principal route into the interior of China.

From Hankow, junks could proceed north-westward on the Han River into Shensi. To some extent also the Grand Canal continued to link the lower Yangtze valley with the North China plain. But North China was much less served with navigable waterways than the south. Here the large-wheeled North China carts and pack animals moved over dust and mud tracks, which constant traffic in the loess regions of Honan, Shansi, and Shensi had sometimes cut down ten or more feet below the surface of the surrounding countryside. The major traditional trade routes from Peking followed a difficult course overland to Shansi, and via Kalgan across Mongolia to Kiakhta on the Russian border, with branches westward to Shensi and Kansu. Where water routes were not available, as in much of North China, the movement of goods was slow and expensive.[27] Overland freight costs by cart, wheelbarrow, pack animal or on the backs of porters are estimated to have been two to five times higher per ton mile than freight charges by junk.

The nineteenth-century commercial system, in spite of its high level of traditional development, was of course not yet a "modern" market economy. While a few high-value commodities, as I have indicated, might have carried by water throughout the empire, it would be incorrect to speak of a national market even for these. Commerce tended to be contained within a large number of hierarchically arranged cells, as a result of friction created by certain factors. These were a bimetallic silver-copper standard with multiple local currencies, high-cost transportation (in money and time), the comparative rarity of credit advances against commodities, the absence of a commercial banking system for the mutual clearing of indebtedness, and the omnipresence of numerous petty middlemen with vested interests in the traditional structure of trade. Each cell bustled with petty commerce and, to use Sol Tax's phrase, "penny capitalism," but they were connected only by a traffic of semi-luxury goods and the outflow of silver and some grains in the form of taxes to the administrative hierarchy above.

Foreign observers in the second half of the nineteenth century, after the establishment of the likin tax in 1853 to finance the suppression of the Taiping rebels, were wont to see this levy on internal trade (which admittedly was sometimes capriciously administered) as the principal obstacle to their own trade and to the commercial integration of China.[28] But compared with freight and handling markups of 15 to 100 per cent, it appears unlikely that the common likin rate of 2 per cent at each tax station had more than a small effect on the total amount and direction of internal trade. The British, as I have stated earlier, found it difficult to sell Lancashire cloth in the interior of China because domestic handicraft weaving offered effective competition. The marketing structure and size of China's domestic commerce were constrained not primarily by burdensome official exactions, but by the limitations of pre-modern transportation and communications.

By the end of the Manchu dynasty in 1911, there was a small but noticeable change in the commercial system at its outer fringes. While, as I shall argue, it remained essentially intact, it is, after all, common sense that the late-Ch'ing economy was influenced by the progressive opening of treaty ports and the expansion of foreign trade. The trade data compiled by the foreign-administered maritime customs are almost the only substantial long-term historical statistics for modern China. But even these generally excellent data have shortcomings. To 1887, imports from Hong Kong were not included, and free on board (F.O.B.) and cost, insurance, and freight (C.I.F.) values were not used so that export values were understated while imports were overstated. Moreover, the trade was measured in silver haikwan (maritime customs) taels in an era when silver was steadily declining in

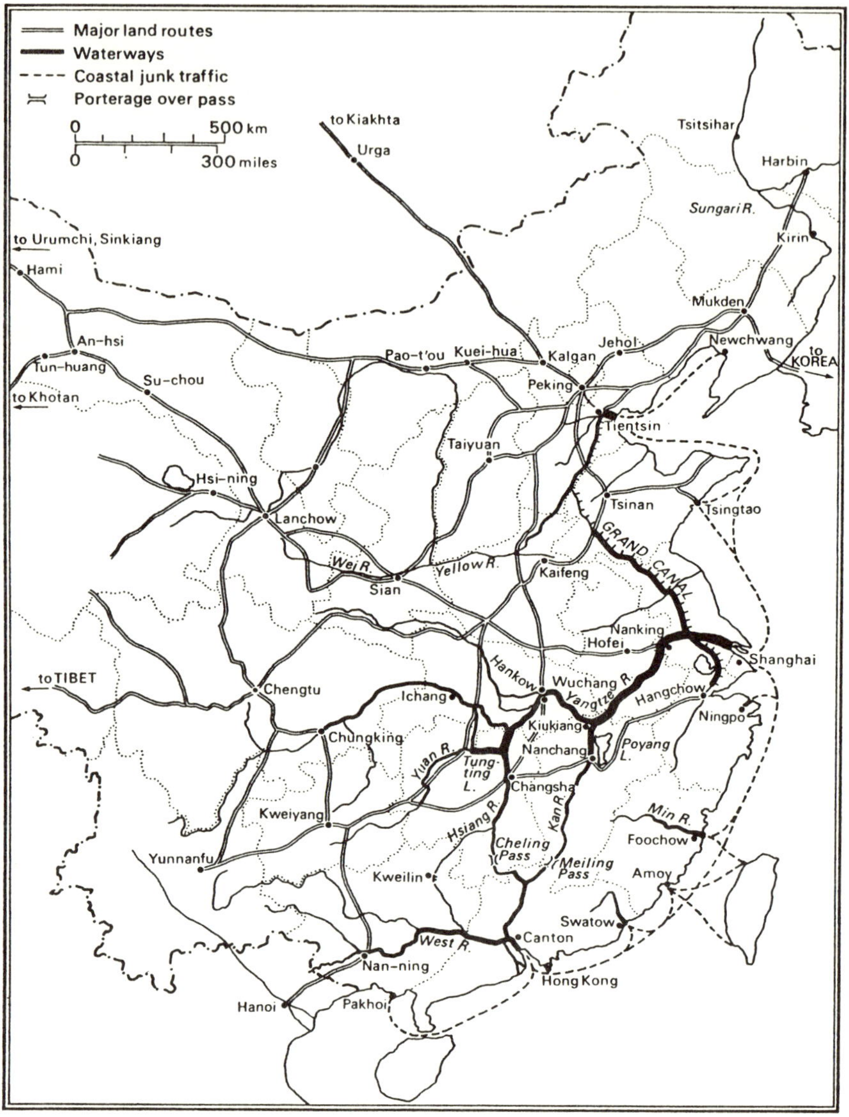


Map 2. Trade routes

terms of gold with the result that the recorded value of the trade was inflated as compared with its gold value or its actual quantity. Table 16 presents values in current haikwan taels and index numbers of China's foreign trade for the period 1870–1911.

In current haikwan taels the total volume of trade increased more than sevenfold from 1870 to 1911. As already indicated, silver values inflate the actual growth of trade: in terms of quantity, imports increased 312 per cent and exports 307 per cent during these four decades. The growth of total trade measured in current values was relatively slow until the 1890s, with the most rapid increase coming in the first decade of the twentieth century. The quantity indices indicate that the growth of imports was fairly steady (the great spurt in 1905–06 was a direct consequence of the Russo-Japanese War and should be discounted) while exports, which were relatively stationary in the 1890s, increased rapidly in the last few years of the dynasty. Bean and bean product shipments, primarily from Manchuria, account for much of this export spurt. If the pre-1888 trade data are adjusted to measure imports at cost, insurance and freight values and exports at free on board values, and an allowance is made for opium and others "smuggled" from Hong Kong, China's foreign trade probably showed an export surplus from 1870 to 1887. From 1888 to 1900, imports moderately exceeded exports by an annual average of 40,876,000 haikwan taels. After 1900, the import excess became substantially larger, the average annual excess for 1901–11 growing to 121,377,000 haikwan taels. Part of this adverse trade balance was offset by remittances homeward by overseas Chinese, and up to 1900 by a small net export of gold and silver. The remainder was financed by an inflow of capital—including investment in industry after 1895 as described above, and loans to the Ch'ing government which I shall discuss later.

Opium, mainly from India, ranked as the most important single Chinese import until 1890 when it was surpassed by cotton piece goods. Cotton cloth and yarn together after 1890 accounted for about one-third of China's imports by value. The cotton trade and its effect on the Chinese economy have already been discussed in connection with the handicraft industry. Cereals and other foodstuffs were imported largely to supply the large coastal cities in quantities which appear to have fluctuated with localized harvest supply conditions rather than the general quality of the harvest; this trade reflects both the growth of these cities and the heavy transportation and marketing costs for domestic grains grown outside their immediate

TABLE 16
VALUES AND INDEX NUMBERS OF CHINA'S FOREIGN TRADE, 1870–1911
(ALL INDICES: 1913 = 100)

| | Value in current haikwan taels (1,000) | | | | Indices of value of total trade | | Indices of quantity | | Net barter terms of trade |
|---|---|---|---|---|---|---|---|---|---|
| | Net Imports | Exports | Total | Trade balance | Current values | "Real" values* | Imports | Exports | (import prices/ export prices) |
| 1870 | 63,693 | 55,295 | 118,988 | – 8,398 | 12.2 | — | 25.9 | 33.3 | 76.5 |
| 1871 | 70,103 | 66,853 | 136,956 | – 3,250 | 14.1 | — | 28.1 | 39.4 | 75.9 |
| 1872 | 67,317 | 75,288 | 142,605 | + 7,971 | 14.6 | — | 27.9 | 43.3 | 71.1 |
| 1873 | 66,637 | 69,451 | 136,088 | + 2,814 | 14.0 | — | 27.3 | 39.1 | 70.8 |
| 1874 | 64,361 | 66,713 | 131,074 | + 2,352 | 13.5 | 20.7 | 31.5 | 40.1 | 62.8 |
| 1875 | 67,803 | 68,913 | 136,716 | + 1,110 | 14.0 | 21.0 | 33.8 | 42.2 | 65.3 |
| 1876 | 70,270 | 80,851 | 151,121 | +10,581 | 15.5 | 21.6 | 36.3 | 42.8 | 54.4 |
| 1877 | 73,234 | 64,445 | 140,679 | – 5,789 | 14.5 | 21.9 | 36.1 | 40.8 | 65.2 |
| 1878 | 70,804 | 67,172 | 139,976 | – 3,632 | 14.2 | 20.5 | 34.9 | 41.4 | 66.3 |
| 1879 | 82,227 | 72,281 | 154,508 | – 9,946 | 15.9 | 22.0 | 40.8 | 43.2 | 63.9 |
| 1880 | 79,293 | 77,884 | 157,177 | – 1,409 | 16.1 | 23.7 | 36.2 | 47.2 | 69.7 |
| 1881 | 91,111 | 71,453 | 163,364 | –20,458 | 16.8 | 23.3 | 40.8 | 43.5 | 72.8 |
| 1882 | 77,715 | 67,337 | 145,052 | –10,378 | 14.9 | 21.3 | 36.4 | 45.9 | 76.7 |
| 1883 | 73,568 | 70,198 | 143,766 | – 3,370 | 14.8 | 22.0 | 35.0 | 47.2 | 75.1 |
| 1884 | 72,761 | 67,148 | 139,909 | – 5,613 | 14.4 | 21.1 | 34.5 | 50.6 | 83.6 |
| 1885 | 88,200 | 65,006 | 153,206 | –23,194 | 15.7 | 23.1 | 40.5 | 47.6 | 83.3 |
| 1886 | 87,479 | 77,207 | 164,686 | –10,272 | 16.9 | 24.2 | 35.3 | 54.2 | 91.4 |
| 1887 | 102,264 | 85,860 | 188,124 | –16,404 | 19.3 | 28.4 | 41.6 | 41.2 | 62.4 |
| 1888 | 124,783 | 92,401 | 217,184 | –32,382 | 22.3 | 34.3 | 50.3 | 43.6 | 62.7 |
| 1889 | 110,884 | 96,948 | 207,832 | –13,936 | 21.3 | 31.4 | 44.0 | 45.2 | 63.0 |
| 1890 | 127,093 | 87,144 | 214,237 | –39,949 | 22.0 | 32.4 | 54.8 | 42.0 | 59.8 |
| 1891 | 134,004 | 100,948 | 234,952 | –33,056 | 24.1 | 35.5 | 60.8 | 47.9 | 56.1 |
| 1892 | 135,101 | 102,584 | 237,865 | –32,517 | 24.4 | 34.9 | 59.9 | 49.8 | 58.8 |
| 1893 | 151,363 | 116,632 | 267,995 | –34,731 | 27.5 | 38.8 | 59.4 | 57.2 | 67.0 |

| | | | | | | | | | |
|---|---|---|---|---|---|---|---|---|---|
| 1894 | 162,103 | 128,105 | 290,208 | –33,998 | 29.8 | 40.3 | 45.3 | 60.1 | 91.1 |
| 1895 | 171,697 | 143,293 | 314,990 | –28,404 | 32.4 | 45.6 | 45.8 | 66.3 | 96.4 |
| 1896 | 202,590 | 131,081 | 333,671 | –71,509 | 34.3 | 47.6 | 53.2 | 56.4 | 91.0 |
| 1897 | 202,829 | 163,501 | 366,330 | –39,328 | 37.6 | 47.6 | 49.7 | 61.6 | 85.7 |
| 1898 | 209,579 | 159,037 | 368,616 | –50,542 | 37.9 | 45.1 | 51.3 | 63.4 | 91.2 |
| 1899 | 264,748 | 195,785 | 460,533 | –68,963 | 47.3 | 50.9 | 69.2 | 62.5 | 68.5 |
| 1900 | 211,070 | 158,997 | 370,067 | –52,073 | 38.0 | 43.7 | 49.5 | 54.9 | 82.3 |
| 1901 | 268,303 | 169,657 | 437,960 | –98,646 | 45.0 | 55.5 | 62.5 | 59.8 | 85.4 |
| 1902 | 315,364 | 214,182 | 529,546 | –101,182 | 54.5 | 56.1 | 70.9 | 65.1 | 82.6 |
| 1903 | 326,739 | 214,352 | 541,091 | –112,387 | 55.6 | 54.0 | 65.1 | 59.8 | 85.5 |
| 1904 | 344,061 | 239,487 | 583,548 | –104,574 | 59.9 | 60.6 | 69.2 | 64.0 | 94.1 |
| 1905 | 447,101 | 227,888 | 674,989 | –219,213 | 69.3 | 62.5 | 96.6 | 62.5 | 89.8 |
| 1906 | 410,270 | 236,457 | 646,727 | –173,813 | 66.4 | 66.4 | 95.3 | 64.6 | 83.2 |
| 1907 | 416,401 | 264,381 | 680,782 | –152,020 | 69.9 | 67.2 | 88.7 | 67.1 | 84.3 |
| 1908 | 394,505 | 276,660 | 671,165 | –117,845 | 68.9 | 62.7 | 72.7 | 73.0 | 101.4 |
| 1909 | 418,158 | 338,993 | 757,151 | –79,165 | 77.8 | 70.1 | 77.1 | 92.9 | 105.1 |
| 1910 | 462,965 | 380,833 | 843,789 | –82,132 | 86.7 | 85.0 | 79.2 | 102.9 | 111.7 |
| 1911 | 471,504 | 377,338 | 848,842 | –94,166 | 87.2 | 82.3 | 80.9 | 102.1 | 111.7 |

* Total trade in current values divided by index of wholesale prices.

*Sources:* Yang Tuan-liu, *Statistics of China's foreign trade,* tables 1-3; Nankai Institute of Economics, *Nankai index numbers, 1936,* pp. 37-38; and Chi-ming Hou, *Foreign investment and economic development in China, 1840–1937,* pp. 194-98, for pre-1904 terms of trade.

hinterlands. The percentage distribution of China's principal imports is given in table 17, and exports are shown in table 18.

Silk and tea, which had been China's most important exports before the Treaty of Nanking, continued to occupy this position until the end of the Ch'ing dynasty. Their combined relative position in the export trade was, however, a diminishing one. Tea exports fell largely because of the inability of exporters in China to enforce quality standards among producers and middlemen in the face of growing Indian and Japanese competition. While the large absolute quantities of silk piece goods exported suggest the continued strength of a major rural handicraft industry, the new importance of bean oil, leather, flour, egg and egg products, and to a lesser extent ginned cotton exports, reflects the establishment from the turn of the century of numerous small handicraft workshops in the larger and medium-sized urban centers.

Hong Kong's large nominal share in China's foreign trade, combined with the lack of data before 1932 on goods shipped from and to Hong Kong, prevent an accurate statement of the proportions of trade with each foreign country. Table 19 presents an unadjusted percentage distribution of China's foreign trade for selected years, 1871–1911, while table 20 represents H. B. Morse's estimate for the Imperial Maritime Customs of the distribution of trade, which treats Hong Kong as a Chinese port and apportions its imports and exports among the several major trading countries. The United Kingdom was China's most important trading partner until the end of the nineteenth century—and on into the twentieth century if the entire British empire is considered. British predominance in the import trade is most notable, and as already indicated is accounted for by cotton piece goods from Lancashire and yarn and opium from India. The total British share, while it remained the largest, was a declining one. From the 1890s Japanese trade, spurred on by the provisions of the Shimonoseki Treaty and by Japan's post-1900 role in Manchuria, grew rapidly. The American and Russian shares in China's trade were also in general increasing ones.

Two general observations about the foreign trade which has just been described are pertinent here. First, although it was a growing commerce, as late as 1913 China's world trade per head of population (in US dollars: imports, \$0.94; exports, \$0.67; total, \$1.61) was the *lowest* of eighty-three countries for which League of Nations data were compiled. It is possible that the 1913 population of China was overstated in these estimates; but

TABLE 17
PERCENTAGE DISTRIBUTION OF CHINA'S PRINCIPAL IMPORTS, 1870-1910

| | Total value (HK taels 1,000) | Total % | Opium % | Cotton piece goods % | Cotton yarn % | Cereals, flour % | Sugar % | Tobacco % | Coal % | Kerosene % | Metals and minerals % | Machinery* % | Railway† materials, vehicles % | All other % |
|---|---|---|---|---|---|---|---|---|---|---|---|---|---|---|
| 1870 | 63,693 | 100 | 43.0‡ | 28.0 | 3.0 | 0.04 | 0.1 | — | 0.09 | — | 5.8 | — | — | 19.97‡ |
| 1880 | 79,293 | 100 | 39.3 | 24.9 | 4.6 | 0.1 | 0.4 | — | 1.2 | — | 5.5 | — | — | 24.0 |
| 1890 | 127,093 | 100 | 19.5 | 20.2 | 15.3 | 9.6 | 0.9 | — | 1.6 | 3.2 | 5.7 | 0.3 | — | 23.7 |
| 1900 | 211,070 | 100 | 14.8 | 21.5 | 14.3 | 7.0 | 3.0 | 0.5 | 3.1 | 6.6 | 4.7 | 0.7 | — | 23.8 |
| 1910 | 462,965 | 100 | 12.0 | 14.7 | 13.6 | 7.7 | 4.8 | 2.0 | 1.8 | 4.7 | 4.3 | 1.5 | 3.8 | 29.1 |

* Not recorded separately before 1886 † Not recorded separately before 1903 ‡ Estimated

*Sources:* Yang Tuan-liu, *Statistics of China's foreign trade*, table 5, pp. 15-25, table 9, pp. 43-48; Yu-kwei Cheng, *Foreign trade and industrial development of China*, p. 19.

TABLE 18
PERCENTAGE DISTRIBUTION OF CHINA'S PRINCIPAL EXPORTS, 1870-1910

| | Total value (HK taels 1,000) | Total % | Tea % | Silk, silk goods % | Seeds, oil % | Beans % | Hides, leather, skins % | Raw cotton % | Wool % | Coal % | Eggs, egg products % | Flour % | All other % |
|---|---|---|---|---|---|---|---|---|---|---|---|---|---|
| 1870 | 55,295 | 100 | 49.9 | 38.8 | 1.2 | 1.2 | — | 0.5 | — | — | — | 0.3 | 8.1 |
| 1880 | 77,884 | 100 | 45.9 | 38.0 | 0.1 | 0.2 | 0.5 | 0.2 | 0.4 | — | — | 0.2 | 14.5 |
| 1890 | 87,144 | 100 | 30.6 | 33.9 | 0.6 | 0.4 | 1.4 | 3.4 | 1.6 | — | — | 0.3 | 27.8 |
| 1900 | 158,997 | 100 | 16.0 | 30.4 | 2.5 | 1.9 | 4.3 | 6.2 | 1.9 | — | — | 0.8 | 36.0 |
| 1910 | 380,833 | 100 | 9.4 | 25.4 | 8.4 | 5.6 | 5.3 | 7.4 | 2.5 | 1.5 | 1.1 | 1.5 | 32.0 |

*Sources:* Yang Tuan-liu, *Statistics of China's foreign trade*, table 5, pp. 15-25, table 9, pp. 43-48; Yu-kwei Cheng, *Foreign trade and industrial development of China*, p. 19.

TABLE 19
PERCENTAGE DISTRIBUTION OF CHINA'S FOREIGN TRADE WITH PRINCIPAL TRADING PARTNERS, 1871-1911

| | Imports from | | | | | Exports to | | | | |
|---|---|---|---|---|---|---|---|---|---|---|
| | 1871-73 | 1881-83 | 1891-93 | 1901-03 | 1909-11 | 1871-73 | 1881-83 | 1891-93 | 1901-03 | 1909-11 |
| Hong Kong | 32.5 | 36.2 | 51.2 | 41.6 | 33.9 | 14.7 | 25.4 | 39.3 | 40.8 | 28.2 |
| Great Britain | 34.7 | 23.8 | 20.4 | 15.9 | 16.5 | 52.9 | 33.3 | 11.3 | 4.8 | 5.1 |
| Japan* | 3.7 | 4.9 | 4.7 | 12.5 | 15.5 | 1.7 | 2.4 | 7.2 | 12.5 | 15.9 |
| United States | 0.5 | 3.7 | 4.5 | 8.5 | 7.1 | 14.1 | 12.4 | 9.8 | 10.2 | 9.0 |
| Russia | 0.2 | 0.2 | 0.6 | 0.8 | 3.5 | 3.3 | 7.3 | 8.6 | 5.5 | 12.5 |
| Germany† | — | — | — | — | 4.2 | — | — | — | — | 3.1 |
| France† | — | — | — | — | 0.6 | — | — | — | — | 10.7 |
| Others | 28.4 | 31.2 | 18.6 | 20.7 | 18.7 | 13.3 | 19.2 | 23.8 | 26.2 | 15.5 |
| Total | 100.0 | 100.0 | 100.0 | 100.0 | 100.0 | 100.0 | 100.0 | 100.0 | 100.0 | 100.0 |

* includes Taiwan from 1895 † included in "Others" before 1909-11

*Source:* Yen Chung-p'ing, et al., comps., *Chung-kuo chin-tai ching-chi shih t'ung-chi tzu-liao hsuan-chi* (Selected statistics on China's modern economic history), tables 7-8, pp. 65-66.

even in the unlikely case that per capita foreign trade was double the figures given above, China would still be near the very bottom of the list of eighty-three. Professor Kuznets' studies have indicated that a negative correlation is to be expected between a country's size and its foreign trade as a proportion of national income. In the case of China this size factor was reinforced by an economic system with substantially autarchic economic cells, sustained by a relatively unchanging transport system.

The second observation is that, by and large, the inland distribution of foreign goods and, to a somewhat lesser extent, the assembly of exports were dominated by Chinese merchants and operated through the traditional channels of trade. "There is at present not a single Western merchant engaged in the cotton-goods import trade in the whole Yangtze Valley, except in Shanghai: English capital has been withdrawn from ports like Hankow, and has never been invested in the new ports like Ch'ungking," reported the Lancashire mission to China of 1896–97.[29] Eleven large Chinese dealers in Hankow regularly bought imported cloth and yarn in Shanghai through their agents. They then resold the goods to Hankow retailers and to merchants from lower level markets in Hunan and Honan who came to Hankow for their supplies. In 1896, there were five European firms in Chungking; only one of these dealt in imported cotton goods, China's most important import, and that was in a small way. The cotton trade in Chungking was in the hands of twenty-seven Chinese firms who, together with three firms in Chengtu and one in Chia-ting, each August sent their agents (often partners of the several firms) to Shanghai where they resided until May while they purchased and shipped cloth and yarn to Chungking. Lower level markets in Szechwan were supplied by local merchants who bought on credit from the Chungking dealers. In South China, agents or partners of firms in such relatively small centers as Linanfu in Yunnan bought directly from British importers in Hong Kong, the goods being shipped via Haiphong and entering China at Mengtze. While in the 1860s and into the 1870s branches of foreign firms, especially British, handled much of the importation of cotton goods into such ports as Hankow, these branches in the smaller treaty ports—which were the urban markets for large regional trading areas—were unable to develop permanent direct ties with rural Chinese distributors even at the central market level, not to speak of intermediate or basic markets. The Chinese firms with whom they dealt in Chinkiang or Hankow were located at the apex of the traditional marketing structure and had the advantage of local know-how and long-standing connections with lower level markets. Increasingly firms like those in Chungking mentioned above preferred to buy directly in Shanghai or Hong Kong where the selection of goods was larger and where they might benefit from competition among importers and frequent auction sales. Chinese and foreign steamship companies on the Yangtze were highly competitive and offered as favorable terms to Chinese merchants as to foreign. And, moreover, the Chefoo Convention of 1876 formalized the right of Chinese shippers transporting imported goods to obtain transit passes and thus nominal equality of taxation with the foreigner. It is perhaps only a small exaggeration, regarding the importation and distribution of the major staples of commerce, to describe the foreign trading firms in China as having been gradually transformed into Shanghai and Hong Kong commission agents serving the established Chinese commercial network. For some proprietary goods or those representing an advanced technology, networks of Chinese agents under direct foreign supervision were established from about the turn of the century. Some of the increasing Japanese trade after the Sino-Japanese War was also distributed by direct methods. But the bulk of the distribution of imports remained in Chinese hands.

TABLE 20
PERCENTAGE DISTRIBUTION OF CHINA'S FOREIGN TRADE (INCLUDING HONG KONG) WITH PRINCIPAL TRADING PARTNERS, 1899–1905

| | Imports from | | | Exports to | | |
|---|---|---|---|---|---|---|
| | average 1899–1903 | 1904 | 1905 | average 1899–1903 | 1904 | 1905 |
| Great Britain | 20.13 | 23.92 | 23.53 | 8.60 | 7.72 | 6.97 |
| British Dominions, etc. | 28.33 | 26.54 | 23.81 | 13.98 | 12.49 | 12.44 |
| (Total British empire) | (48.46) | (50.46) | (47.34) | (22.58) | (20.21) | (19.41) |
| Japan* | 18.26 | 18.06 | 16.13 | 12.70 | 15.51 | 14.03 |
| United States | 10.95 | 9.20 | 18.11 | 12.92 | 16.09 | 15.47 |
| Russia | 2.54 | 4.31 | 3.49 | 13.59 | 13.24 | 14.83 |
| Germany | 5.50 | 5.90 | 5.08 | 3.39 | 4.05 | 4.41 |
| France | 0.80 | 0.56 | 0.46 | 19.35 | 16.97 | 16.52 |
| Others | 13.32 | 11.51 | 9.40 | 15.47 | 13.93 | 15.33 |
| Total | 100.00 | 100.00 | 100.00 | 100.00 | 100.00 | 100.00 |

* includes Taiwan.

*Source:* Calculations by H. B. Morse in China, Inspectorate-General of Customs, *Returns of trade and trade reports, 1906*, pt. 1, p. 46.

The Chinese demand for imported goods was thus a limited one, and beyond the treaty ports this demand was supplied almost entirely through the traditional Chinese marketing system. On the export side the situation was similar, but there are indications of a somewhat greater foreign participation. The inability of foreign exporters in the treaty ports to exercise any quality control in the assembly of the annual tea crop was a major factor in the relative decline of China teas in foreign markets in the face of Indian, Ceylonese, and Japanese competition. On the other hand, foreigners played a direct role at least in the earlier development of the supply of such new exports as hog bristles, hides and leather, and eggs and egg products.

The stability of the traditional marketing system was, as I have stated, directly related to the technology and cost of transportation. By 1911 steamships and steam launches and the railroad had penetrated the interior of China only to a very limited extent. In 1865, the Ch'ing government prohibited the traffic of foreign steam launches in inland waters which had been tolerated during the Taiping Rebellion. But foreign- and Chinese-owned steam shipping among the treaty ports including those on the Yangtze, which was permitted by the treaties, expanded from the 1870s. In 1874, 17 American, 11 British, and 6 Chinese steamers were carrying freight on the Yangtze River and between Shanghai and other treaty ports. By 1894, 76 vessels owned by the China Merchants' Steam Navigation Co. and at least 51 owned by two British companies were in service on these routes. Smaller Chinese-owned steam launches were also beginning to ply between the treaty ports and inland cities not open to foreign traffic. The spread of the steam launch is apparent from the falling average tonnage of Chinese-owned steam vessels registered with the Imperial Maritime Customs: 1882, 737 tons; 1892, 247 tons; 1900, 35 tons. In 1898, in "compensation" for China's refusal to accept Great Britain's offer of a loan, the British government forced Peking to permit foreign-flag steamers to trade at the inland ports from which they had been excluded since 1865. By 1903, 614 Chinese and foreign steamers had registered for inland trade, a number which increased to 977 in 1909, 1,030 in 1910 and 1,130 (936 Chinese and 194 foreign) in 1913. These small river steamers brought cheaper and more rapid transportation to the traditional trade routes on the tributaries of the Yangtze and West rivers (360 of the total in 1909 were registered at Shanghai, 72 at Hankow and 277 at Canton), but they remained vastly overshadowed in numbers and total tonnage by the thousands of junks and rafts of all sizes which continued to carry the bulk of the inland trade.[30]

Similarly, although 9,244 kilometers of trunk and branch railway lines had been completed by 1917 (including 288 kilometers before 1895), the railway had only a limited impact upon the late-Ch'ing economy and commercial system—as opposed to its very considerable political consequences for the ultimate fate of the Manchu dynasty. China's pre-1912 railways affected the economy and marketing system little not only because their total mileage was, after all, extremely small, but also because the bulk of this track was opened only in the last few years of the dynasty. Moreover, such consequences as the railway did have in the first years of the Republic were seriously distorted by endemic civil war which commandeered railway lines for troop transport, diverted revenues to the maintenance of warlord armies, and neglected repairs to the roadbed and rolling stock.

With minor exceptions such as the 199 kilometers from Peking to Kalgan which were built by Chinese engineers largely with the profits of the Peking-Mukden line, China's pre-republican railways were financed mainly by foreign loans and constructed by foreign concessionaires. The Chinese Eastern Railway in Manchuria (1,481 kilometers) and the South Manchurian Railway mainline from Harbin to Dairen (944 kilometers) were completely Russian undertakings with only a thin veneer of Chinese participation; and the Shantung railway from Kiaochow to Tsinan (394 kilometers) was a German financed and operated line. Slightly more than one-third of the total railway mileage in 1912 was in Manchuria, and unquestionably the railway was important for increasing the export of Manchurian soybeans and for the steady growth of cotton goods imports in the first decade of the twentieth century. Harbin was in effect created by the Chinese Eastern Railway, and such ports as Newchwang and Chinwangtao which lacked navigable waterways in their hinterlands were dependent on the railway. The major trunk lines within China proper—the Peking-Hankow railway (1,215 kilometers) and the Tientsin-Pukow railway (1,009 kilometers)—ran from north to south and provided links between the North China plain and the Yangtze valley where only the inadequate Grand Canal had served before. While these two parallel lines were possibly to some degree an uneconomical duplication, in general the routes of the lines completed in this first spurt of railway construction were well located to open new territories as in Manchuria, and to compensate for the absence of navigable waterways in North China. A radial network, centering perhaps at Hankow, would have been theoretically more desirable, but in 1906 when the Peking-Hankow line was completed it was not possible to foresee the duplication of lines for political reasons as in Manchuria in the 1920s, the delay of several decades before Hankow was connected with Canton, and the failure to build westward to Szechwan before 1949. At the end of the Ch'ing dynasty the comment of the customs commissioner at Shasi in Hupei applied to all except the few major centers in North China and Manchuria which were connected by rail: "Shasi has no railway communication, and, being the center of a most extensive system of natural and artificial waterways, can dispense with any for many years."[31]

Though it may be contrary to the more common view, it does appear that the foreign merchant in late-Ch'ing China increasingly served rather than controlled the Chinese commercial system. The actual process of importing and exporting, however, which was conducted primarily at Shanghai and Hong Kong, remained almost completely in foreign hands until the 1920s. The principal link between the foreign merchant who spoke no Chinese and his customer or supplier from Chungking or Hankow who spoke no English was the comprador. While nominally employees of foreign firms, many compradors were traders on their own account in the goods handled by their employers. Their role in purchasing from Chinese dealers in exports and in arranging credit for buyers of imports provided unique opportunities to influence the flow of trade inward and outward—and to profit therefrom. Many of the original investors in Chinese-owned shipping, financial, and manufacturing enterprises were men who had grown wealthy as compradors of the leading foreign firms in Shanghai. The increase in the number of Chinese- and Japanese-owned export-import houses after 1911 (the Japanese apparently made greater efforts than the British or Americans to acquire some competence with the Chinese language) reduced the overall significance of the compradors as the link between foreign trade and the Chinese marketing system. In a somewhat truncated form, however, the institution lingered on.

Continued foreign dominance of the export-import process in the treaty ports was sustained by the role of foreign banks in China in financing foreign trade. From 1848, when the Oriental Banking Corporation established an office in Shanghai, the British enjoyed for forty years a virtual monopoly of modern-style banking in China. The two most important British-controlled firms were the Chartered Bank of India, Australia and China, whose first Chinese branch was opened in 1857, and the Hongkong and Shanghai Banking Corporation, which was established in 1865. German, Japanese, Russian, French, and American competitors began to appear

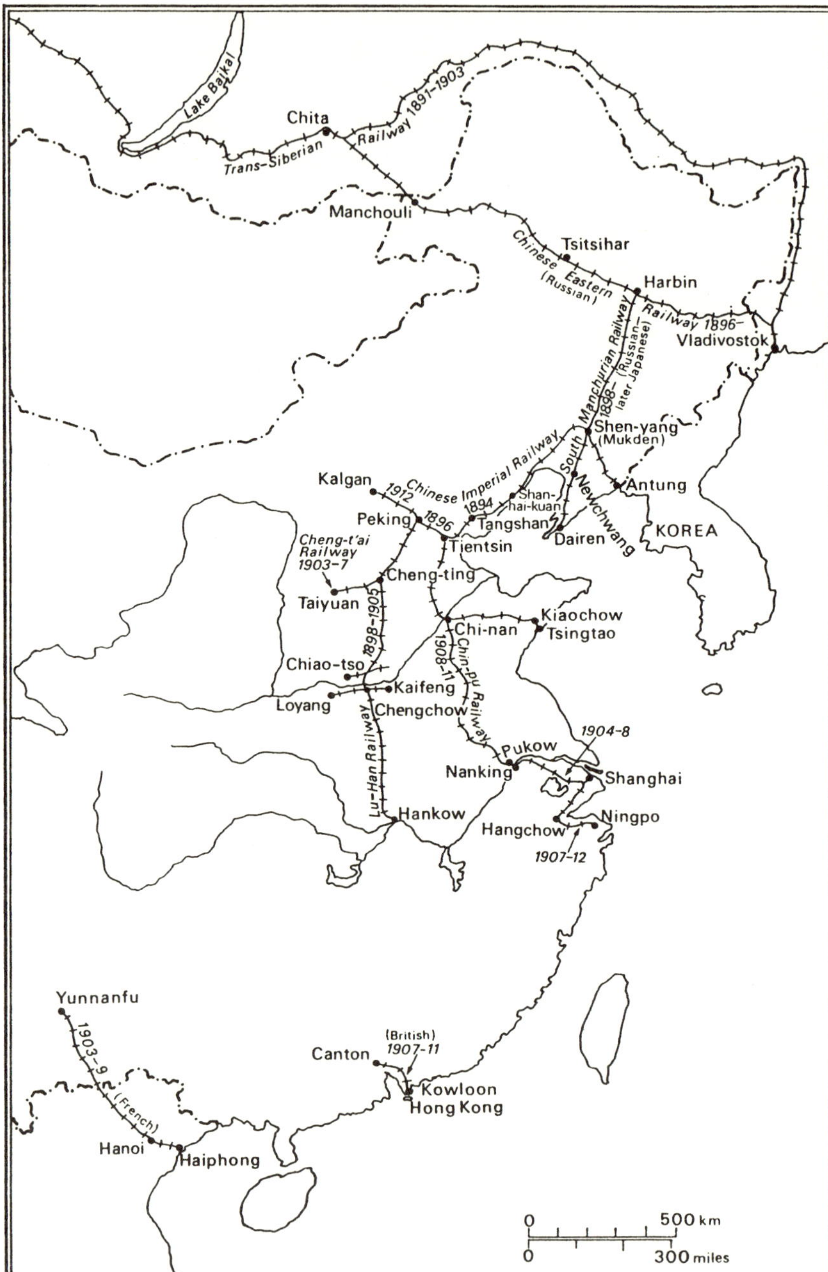


Map 3. Railway building, late Ch'ing

in the 1890s. Most of the advances of the foreign banks for financing imports and exports were made to foreign firms; direct loans to Chinese merchants were limited. Short-term credits were, however, allowed to "native banks" which in turn loaned funds to Chinese merchants. In effect, the foreign banks by virtue of their monopoly of the financing of foreign trade also controlled the foreign exchange market. They were the channel through which the flow of silver to and from China took place, and they determined the fluctuating gold price of silver. Until 1935 the official exchange rate in the Shanghai market was based on the daily quotations of the Hongkong and Shanghai Bank.

The first Chinese modern bank, the Chung-kuo t'ung-shang yin-hang (known before 1911 as the Imperial Bank of China), was established by Sheng Hsuan-huai in 1896, but no Chinese bank played a significant role in the financing of foreign trade until the Hu Pu Bank established in 1904 had evolved into the Bank of China in the Republican period. Between 1896 and 1911 sixteen modern-style Chinese banks were opened (of which only seven survived up to the 1930s). All their main offices and branches were located in the larger cities; and they maintained only small and indirect connections with the trade of the interior in the form of short-term advances to inland "native banks." Modern commercial banking did not begin to penetrate the traditional marketing system until the 1920s and 1930s, while its total influence was meager at best even after World War II. The bulk of local commerce in late-Ch'ing China, to the degree that it depended upon external credit at all, continued to be financed by old-style banks—one further indication that, other than in the major treaty ports, the structure of trade and the institutions which facilitated it had not changed greatly by 1911 from what they had been half a century before.[32]

## 5. Government and the Economy

The consequences of the Ch'ing political system for the Chinese economy have often been stated in terms of excessive and capricious taxation, omnipresent corruption, and a general disdain for commerce and the merchant. These are not matters simply to be disregarded—the ideological posture of "exalting agriculture and disparaging commerce" in particular requires examination that I cannot give it here. The fact is, however, that within the constraints of the traditional technology, as earlier sections of this chapter have demonstrated, late-Ch'ing China was possessed of a complex, commercialized, "developed" economy. Over the span of two centuries it had been able to support a growing population, had facilitated the "pacification" of immense territories beyond the boundaries of China proper, and until the late eighteenth century (with the exception of the Rebellion of the Three Feudatories in 1673–81) had seen an unusually lengthy era of internal peace, relative prosperity and effective rule. In modern terms the tax burden on the population, while sometimes capriciously administered, was light. Depravity found its place in China as in other societies, but much of what appeared to the treaty-port observer as "corrupt" represented the foreigner's inability to understand the informal but institutionalized *lou-kuei* ("customary exactions") which interpenetrated the highly rationalized fiscal system set forth in the official statutes of the dynasty. If the merchant was devalued in the official ideology and sometimes inordinately pressed for "contributions" to the government, this does not negate the fact that he might be rich. The average annual profit of the Liang-Huai salt transport monopoly in the eighteenth century was perhaps 5 million taels, which was shared by thirty principal transport merchants and some two hundred lesser dealers; an additional profit of 2 million taels was divided annually among some thirty factory merchants. The merchant might also be powerful, in particular within the rural marketing structure where the local elite in and out of office invested in commerce or usury through the merchant's auspices. In addition a merchant might be fortunate. His sons and grandsons, with ample leisure and strict instruction—and perhaps a purchased initial degree—might themselves enter the political elite. In short, for the maintenance, extension and prosperity of the traditional economy at a relatively constant level of per capita output, the ideology and administration of the state were at least neutral factors and almost never, except in recurrent periods of dynastic decay, major obstacles.

If, however, one's point of reference is economic development—either in the sense of increasing per capita national product or in the sense of industrialization (that is, the rapid growth of a modern manufacturing sector with or without an immediate increment in per capita product), then undoubtedly the late-nineteenth-century Chinese government was incapable of supplying positive assistance. Ideology, traditional fiscal practices, and the patterns of revenue and expenditure, were all obstacles to suitable action.

In the first spurt of industrialization in the more "backward" countries of Europe, Russia in the 1890s for example, as Professor Gerschenkron has shown,[33] the state budget substituted for deficient market demand and capital supply, which were sharply limited by the poverty of the agricultural sector. A similar role was played by the credit-creating operations of the industrial banks in less "backward" countries such as Germany and France. Neither alternative was available in late-Ch'ing China. As we have seen, apart from the important role of modern foreign banks in financing international trade, the pre-1911 banking system of China was almost entirely limited to transfer banks of the Shansi bank type and to local "native banks." The directors of China's first modern bank, the semi-official Imperial Bank of China, were primarily concerned with gaining control of the lucrative transfer of government funds between the provinces and Peking. When this project failed, they turned completely to conventional commercial banking. Neither of the two relatively small government banks established later (the Bank of Communications founded in 1908; and the Hu Pu Bank founded in 1904 and reorganized as the Ta-Ch'ing Bank in 1908) was intended to make industrial loans.

The failure of the Ch'ing government to promote a modern banking system which could foster industrial investment ultimately stemmed from the same causes which made it unable to invest in economic development from its own budget. In brief, the fiscal system of the central government like other aspects of its administration was quite superficial. Even in normal times the imperial bureaucracy, although highly centralized in its formal organization, did not penetrate very deeply into Chinese society including those aspects of society which constituted the economy. The central government normally confined its economic role to claiming its share of a relatively fixed economic product and to providing the internal order and external defenses which would permit that product to be reproduced from one year to the next. This was of course in accordance with the main stream of the Confucian political ideology. But at various times in the two millennia of empire the more activist Legalist strain in the Confucian-Legalist ideological amalgam which supported the imperial system had been drawn upon for departures from economic passivity, notably in the "reforms" of Wang Mang and Wang An-shih. Such departures, however, were perhaps particularly difficult for the ultra-conservative Manchu dynasty, always conscious of its foreign origin and determined to demonstrate its mandate by upholding Confucian orthodoxy. Thus as land under cultivation increased (until about 1800) and as the population grew slowly and unevenly (except for probable losses during the mid-nineteenth century rebellions), the total economic product of course grew in size. But for the central government, economic growth by the accretion of more units of roughly the same mix of factors of production was not an opportunity to increase its revenues and its participation in the economy. In 1712 the official rates for the most important imperial revenue, the land tax, were fixed in perpetuity by the K'ang-hsi Emperor; the provincial quotas due to Peking were to be raised only as new land was opened to cultivation and added to the tax rolls, increments which the provinces rarely recorded in their reports to the capital.

TABLE 21
ESTIMATED ANNUAL REVENUE AND EXPENDITURE
OF THE CENTRAL GOVERNMENT IN THE EARLY 1890S
(*K'u-p'ing* or treasury taels)

| | |
|---|---|
| *Revenue* | |
| land tax | 25,088,000 |
| grain tribute | 6,562,000 |
| salt gabelle (including salt likin) | 13,659,000 |
| likin on merchandise | 12,952,000 |
| maritime customs (1893) | 21,989,000 |
| native customs | 1,000,000 |
| duty and likin on domestic opium | 2,229,000 |
| miscellaneous taxes, sale of degrees, "contributions," etc. | 5,500,000 |
| Total | 88,979,000 |
| *Expenditure* | |
| central government administration, imperial household, stipends to Manchu garrisons | 19,478,000 |
| maritime customs administration | 2,478,000 |
| public works | 1,500,000 |
| modernized armies, coastal defense | 8,000,000 |
| defense of Manchuria | 1,848,000 |
| civil and military administration of Kansu and Central Asia | 4,800,000 |
| Northern Fleet | 5,000,000 |
| Southern Fleet | 5,000,000 |
| railway construction | 500,000 |
| grants-in-aid to Kwangsi, Kweichow, and Yunnan | 1,655,000 |
| Provincial administration, provincial troops | 36,220,000 |
| Principal and interest payments on foreign loans | 2,500,000 |
| Total | 88,979,000 |

*Source:* George Jamieson, *Report on the revenue and expenditure of the Chinese empire.*

However, as we shall see, it is evident that provincial and local tax collections retained their flexibility and flourished with the increasing size of the national product. Yet from the point of view of possible economic development as opposed to maintenance of an economic equilibrium, these new resources were completely neutralized. It remained an ideological possibility, even though remote, within the central government bureaucracy that Legalist *raison d'état* might be revived and motivate programs of economic development, To a limited extent this was done by the "self-strengtheners" of the late nineteenth century, such as Li Hung-chang, Chang Chih-tung, and Sheng Hsuan-huai, by the "reformers" of 1898, and by the late-Ch'ing reform movement after 1901. But local administration was pre-eminently the home of the Confucian "general will" until nearly the end of the dynasty. This was broader and more diffuse than the interest of the bureaucratic state *per se,* and reflected the preoccupation of the local elite with maintaining unchanged a society that was truly theirs. These people had been educated in and sustained by the Confucian ideal of rule by moral example. Although the "general will" was increasingly penetrated by anti-imperialist nationalism after 1900, this did not extend to an acceptance of the fiscal burdens of economic development. No effective initiatives for economic change could be expected here. Hence my attention in what follows to the disabilities of the central government—a weak branch to be sure, but none other offered even a foothold.

The statutory receipts recorded by the Peking government did not change significantly between 1712 and the third quarter of the nineteenth century. (For selected years the total central government receipts were: 1725, 36,106,483 taels; 1753, 39,767,292 taels; 1812, 43,343,978 taels; 1841, 38,600,750 taels.) Land tax supplied 75 to 80 per cent of the total. Provincial and local collections, however, continued to increase notwithstanding the freezing of land tax rates by the K'ang-hsi Emperor. Three principal devices were utilized to enlarge actual collections beyond the nominal quotas due to the central government. The first was a "meltage" fee (*hao-hsien*), in theory assessed to compensate for remittances in silver of less than the required purity and for losses in melting and casting silver ingots. In practice these losses were minimal; the meltage fee was in fact a tax increase beyond the rates sanctioned by K'ang-hsi. In 1724, this surtax received formal imperial recognition and in part was remitted to Peking for payment to officials as an annual bonus to "foster their honesty" (*yang-lien*), that is to compensate for inadequate salaries. The bulk of the collection, however, remained outside Peking's control. Secondly, local officials added a conventional sum for expenses of collection to the bill submitted to taxpayers. The third device was the relative freedom with which local magistrates set the exchange rates between nominal assessments in grain or silver and the number of copper cash per picul of grain or tael of silver which they would accept in full payment of the tax due.

In the mid-nineteenth century two major sources of revenue were added to the traditional land tax, salt gabelle and customs duty. The establishment of the foreign-operated Imperial Maritime Customs after 1854 regularized the collection of duties on foreign trade and channeled these receipts to the Peking government rather than to the provinces. The second new impost, in contrast, was almost entirely outside Peking's control. This was the likin (*li-chin*) which was originally instituted by provincial officials to finance their campaigns against the Taipings. It was first levied in 1853 in Kiangsu as an internal transit tax on grain passing through the Grand Canal. By 1862 it had been applied to nearly all commodities and had been adopted by nearly every province. In some cases likin was collected not only along the route of transit but also as a production tax at the point of origin or as a sales tax at the destination. The rate varied widely, from 1 to 10 per cent *ad valorem,* with the most common rate about 2 per cent at each tax barrier. Of the likin collections on merchandise reported annually by the provinces to the Hu Pu (Board of Revenue), only about 20 per cent was disposed of by the central government, the balance remaining under the *de facto* control of the provinces. The unreported collection, of unknown size, was also of course retained locally.

In addition some small and temporary increases in receipts from the salt gabelle and miscellaneous taxes were realized as a result of constant prodding by the Hu Pu in the 1870s and 1880s to meet the costs of a continuing series of crises: rebellion in Central Asia, the Ili dispute with Russia, the Sino-French War, floods and famines. The nearly doubled imperial revenue of the 1880s and 1890s as compared with mid-century receipts was, however, almost entirely accounted for by maritime customs duties and likin. For the immediate financing of such emergencies as Tso Tsung-t'ang's military expeditions and "pacification" of the north-west, to which traditional fiscal system was incapable of responding rapidly, the government was forced to turn to foreign loans. Before 1894 nine loans totaling 40 million taels were concluded, mostly for military expenses. These funds were advanced by foreign firms in the treaty ports, not foreign governments. By the outbreak of the Sino-Japanese War, 33 million taels in principal and interest had been repaid, largely from maritime customs revenue.

Table 21 shows estimates of Peking's revenue from all sources and of the major items of expenditure in a typical year in the early 1890s. The revenue figures do not represent actual remittance of tax receipts to the capital; they are the amounts reported to the Hu Pu yearly (in two installments). They were then stored in money or in kind in the several provincial treasuries to await allocation by the Hu Pu. No composite budget of income and expenditure was prepared by the central treasury. (One of the unrealized projects of the reformers was the establishment of a regular national budget.) Rather, items of recurring expenditure had gradually come to be charged piecemeal against the yields of specific taxes in particular provinces. Eventually one part of the reported total was retained by the provinces to cover local civil and military expenses for the ensuing period, a second portion was remitted to Peking (or elsewhere at the direction of the Hu Pu), and in some cases a third part was transferred as grants-in-aid to other provinces. The fiscal system was oriented to short-range operations and the weight of traditional practices made it incapable of responding rapidly to emergency needs. As a result of the Taiping and other mid-century rebellions Peking's control of the revenue sources of the empire had been weakened and the fiscal system was severely strained. In contrast to the last seventeen years of the dynasty, however, with the assistance of new revenues the government's civil and military expenditures until 1894 were met without major borrowing from abroad, and the normal income was stretched to amortize the costs of the relatively modest foreign loans that were made. Little, of course, was realized from the substantial investment in a modernized navy and foreign-style armies, as the meager results of the pre-1895 *yang-wu* (foreign matters) military and industrial projects testify.

As already noted, the revenue reported annually to Peking represented only a portion of the total tax collection of the empire. The share of the potential fiscal resources of the country which the central government could control was largely inelastic. It had no chance to increase revenue from the growth of foreign trade, because tariff rates could not be changed without the unanimous consent of the treaty powers, and it had only a limited ability to manipulate the salt gabelle and various minor taxes. Several estimates of total national tax revenues have been made; while none is more than an intelligent guess so far as the absolute total is concerned, collectively they are strong evidence that the total annual tax collection at all levels in the last decade of the Manchu dynasty was more than twice the amount reported to Peking. A recent examination of the provincial *Ts'ai-cheng shuo-ming-shu* (Descriptions of financial administration), which are the reports of the Financial Reorganization Bureaux set up by imperial decree in each of the provinces in 1909, suggests that the total tax revenue for 1908 was 292 million taels.[34] H. B. Morse in his account of revenue and expenditure in *The trade and administration of the Chinese empire* offers a minimum total of 284,154,000 taels for the early 1900s apportioned as follows: imperial administration, 99,062,000 taels; provincial administration, 142,374,000 taels; local administration, 42,718,000 taels. Finally, the imperial "budget" for 1911 prepared by the Tzu-cheng yuan (Consultative Assembly) estimated total central and provincial income at 301,910,297 taels (including, it may be noted, likin collections of 44,176,541 taels which should be compared with the 12-15 million taels reported annually by the provinces, and non-tax revenues of 92 million taels). In contrast to Meiji Japan, where the land-tax revision of 1873 brought the major revenue sources of the country under the direct control of the new central government, the late-Ch'ing government was ideologically and politically incapable of extending its control of the revenue.

If we assume that total collections in the latter part of the dynasty were about 250 million taels and that Peking's share came to 100 million taels, what part of the national income was available for government expenditure? Only the crudest estimate is of course possible in the absence of reliable national income data. If Chang Chung-li's "rough estimate of the annual gross national product in the 1880s" is adjusted for its understatement of the agricultural product, GNP in the late-nineteenth century may have been about 3,338,757,000 taels (see table 1 above). Total government revenue would then come to 7.5 per cent of GNP and the Peking government's share to 3 per cent.[35] These proportions are, as I have acknowledged, subject to a very wide margin of error. With this caveat in mind, it is instructive to note that proportions of this general order of magnitude for the share of government consumption in GNP are also to be found in several Western European countries and in the United States in the mid nineteenth century.[36] Economic development in these less "backward" countries was set in motion without any major direct assistance from the government budget.

The contrast with China of course lies in the greater quantity and quality, within the Western governments' total consumption, of expenditures for health and education and for general administrative, legislative and adjudicative services (including commercial and marketing services) which fostered a climate in which the private sector could profitably invest in new enterprises. China's problem was thus not only that a manifestly small proportion of GNP was subject to government control, and that only 40 per cent of even that total was available to the central authorities. Of equal and perhaps greater consequence was the fact that almost all of the increase in central government expenditure was for military purposes, mainly to suppress internal rebellion but also in response to a number of minor external crises. This was so even though this expenditure doubled in the course of the nineteenth century—compare table 21 with the examples cited of annual receipts for selected earlier years. Government services, such as they were, were not significantly augmented; nor was there any important departure from their traditional limitation, which was the maintenance of order and the collection of taxation with which to support the emperor and his bureaucracy. Perhaps the Ch'ing government—aroused now by anti-imperialist nationalism—after 1900 was ideologically prepared to do more. But both political weakness and fiscal stringency kept actual expenditures on such items as the new school system and industrial promotion to a low level.

After 1895 the triple demands of indemnity payments, servicing large foreign loans, and military expenditure wrecked the rough balance between income and outlay which Peking had precariously maintained until that time. Even as the prevalent ideological note was changing from "exalt agriculture and disparage commerce" to "enrich the nation and strengthen its military power," the imperial government was without the facilities to reverse the largely passive economic role it had hitherto assumed, even if it had wanted to do so. And despite the rise of nationalism, conservative resistance to change including modern economic growth remained strong until the end of the dynasty.

Between 1894 and 1911 the Ch'ing government contracted for loans from foreign lenders amounting to 746,220,453 *k'u-p'ing* taels. Of this total 330,587,160 taels was accounted for by loans for railway construction which were to be repaid from the revenue of the lines themselves. While the several contracts granted the foreign mortgagees *de facto* operating privileges and handsome commissions on the purchase of material, repayment of principal and interest on the railway loans did not represent a direct burden on the ordinary budget of the central government. Relatively small amounts were borrowed for industrial purposes (25,517,349 taels), to finance telegraph lines and equipment (5,452,783 taels), and for miscellaneous uses (647,812 taels). The industrial loans consisted mainly of advances by Japanese creditors to the semi-official Hanyehping Coal and Iron Co. Hanyehping was unable to repay these loans and fell deeper and deeper into debt to the lenders, thus providing the pretext for the inclusion of formal recognition of Japanese control over the company in the Twenty-one Demands of 1915.

TABLE 22
MILITARY AND INDEMNITY LOANS, 1894–98

| | Face amount (in *k'u-p'ing tael equivalents*) | Underwriter | Security |
|---|---|---|---|
| 7% Silver Loan of 1894 | 10,000,000 | Hongkong and Shanghai Bank | maritime customs |
| 6% Sterling Loan of 1895 | 18,653,961 | Hongkong and Shanghai Bank | maritime customs |
| 6% Gold Loan of 1895 | 6,217,987 | Arnhold, Karberg & Co. (for National Bank für Deutschland) | Kiangsu salt likin/ maritime customs |
| 6% Gold Loan of 1895 | 6,217,987 | Cassel Bank | maritime customs |
| 4% Gold Loan (Franco-Russian) of 1895 | 98,968,370 | Syndicate of Paris and St. Petersburg banks | maritime customs |
| 5% Sterling Loan (Anglo-German) of 1896 | 97,622,400 | Hongkong and Shanghai Bank/Deutsch-Asiatische Bank | maritime customs |
| 4½% Gold Loan (Anglo-German) of 1898 | 112,776,780 | Hongkong and Shanghai Bank/Deutsch-Asiatische Bank | likin/salt likin/ maritime customs |
| Total | 350,457,485 | | |

*Source*: Hsu I-sheng, *Chung-kuo chin-tai wai-chai shih t'ung-chi tzu-liao, 1853–1927* (Statistical materials on the history of China's foreign loans, 1853–1927), pp. 28-31.

Apart from the large sums for railway construction, the funds were borrowed principally for the military costs of the Sino-Japanese War (119,838,648 taels) and to finance the large war indemnity which China was required to pay to the victor (263,176,701 taels). These totals include several short-term advances; the seven major long-term military and indemnity loans are shown in table 22. Payment of principal and interest on these loans required an annual outlay of some 20 million taels in addition to the normal annual expenditure summarized in table 21. From where did these funds come? All but two of the loans in table 22 were entirely secured on the maritime customs revenue. The Arnhold Karberg loan of 1895 was secured as a first charge on the salt likin of Kiangsu and as a second charge on the customs revenue. The 1898 Anglo-German loan was secured on the unencumbered portion of the customs revenue (which in view of the earlier loans was small in 1898) and on the revenue of seven salt and likin collectorates in the Yangtze basin which were placed under the supervision of the Inspector-General of Customs. This, however, is only the beginning of the matter. Customs revenue between 1890 and 1900 remained fairly stable at about 22-23 million taels per annum. Its allocation to service the foreign debt left the Hu Pu with a substantial deficit in its regular accounts—at least 1,6,700,000 taels in 1900 according to the Board's estimate. Ultimately the loan payments were made by increasing salt prices several times, reducing some salaries and emoluments, raising the tax on domestic opium, increasing market taxes and other miscellaneous levies, enlarging slightly the likin remitted to Peking, and so on—all traditional measures, and each the result of a protracted negotiation with the provincial authorities. The payments were made as scheduled, but until 1902 the fiscal system was in chaos. Of some interest is an attempt to float a public domestic loan—China's first—in 1898: 100 million taels of "Sincerity Bonds" paying 5 per cent and redeemable in twenty years were offered. Perhaps as much as 10 million taels' worth of bonds were sold before cries of extortion by the local elite and merchants brought the experiment to a close. There was little public confidence in the "full faith and credit" of the Ch'ing government and no banking system to absorb government bonds at a huge discount as was so often done in the Republican era.

On top of the annual requirements for the service of the loans listed in table 22, from 1902 at least an equal amount had to be found to meet the annual Boxer indemnity payments. In the last years of the dynasty, loan service and Boxer payments together came to 46-47 million taels per annum. Part of the added outlay was obtained from increased customs revenue collections after the 1902 tariff revision and from the receipts of native customs stations placed under the Inspectorate of Customs by the Boxer protocol. It is instructive, however, that three-quarters of the Boxer payments until the fall of the dynasty were met by regular annual remittances by the provinces of land tax, salt and likin funds above the quotas shown in table 21. The extraction by Peking from the provinces—in spite of strong protests and without the inconclusive bargaining of 1895–1901—of more than 18 million taels annually which had previously been outside its control was of course only possible in the extraordinary circumstances of a *de facto* occupation of North China by foreign armies. But this and the other funds raised more fitfully are evidence that the late-Ch'ing economy was not without some potential for savings. The missing factors were both the ideological sanction and the political power to mobilize this potential for productive investment.

A total of 476,982.,000 taels in principal and interest was paid between 1895 and 1911 to foreign creditors on account of the Boxer indemnity and the three loans (Russo-French, two Anglo-German) from which the war indemnity to Japan was met. This represented a large net drain on China's available resources. (If the four military loans were included, payments would rise to 547,552,066 taels, but let us allow that military expenditure is an essential service and does not represent a net loss of resources in the sense that an indemnity does.) The sum of 476,982,000 taels is one-and-a half times as much as the total amount borrowed from foreign lenders for railway construction before 1912. It is more than twice the size of the total initial capitalization of all the foreign, Sino-foreign and Chinese-owned manufacturing enterprises established between 1895 and 1913. Apart from the growth of maritime customs revenue in the dynasty's last decade, this enormous outflow of funds from the Chinese economy came ultimately from increased taxes on the population levied by local collectors and remitted to the central government for payment to foreign creditors.

The Ch'ing did not fall, however, primarily because the populace rose up against excessive taxation. Quite the contrary. By 1911 both its political and its fiscal resources were equally superficial and superfluous. When the Peking government after 1900 slowly began to break through the ideological resistance to engaging in "national development" in its various aspects, it not only lacked the political control required (though it set out to get it); it was also saddled with foreign debts which preempted the fiscal resources with which it might have got started. But the process of acquiring these debts had been the blunt, educative instrument which had led the government to begin to broaden its objectives. So there is, perhaps, in all of this an element of tragic inevitability.

Slowly and on a very small scale, the "traditional" Chinese economy had begun to change in the second half of the nineteenth century. The changes were not, however, of the kind to encourage the expectation either that the economic system would be radically restructured ("modernized," "industrialized") with the mere passage of a few decades, or that the basically unaltered economy had a capacity to continue the growth along traditional lines which it had displayed until about 1800. The plain facts are that by the mid-nineteenth century, if not earlier, China's economy had reached the limits of development possible with the technology (mechanical and organizational) at its disposal, and that by 1911 very little new ("advanced," "modern") technology had been imported and adopted or generated internally. Neither the state nor the private sector, moreover, was ideologically and fiscally competent to promote "economic development" as a priority policy.

On the other hand, in spite of sectoral and local strains, by the end of the Ch'ing dynasty there was little to suggest that this economic system was in mortal agony, ripe to be overthrown and discarded. Much of the population lived close to—but still at a distance from, it is important to state—a minimum level of subsistence. Social disorder and class conflict were endemic. But rather than being symptoms of fundamental systemic malignancies, this turbulence seems to have oscillated in scope and intensity with the occurrence of temporary and largely random crises exogenous to the economic system itself: flood and drought, seasonal crop failures, banditry and civil war, foreign incursions, official corruption. Eventually, in the absence of technological advancements, the inexorable pressure of population on land could be expected to threaten the viability of the whole economy. A confrontation of this magnitude was, however, not yet on the agenda at the beginning of the twentieth century. In "normal"' years the population, rural and urban, could be provided for, however poorly.

As it happened the ideological and political components of the *ancien régime* collapsed and were discarded earlier than those that may be properly described as economic. When new political forces turned consciously to the task of economic development, they perhaps overconfidently assumed that the traditional economy too had been substantially undermined in the revolutionary century before 1949. They thought there was nothing inherent in the basic values or structure of the Chinese economy which would prevent rapid economic growth once the onerous fetters on the people's strength had been removed. That hope continues to haunt Peking.

# II. Economic Trends in the Republic, 1912–49

## 1. Introduction: An Overview

To survey the history of the Chinese economy from the end of the Manchu dynasty to the establishment of the People's Republic is inevitably to tell a tale in a minor key. The years prior to 1949 saw no "take-off" towards sustained growth of aggregate output and the possibility of increased individual welfare that might accompany it. At best, the great majority of Chinese merely sustained and reproduced themselves at the subsistence level to which, the callous might say, they had long since become accustomed. In the bitter decade of war and civil war which began in the mid-1930s, the standard of life for many fell short even of that customary level.[1]

A cautious weighing of what little is definitely known suggests that aggregate output grew only slowly during 1912–49, and that there was no increase in per capita income. Nor was there any downward trend in average income. Although a small modern industrial and transport sector, which first appeared in the late nineteenth century, continued to grow at a comparatively rapid rate, its impact was minimal before 1949. The relative factor supplies of land, labor, and capital remained basically unaltered. The occupational distribution of the population was hardly changed; nor in spite of some expansion of the urban population was the urban-rural ratio significantly disturbed during these four decades. While some new products were introduced from abroad and from domestic factories, quantitatively they were a mere dribble, and they scarcely affected the quality of life. Institutions for the creation of credit remained few and feeble; the organization of a unified national market was never achieved. Foreign trade was relatively unimportant to the majority of the population. Throughout rural

China a demographic pattern of high birth rates and high death rates persisted. Economic hardship, in rural China in particular, was endemic, and probably grew more critical after the outbreak of war in 1937. Yet in the absence of a profound transformation of values in a significant portion of the elite leadership of Chinese society, which led ultimately to the harnessing of this distress to political ends not directly determined by the processes of the economy itself, there is no good reason to believe that the economic system would either have collapsed catastrophically or advanced rapidly towards modern economic growth. As a system, China's economy which was "pre-modern" even in the mid-twentieth century ceased to be viable only after 1949—and then as a consequence of explicit political choice by the victorious Communist Party and not primarily as a result of lethal economic contradictions.

While the quantitative indicators do not show large changes during the republican era, China in 1949 was nevertheless different from China in 1912. The small industrial and transport sector and, perhaps even more, the reservoir of technical skills and of experience with complex economic organizations—the hundreds of thousands of workers, technicians, and managers who had themselves "become modern"—provided a base upon which the People's Republic could and did build.

As a crude first approximation, the Chinese economy prior to 1949 may be described as consisting of a large agricultural (or rural) sector encompassing approximately 75 per cent of the population and a much smaller non-agricultural (or urban) sector with its principal base in the semi-modern treaty-port cities. Rural China grew the agricultural products which constituted 65 per cent of national output, and also made use of the handicrafts, petty trade, and old-fashioned transport. To the urban sector was attached, with ties of varying strength, an agricultural hinterland. It was located mainly along rivers and railways leading to the ports, and may be differentiated from the mass of rural China by the greater degree to which it traded with the coastal and riverine cities of the urban sector.

The agricultural sector was composed mainly of 60 to 70 million family farms. Perhaps one-half were owner-operated, one-quarter were farmed by part-owners who rented varying portions of their land, and the remaining quarter was cultivated by tenant farmers. These families lived in the several hundred thousand villages that filled most of the landscape of the arable parts of China. In the course of the first half of the twentieth century the average size of these farms decreased as the growth of population exceeded the increments to arable land. Only a few areas in rural China (in the regions of dense population) lacked agglomerated settlements—parts of Szechwan, for example, where scattered farmsteads were the norm. The typical landscape was dotted with clusters of houses arranged along one or more streets that were surrounded by the village fields. So closely spaced were the villages in the areas of densest settlement that one was usually within sight of another. In response to local disorder in the nineteenth century many villages, first in North China and then also in the south, had erected protective walls so that the village was defined in terms of the inhabitants living within its earthen or brick ramparts. This definition proved compatible with the lineage system insofar as many village populations shared the same or a small number of different surnames. The boundaries between the fields of the residents of one village and those owned by its closest neighbors were not, however, so unambiguously distinguishable. In the course of time farm land changed hands, and it was not unusual for the mortgagee (and possible eventual owner) of property in village A to be a resident of village B, or even of village X at some distance removed from A.

This indeterminacy of village boundaries began to change only in the latter part of the nineteenth century when increased tax demands by hsien (county) governments made it essential that the villages be concerned about the precise areas in which the new levies would be collected. Even in the twentieth century, while more formal village organizations were elaborated, the rural village was usually not an effective political unit, certainly not for the purpose of organizing its human and material resources for economic development. Indeed, the frequent inability of higher levels of government before 1949 to penetrate into the basic "natural" units of Chinese society except to collect taxes was one factor perpetuating China's traditional economy into the middle of the twentieth century.

Household and village were natural social units, not imposed by the state as the revived *pao-chia* (registration and police) system was from the 1920s onwards; but the peasant's horizon was not bounded by them. The normal limits of social interaction were not the village boundaries, but rather the borders of a higher order community composed of several (a dozen or more) villages and the market town which served them. A high proportion of China's farm households produced all or much of their own food, but grains, cash crops, local agricultural specialties, as well as the products of household handicraft—perhaps 30 per cent by value of farm

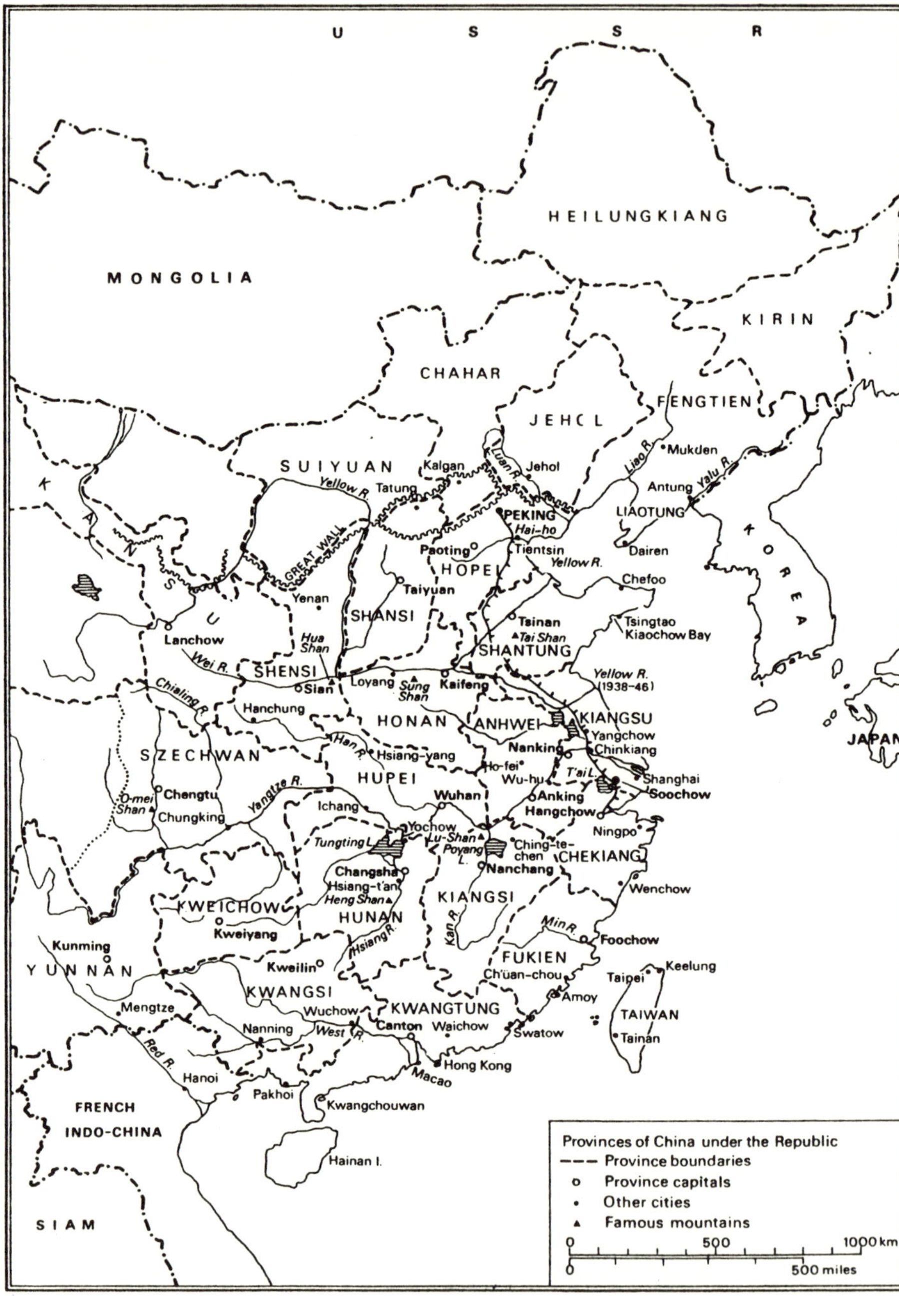


Map 4. Provinces of China under the Republic

output—were regularly marketed. The peasant sector in fact consisted of a large number of local market areas, each one roughly defined by a radius equal to the distance which a peasant buyer or seller and his products might cover on foot in one day.

The markets were normally periodic rather than continuous, occurring every few days according to one of several scheduling systems that were characteristic of different regions in China. Skinner, who refers to these basic units as "standard marketing areas" (SMA), has suggested that "the rural countryside of late traditional China can be viewed as a grid of approximately 70,000 hexagonal cells, each an economic system focused on a standard market."[2] The bulk of the trading in standard markets consisted of a horizontal exchange of goods among peasants. To some extent there was an upward flow out of the SMA of handicraft items and local agricultural specialties; the principal outflow of staples, however, consisted of tax grains to the government level of the economy. Increasingly in the late-nineteenth and twentieth centuries the SMA was the ultimate destination of new commodities either manufactured in the treaty ports or imported from abroad.

To the limited extent that rural China began to produce staples for export, including technical crops for the treaty-port factories, these tended to move in new commercial channels alternative to the traditional periodic markets. In the agricultural hinterland of the east coast treaty ports, in particular, a modern town economy developed alongside the periodic-marketing economy. But in the vast area of rural China the traditional market structure was flourishing with few signs of decay right down to 1949, a strong indication that the rural economy had not been substantially transformed. The peasant household in the mid-twentieth century probably depended more on commodities not produced by itself or by its neighbors than was the case 50 years earlier. But, because there was little real improvement in transportation at the local level, the primary marketing area was not enlarged so as to bring about a radical replacement of standard markets by modern commercial channels organized around larger regional marketing complexes.

Non-agricultural, or "urban," does not necessarily imply "modern." At the beginning of the nineteenth century perhaps as many as 12 million people, 3 to 4 per cent of the then 350 million Chinese, lived in cities with populations of 30,000 or more. With few exceptions, these cities were primarily administrative centers—the national capital, Peking, with nearly one million inhabitants, major provincial capitals, and the largest prefectural (*fu*) cities. Some were simultaneously important centers of inter-provincial and inter-regional commerce like Nanking, Soochow, Hankow, Canton, Foochow, Hangchow, Chungking, Chengtu, and Sian. These cities were the loci of the highest officials of the empire, the major military garrisons, the wealthiest merchant groups, and the most skilled artisans. Their populations included, too, prominent non-official gentry, lesser merchants, the numerous underlings who staffed the government yamens, laborers and transport workers, as well as the little-studied literate stratum of monks, priests, jobless lower-degree holders, failed examination candidates, demobilized military officers, and the like who were part of the "transients, migrants and outsiders"[3] so prominent in the traditional Chinese city. But the patterns of late-Ch'ing city life, political and economic, greatly resembled what they had been under the Sung dynasty, five centuries earlier.

From the mid-nineteenth century onwards, as a consequence of the establishment of a foreign presence in China, the Chinese city began to add modern economic, political, and cultural roles to those which continued from late-traditional times. The total number of urban residents grew slowly in the course of the nineteenth century, at a rate not much greater than total population growth; and then more rapidly between 1900 and 1938, at almost twice the average population growth rate. Cities with populations over 50,000 in 1938 included approximately 27.3 million inhabitants, 5 to 6 per cent of a total population of 500 million. These same cities had had perhaps 16.8 million inhabitants at the turn of the century, 4 to 5 per cent of a 430 million population. The difference suggests an annual growth rate for all large cities of about 1.4 per cent. China's six largest cities—Shanghai, Peking, Tientsin, Canton, Nanking, and Hankow—however, were growing at rates of 2 to 7 per cent per annum in the 1930s.[4]

By the start of the First World War 92 cities had been formally opened to foreign trade and while some of these "treaty ports" were places of minor importance, a high proportion of China's largest cities were among them. (Some notable exceptions were Sian, Kaifeng, Peking, Taiyuan, Wuhsi, Shaoshing, Nanchang, Chengtu). The treaty ports were the termini of the railway lines which began to appear in the 1890s, and of the steam shipping which spread along China's coast and on the Yangtze and West Rivers. Foreign commercial firms opened branches and agencies in the larger treaty ports, and under the provisions of the Treaty of Shimonoseki of 1895, foreigners were permitted to operate manufacturing enterprises (some had done so illegally before 1896). Chinese firms specializing in foreign trade and its adjuncts made their appearance parallel to the arrival of the foreigner. While not restricted to the open ports, most of the small but growing Chinese-owned industrial sector which began to appear in the 1870s was also located in these same cities. In the shadow of the modern factories, Chinese and foreign, handicraft workshops flourished either as subcontractors or, as in the case of cotton weaving, as major customers for the output of the new spinning mills. The processing of exports, too, still largely a handicraft operation, burgeoned in the major port cities. For a small number of urban dwellers, in addition to manufacturing and commerce a number of new occupations in the free professions, in journalism and publishing, and in modern educational and cultural institutions, gradually came into being.

But this modern industrial, commercial and transport sector for the most part remained confined to the treaty ports. Only to a very limited degree did it replace traditional handicrafts, existing marketing systems, or transport by human and animal backs, carts, sampans, and junks. There was almost no spill-over into the agricultural sector, for example, in the form of improved technology (new seeds, chemical fertilizer, modern water control, farm machinery) or more efficient organization (credit, stable marketing, rationalized land use).[5] The fluctuations of world markets for silver or for China's agricultural exports, experienced directly first in the treaty ports, could at times send ripples of influence into the countryside. Overall, however, the peasant sector and the treaty-port economy remained only very loosely linked until 1949.

## 2. Population

Diminishing returns have probably been reached in the manipulation of available Chinese population statistics. The census-registration of 1953–54 which reported a population of 585 million for mainland China, is the nearest to an accurate count of the population of China that has ever been made. This large number is at odds with such estimates as the Kuomintang official figure of 463,493,000 for 1948; but this figure together with several dozen other official and private estimates have been based more on guesswork than was the 1953–54 census, whatever its technical shortcomings.[6] A population of approximately 580 million in 1953 fits quite well a putative

TABLE 23
OCCUPATIONAL DISTRIBUTION, 1933

| | | millions | % of 500 million |
|---|---|---|---|
| Total population | | 500.00 | 100.00 |
| *A. Agricultural population* | | 365.00 | 73.00 |
| 1. Working population, aged 7-64 | | 212.30 | 42.46 |
| a. Agriculture only | | 118.78 | 23.76 |
| b. Joint agriculture and subsidiary occupations | | 93.52 | 18.70 |
| i. Agriculture | = man-labor units apportioned to each part of joint occupations | 86.13 | 17.23 |
| ii. Industry | | 3.61 | 0.72 |
| iii. Trade | | 1.66 | 0.33 |
| iv. Transport | | 1.14 | 0.23 |
| v. Other non-agricultural occupations† | | 0.98 | 0.20 |
| 2. Children under 7 | | 71.21 | 14.24 |
| 3. Students, aged 7 and over | | 5.13 | 1.02 |
| 4. Aged 65 and over | | 10.99 | 2.20 |
| 5. Unemployed or idle, aged 7-64‡ | | 65.36 | 13.07 |
| *B. Non-agricultural population* | | 155.00 | 27.00 |
| 1. Working population, aged 7-64§ | | 46.91 | 9.38 |
| a. Factories | | 1.13 | 0.23 |
| b. Handicrafts | | 12.13 | 1.43 |
| c. Mining | | 0.77 | 0.15 |
| d. Utilities | | 0.04 | 0.01 |
| e. Construction | | 1.55 | 0.31 |
| f. Trade | | 13.22 | 2.64 |
| g. Transport | | 10.16 | 2.03 |
| h. Other non-agricultural occupations | | 7.91 | 1.58 |
| 2. Children | | | |
| a. Under 7 | | 26.33 | 5.26 |
| b. Under 12 | | 43.86 | 8.77 |
| 3. Students | | | |
| a. Aged 7 and over | | 5.74 | 1.15 |
| b. Aged 12 and over | | 0.60 | 0.12 |
| 4. Aged 65 and over | | 4.08 | 0.82 |
| 5. Unemployed or idle‡ | | | |
| a. Aged 7-64 | | 51.94 | 10.39 |
| b. Aged 12-64 | | 39.56 | 7.91 |

* Manufacturing, home industries, mining, utilities, and construction.

† Professional and public service, etc.

‡ Including housewives.

§ Actual age of the working non-agricultural population falls mostly within the range 12-64; the age of 7 is taken as the lower limit merely for the convenience of grouping on the same basis as the agricultural working population.

*Source:* Liu Ta-chung and Yeh Kung-chia, *The economy of the Chinese mainland: national income and economic development, 1933–1959*, pp. 185 and 188, tables 54 and 55.

TABLE 24
DOMESTIC PRODUCT, 1933 (billion 1933 Chinese $)

| Net value added in: | Liu-Yeh | | Ou |
|---|---|---|---|
| 1. Agriculture | 18.76 | | 12.59 |
| 2. Factories | 0.64 | | |
| a. Producers' goods | | 0.16 | 0.38 |
| b. Consumers' goods | | 0.47 | |
| 3. Handicrafts | 2.04 | | |
| a. Identified portion | | 1.24 | 1.36 |
| b. Others | | 0.80 | |
| 4. Mining | 0.21 | | 0.24 |
| 5. Utilities | 0.13 | | 0.15 |
| 6. Construction | 0.34 | | 0.22 |
| 7. Modern transport and communications | 0.43 | | |
| 8. Old-fashioned transport | 1.20 | | 0.92 |
| 9. Trade | 2.71 | | |
| a. Trading stores and restaurants | | 1.75 | 2.54 |
| b. Peddlers | | 0.96 | |
| 10. Government administration | 0.82 | | 0.64 |
| 11. Finance | 0.21 | | 0.20 |
| 12. Personal services | 0.34 | | 0.31 |
| 13. Residential rents | 1.03 | | 0.93 |
| (Less: double counting of banking service) | | | (–0.17) |
| Net domestic product | 28.26 | | 20.32 |
| Depreciation | 1.02 | | 1.45 |
| Gross domestic product | 29.88 | | 21.77 |

*Sources*: Ou Pao-san's 1949 Harvard Ph.D. thesis, "Capital formation and consumers' outlay in China,," pp. 204-11, summarizes the data in his *Chung-kuo kuo-min so-te, i-chiu-san-san-nien* (China's national income, 1933) and takes account of his later revisions. Liu Ta-chung and Yeh Kung-chia, *The economy of the Chinese mainland*, pp. 66, table 8.

average increase of 0.8 per cent per year between 1912 and 1953, such a rate as might be expected from a demographic situation of slow but irregular growth resulting from the difference between high and fluctuating death rates and high but relatively stable birth rates. While no statistical data are available, it appears likely that population growth was sufficiently greater than this average during the Yuan Shih-k'ai presidency (1912–16), the Nanking government decade (1928–37), and the first years of the People's Republic (1950–58) to compensate for the probable negative demographic effects of the warlord period and the Second World War and civil war of 1937–49. Starting with approximately 430 million people in 1912, the population of mainland China in 1933 was some 500 million, and grew to about 580 million in 1953.

Liu and Yeh have made detailed estimates of the occupational distribution of the total population for 1933 (see table 23). Judging from more fragmentary data for individual provinces or cities for the previous two decades, this distribution was largely unchanged during the republican period.

Of a total working population in 1933 of 259.21 million, 204.91 million or 79 per cent actually engaged in farming and 54.3 million (including man-labor units apportioned from joint occupations) or 21 per cent followed non-agricultural pursuits. Of the total population 73 per cent lived in families having agriculture as their main occupation, while 27 per cent were members of non-agricultural families. Although twentieth-century China experienced some industrial growth in the treaty ports, and some development of mining and railway transport, the small numbers engaged in these occupations even in 1933 suggests that the occupational distribution of China's population as a whole had changed little from what it had been at the end of the Ch'ing dynasty. By way of contrast, in the United States only 21.4 per cent of those 10 years old and over gainfully occupied were engaged in agriculture in 1930. To find figures even remotely comparable to those of China in 1933 one would need to look at America in 1820 or 1830 when 70 per cent of the labor force worked in agriculture.

## 3. National Income

Two major independent estimates of China's national income in the republican period have been made by Liu Ta-chung and Yeh Kung-chia, and by Ou Pao-san (Wu Pao-san) (see table 24). The aggregates differ widely—the larger estimate is about 40 per cent greater than the smaller—but the only important difference between the two is value added in agriculture. Both estimates are for 1933 only.

The probably more reliable Liu-Yeh data may be summarized as follows: agriculture of course bulked greatest in the 1933 net domestic product, contributing 65 per cent in 1933 prices. All "industry" (factories, handicrafts, mining, utilities) contributed 10.5 per cent. Trade was third with 9.4 per cent. Other sectors ranked as follows: transport 5.6 per cent; finance, personal service, and rent 5.6 per cent; government administration 2.8 per cent; and construction 1.2 per cent. Another way of stating the composition of national income in 1933 is to note that the modern non-agricultural sectors (very generously defined as factories, mining, utilities, construction, modern trade and transport, trading stores, restaurants and modern financial institutions) contributed only 12.6 per cent of the total. Agriculture, traditional non-agricultural sectors (handicrafts, old-fashioned transport, peddlers, traditional financial institutions, personal services, rent) and government administration accounted for 87.4 per cent. The structure of China's mainland economy before 1949 was also typical of a pre-industrial society when looked at from the expenditure side. By end use, 91 per cent of gross domestic expenditure in 1933 went to personal consumption. Communal services and government consumption together accounted for 4 per cent, while gross investment totaled 5 per cent.

To what degree 1933, a depression year, may be characteristic of the entire republican period is perhaps questionable, but no comparably complete national income estimates for any other year have been attempted. Perkins, however, has converted the Liu-Yeh data into 1957 prices, substituted his own somewhat lower farm output figures,[7] and added estimates for 1914–18 with results that suggest a slowly growing gross domestic product during the republican era, and one which was also changing slightly in composition (table 25).

The absolute values shown in tables 23 and 25 are not comparable because one is stated in 1933 and the other in 1957 prices. In addition, the 1914–18 figures are constructed from plausible guesses as well as true estimates. But the overwhelming predominance of the traditional sectors up to 1949, and the quantitatively small but qualitatively significant changes over four decades which these tables imply, fit very well with other information about the separate sectors of the Chinese economy under the republic presented in the remaining sections of this chapter.[8] Modern manufacturing and mining grew steadily from modest late-nineteenth century beginnings until the outbreak of war with Japan in 1937. In Manchuria this growth continued and even accelerated during the war. Modern transport, railways, and steam ships, experienced a comparable expansion, not replacing traditional communications but supplementing them. A modern financial sector, banking in particular, largely supplanted traditional banking in urban China in the course of the first half of the twentieth century. But even in 1933 Perkins estimates the contribution of the modern sectors (more narrowly defined than in my summary of the Liu-Yeh data in that he excludes modern services) as only 7 per cent of gross domestic product. This was more than twice the 3 per cent of 1914–18 but still minuscule.

The growth of total GDP between 1912 and 1949 therefore, came also from increased output by the traditional sectors, mainly agriculture and handicrafts. Agricultural production grew slowly, but with annual and regional variations due to weather and politico-military circumstances, in the first decades of the twentieth century. The largest increases occurred in newly developed areas such as Manchuria and parts of south-western China. Elsewhere the value of agricultural output was augmented by the increased production of cash crops. For reasons suggested below it is extremely unlikely that total handicraft output, as opposed to its relative share, declined between 1912 and 1949. The contrary is more plausible.

TABLE 25
GROSS DOMESTIC PRODUCT, 1914–18, 1933, 1952 (1957 PRICES)

| Sector | 1914–1918 | | 1933 | | 1952 | |
|---|---|---|---|---|---|---|
| | | | Billion 1957 yuan | | | |
| Manufacturing + * | 8.5 | | 11.77 | | 17.23 | |
| Modern† | | 1.3 | | 4.54 | | 11.11 |
| Agriculture | 29.9 | | 35.23 | | 31.58 | |
| Services | 10.0 | | 12.52 | | 17.07 | |
| Depreciation‡ | — | | 2.19 | | — | |
| GDP | 48.4 | | 61.71 | | 65.88 | |
| | | | Ratio to GDP | | | |
| Manufacturing + | 0.176 | | 0.198 | | 0.262 | |
| Modern | | 0.027 | | 0.074 | | 0.169 |
| Agriculture | 0.618 | | 0.592 | | 0.459 | |
| Services | 0.207 | | 0.210 | | 0.259 | |
| GDP | 1.000 | | 1.000 | | 1.000 | |

* M+ = industry (modern and pre-modern manufacturing, mining and utilities) + transport.

† Modern = factory output, mining, utilities and modern transport.

‡ Not netted out of the individual sectors except for 1955; distributed among the sectors in proportion to their net products in order to calculate the ratios in the lower half of the table.

*Source*: Dwight H. Perkins, "Growth and changing structure of China's twentieth-century economy," in Perkins, ed., *China's modern economy in historical perspective*, p. 117, table 1.

If we compare the estimates of gross domestic product in table 25 with population estimates of 430 million in 1912, 500 million in 1933, and 572 million in 1952, we find per capita GDP in each of these years was on the order of (in 1957 prices) 113, 123, and 115 *yuan* respectively. Given the possibility of potential error in all of this data, the best estimates now available do not show any pronounced upward or downward trend in per capita GDP in the decades covered by this chapter if one omits the 12 years of war and civil war which began in 1937. During this period per capita output and income in some parts of China probably fell sharply. Some notably ar-

OUTPUT AND EMPLOYMENT IN MODERN INDUSTRY, 1933

| | Gross value of output (million 1933 Ch.$) | | | | Number of workers (1,000) | | | |
|---|---|---|---|---|---|---|---|---|
| | China Proper | | | | China Proper | | | |
| | Chinese-owned | Foreign-owned | Manchuria | Total | Chinese-owned | Foreign-owned | Manchuria | Total |
| Producers' Goods | | | | | | | | |
| Lumber | 4.4 | 5.6 | 11.6 | 21.6 | 1.2 | 1.5 | 2.3 | 5.0 |
| Machinery, including transport equipment | 55.4 | 9.9 | 27.2 | 92.5 | 45.7 | 5.2 | 14.4 | 65.3 |
| Ferrous metals and metal products | 29.4 | 1.4 | 18.1 | 48.9 | 15.5 | 0.4 | 11.8 | 27.7 |
| Small electrical appliances | 1.3 | 0.8 | — | 2.1 | 0.7 | 0.3 | — | 1.0 |
| Stone, clay, and glass products | 44.5 | 1.6 | 9.7 | 55.8 | 34.7 | 1.1 | 8.9 | 44.7 |
| Chemicals and chemical products | 58.5 | 10.0 | 19.1 | 87.6 | 5.6 | 2.4 | 4.2 | 12.2 |
| Textile products | 15.3 | — | 1.6 | 16.9 | 4.3 | — | 0.4 | 4.7 |
| Leather | 37.0 | 8.1 | 1.0 | 46.1 | 4.5 | 0.9 | 0.7 | 6.1 |
| Paper, paper products, printing | 72.0 | 10.7 | 3.4 | 86.1 | 42.0 | 3.6 | 0.8 | 46.4 |
| Metal coins | 41.0 | — | — | 41.0 | 0.2 | — | — | 0.2 |
| Total | 358.8 | 48.1 | 91.7 | 498.5 | 154.4 | 15.4 | 43.5 | 213.3 |
| Consumers' Goods | | | | | | | | |
| Wood products | 1.2 | 0.5 | 0.9 | 2.6 | 0.5 | 0.2 | 0.8 | 1.5 |
| Metal products | 12.6 | 1.4 | 1.6 | 15.6 | 4.4 | 0.5 | 0.7 | 5.6 |
| Small electrical appliances | 11.9 | 7.2 | 0.1 | 19.2 | 5.9 | 2.7 | * | 8.6 |
| Chinaware and pottery | 1.3 | 0.2 | 0.7 | 2.2 | 1.3 | — | 1.9 | 3.2 |
| Chemicals and chemical products | 65.3 | 17.2 | 4.4 | 86.9 | 38.4 | 7.3 | 4.9 | 50.6 |
| Textile products | 605.4 | 257.8 | 70.6 | 933.8 | 380.1 | 104.7 | 38.8 | 523.6 |
| Clothing and attire | 101.1 | 4.6 | 3.4 | 109.1 | 101.7 | 2.0 | 3.5 | 107.2 |
| Leather and rubber products | 36.2 | 2.2 | — | 38.4 | 15.1 | 0.7 | — | 15.8 |
| Food products | 436.3 | 39.1 | 158.7 | 634.1 | 51.2 | 8.6 | 21.6 | 81.4 |
| Tobacco products, wine, liquor | 124.9 | 117.3 | 36.0 | 278.2 | 20.3 | 19.0 | 8.4 | 47.7 |
| Paper products | 2.9 | 0.5 | 7.9 | 11.3 | 1.8 | 0.2 | 4.7 | 6.7 |
| Miscellaneous | 13.5 | 1.3 | 0.7 | 15.5 | 8.1 | 1.8 | 0.7 | 10.6 |
| Total | 1,412.6 | 449.3 | 285.0 | 2,146.9 | 628.8 | 147.7 | 86.0 | 862.5 |
| Overall | 1,771.4 | 497.4 | 376.7 | 2,645.4 | 783.2 | 163.1 | 129.5 | 1,075.8 |

* Less than 100 workers.

*Source:* Liu Ta-chung and Yeh Kung-chia, *The economy of the Chinese mainland*, pp. 142-43 and 426-28.

ticulate groups were adversely affected, especially teachers and government employees on fixed salaries which did not keep up with the level of inflation; but urban workers fared relatively well after the war and before the final collapse of 1948–49.

In the wake of the Japanese invasion North China saw a crippling of farm production and a breakdown of the commercial links between town and countryside. During the civil war of 1946–49 agricultural and commercial conditions were probably worse in that region, where the fighting was centered, than elsewhere in China. After 1940 crop production began to decline in unoccupied China, and averaged about 9 per cent below 1939 for the remainder of the war. The introduction of a land tax in kind and compulsory grain purchases in 1942, together with accelerated military conscription which caused severe labor shortages, appear to have reduced the real income of peasants. But industrial production in Nationalist-controlled areas in the interior, beginning from a low base, grew until 1942 or 1943. In the post-war period, the resumption of inflation in 1946 and its runaway character during 1948–49 had much more serious consequences in the coastal, urban sector than in the rural interior of South and West China where total output probably changed little although flows of food and agricultural raw materials to the cities were curtailed as the value of the currency precipitously declined.[9]

It is possible that the income of a significant part of the population was declining while average per capita GDP remained constant or rose slightly. But in the rural areas and among the majority farming population "there is no convincing evidence that landlords were garnering an increasing share of the product during the first half of the twentieth century. The limited available data, in fact, suggest that the rate of tenancy might even have declined slightly, and that in periods of political turmoil landlords often had difficulty collecting their rents."[10]

Allegiances were certainly changed during 1937–49, but even then not primarily because the economy could not support China's population at the prevailing (and low) standard of living in the absence of severe man-made or natural disasters. The rapid recovery which by 1952 had returned output to peak pre-1949 levels was based almost entirely on the success of a new and effective government in restoring the production of existing enterprises, not on new investment. For the rest of the four decades before 1949, civil war in the 1920s and early 1930s, droughts (for example, in 1920–21 in North China), floods (for example, of the Yangtze River in 1931), and other natural disasters indeed undermined the general welfare of the Chinese people, but not necessarily their material welfare, a distinction of substantial importance. Even a slightly rising income is poor compensation for the heightened personal insecurity occasioned by political turmoil and warfare, while on the contrary a low but stable per capita income may be acceptable if offered in a context of greater personal and national security.

## 4. Industry

In describing the Chinese economy in the closing years of the Ch'ing dynasty, we noted that at least 549 Chinese-owned private and semi-official manufacturing and mining enterprises using mechanical power were inaugurated between 1895 and 1913. The total initial capitalization of these firms was Ch.$120,288,000.[11] In addition, 96 foreign-owned and 40 Sino-foreign enterprises established in the same period had an initial capitalization of Ch.$103,153,000. This was of course only a crude estimate, from a variety of contemporary official and non-official sources.

Two similar tabulations, which exclude modern mines but include arsenals and utilities, suggest an appreciable expansion of Chinese-owned modern industry during and immediately following the First World War. The first notes 698 factories with an initial capitalization of Ch.$330,824,000 and 270,717 workers in 1913, while the second, 1,759 factories with an initial capitalization of Ch.$500,620,000 and 557,622 workers in 1920.[12] Concentration on war production by the European powers and the shipping shortage reduced the flow of exports to China and provided an enhanced opportunity for Chinese-owned industry to expand. While orders for equipment were placed earlier—capital goods still came mainly from abroad—the opening of most new plants had to await the end of the war and the actual arrival of the machinery ordered.

Foreign-owned and Sino-foreign enterprises also increased during the first decade of the republic, but little direct investment occurred between 1914 and 1918. The largest increments came immediately after the First World War when, for example, revisions of the Chinese tariff in 1918 and 1922, raising the import duty on the finer count yarns which Japan had been exporting to China. served as an inducement for Japan to open new textile mills in China.

Like both the Chinese- and foreign-owned factories established in the latter part of the Ch'ing dynasty, factories (and mines) opened in the second decade of the twentieth century were heavily concentrated in Shanghai and Tientsin, and in other places in Kiangsu, Liaoning, Hopei, Kwangtung, Shantung, and Hupei, that is, mainly in the coastal and Yangtze valley provinces.[13]

The first and only industrial census in republican China, for the year 1933, was made by investigators of the Institute of Economic and Statistical Research under the direction of D. K. Lieu (Liu Ta-chün). It was based on statistical information gathered directly from factory managers and, apart from its exclusion of all foreign-owned firms, as well as Manchuria, Kansu, Sinkiang, Yunnan, Kweichow, Ninghsia, Tsinghai, Tibet, and Mongolia (none of these except Manchuria had any significant number of modern factories), is considered to be fairly reliable. Published in 1937 Lieu's survey recorded 2,435 Chinese-owned factories capitalized at Ch.$406,926,634 with a gross output valued at Ch.$1,113,974,413 and employing 493,257 workers.[14] These factories were concentrated in the coastal provinces, and especially in Shanghai which accounted for 1,186 of the plants surveyed. More than 80 per cent of Chinese-owned industry in 1933 was located in the eastern and southeastern coastal provinces and Liaoning in Manchuria; and this proportion would be higher still if foreign-owned establishments (which were, of course, limited to the treaty ports) were included in the estimate.

In his study of China's national income in 1933 Ou Pao-san supplemented Lieu's survey by adding estimates for foreign-owned factories in China proper and for factories in Manchuria and the other omitted provinces. His revised estimate reported a total of 3,841 factories (3,167 Chinese-owned and 674 foreign-owned), with a gross output valued at Ch.$2,186,159,000 (Chinese: $1,415,459,000; foreign: $770,700,000) and employing 738,029 workers.[15]

Liu Ta-chung and Yeh Kung-chia have provided a further revision of Lieu's survey in table 26, which shows the gross value of output and the number of workers in the several branches of China's modern industrial sector in 1933. Manufacturing establishments using mechanical power, regardless of the number of workers in each, in China proper and Manchuria produced a gross output valued at Ch.$2,645,400,000 in 1933 and employed a total of 1,075,800 workers. Although Liu-Yeh, in contrast to Lieu and Ou, exclude utilities from their estimate, their totals are substantially

TABLE 27

RELATIVE QUANTITIES OF OUTPUT OF SELECTED INDUSTRIAL PRODUCTS, ELECTRIC POWER, AND COAL IN KUOMINTANG-CONTROLLED AREAS, 1933, 1938-46 (1933=100)*

| | 1933 | 1938 | 1939 | 1940 | 1941 | 1942 | 1943 | 1944 | 1945 | 1946 |
|---|---|---|---|---|---|---|---|---|---|---|
| Coal | 100 | 47 | 55 | 57 | 60 | 63 | 66 | 55 | 52 | 182 |
| Pig-iron | 100 | 153 | 182 | 130 | 184 | 278 | 203 | 116 | 140 | 90 |
| Steel | 100 | 3 | 4 | 5 | 7 | 10 | 23 | 45 | 61 | 52 |
| Electric power | 100 | 14 | 17 | 21 | 24 | 26 | 27 | 29 | 37 | 683 |
| Cement | 100 | 5 | 11 | 11 | 6 | 9 | 8 | 9 | 9 | 65 |
| Alkalis | 100 | 1 | 1 | 2 | 3 | 3 | 5 | 9 | 5 | 93 |
| Sulphuric acid | 100 | 3 | 2 | 8 | 10 | 13 | 12 | 15 | 5 | 138 |
| Hydrochloric acid | 100 | 8 | 6 | 11 | 10 | 32 | 29 | 32 | 26 | 233 |
| Alcohol | 100 | 90 | 241 | 1,362 | 1,605 | 2,340 | 2,289 | 2,180 | 4,814 | 3,673 |
| Gasoline | 100 | — | 1 | 12 | 35 | 316 | 537 | 675 | 718 | 842 |
| Cotton yarn | 100 | 1 | 2 | 2 | 7 | 7 | 7 | 7 | 4 | 95 |
| Flour | 100 | 2 | 3 | 5 | 7 | 7 | 6 | 4 | 3 | 117 |

* The geographic coverage differs significantly between 1933 and 1946, on the one hand, and the intervening years on the other; and also differs somewhat from year to year 1938-43.

*Source:* Yen Chung-p'ing, *Chung-kuo chin-tai ching-chi shih t'ung-chi tzu-liao hsuan-chi* (Selected statistical materials on modern Chinese economic history), pp. 100-101.

higher. This results in part from their broader definition of a factory, from better coverage of Manchuria, and from the utilization of sources other than Lieu's survey for their cotton yarn, cotton cloth, cement, pig iron, and steel data.

For the remaining years before 1949 strictly comparable data are unavailable, in particular there are none on the total value of output. The Ministry of Economic Affairs of the Nationalist Government reported in 1937 that as of that year 3,935 factories (excluding mines but including utilities and arsenals) had registered with the ministry under the Factory Law. They employed 457,063 workers and had a total capitalization of Ch.$377,938,000.[16] Of the 3,935 plants, 1,235 (31 per cent) were located in Shanghai, 2,063 (52 per cent) elsewhere in the coastal provinces, and 637 (17 per cent) in the interior. Textiles and food products accounted for 55 per cent of the total capitalization of the registered factories. It is unclear to what extent the world depression affected China during the years 1933–36. The sizable wartime damage, the fall in production, and the stagnation of new investment under Japanese occupation in such manufacturing centers as Shanghai, Tientsin, and Wuhan after 1937 can be inferred from local and partial qualitative evidence. Similarly, the efforts of the Nationalist government to develop a manufacturing base, largely war-related industry, in unoccupied China were widely but incompletely reported.

During 1938–40, 448 "factories" and 12,182 "technicians" moved inland to Szechwan, Hunan, Kwangsi, and Shensi along with the retreating Nationalist government and armies. At the beginning of 1943 the Ministry of Economic Affairs in Chungking issued an industrial report which, although it lacks output data, gives some indication of wartime developments in unoccupied China. Of the 3,758 factories with 241,662 workers reported, 590 were in existence in 1937, and 3,168 were established during 1938–42. Their total capitalization, allowing for a ten-fold increase in the index of prices, was approximately equal to that of Shanghai's Chinese-owned industries in 1933, and the number of workers was also about the same. The majority of these factories were located in Szechwan (1,654), Hunan (501), Shensi (385) and Kwangsi (292), but others were widely dispersed throughout the Kuomintang-controlled areas. In contrast to the consumers' goods orientation of pre-war industry, about 50 per cent (as measured by capitalization) of the new wartime industry manufactured military-related and producers' goods. Another contrast with pre-war industry was the major role of state-owned enterprises in this wartime industrialization—

while only 656 (17 per cent) of the factories recorded were "public enterprises" (*kung-ying*), they represented 69 per cent of the total capitalization, were larger and employed more mechanical power than privately-owned factories, and dominated the producers' goods sector (especially chemicals, metals and machinery).[17]

The pattern of wartime industrialization in Nationalist areas, in particular the emphasis on military-related producers' goods such as chemicals, is apparent from table 27. After 1942 industrial activity in the interior began to slow down, the number of new firms declined sharply, and output not only ceased to rise but actually declined in certain capital goods lines. The principal reasons for this, apart from raw material shortages and inadequate transport, were uncertainty about the post-war fate of these inland industries (everyone was poised to return to Shanghai), and above all else the level of inflation. Hoarding and speculation in commodities became more profitable than manufacturing.

Industrial output in occupied China proper probably stagnated or declined during 1937–45. The evidence is inconclusive. There was apparently a general fall in production during 1937–9. In North China, from 1939 or 1940 to 1943 or 1944, the output of coal, iron and steel, cement, electric power, and chemicals showed an increase, but such consumers' goods industries as cotton and wool textiles and flour remained substantially below pre-war levels. After a sharp decline, the index of the gross value of factory output (in 1939 prices) in North China had returned to the 1933 level by 1942.[18] Shanghai cotton mills, China's most important industrial plants, however, fared badly during the war. Both yarn and cloth output in Chinese-owned mills fell sharply from 1937, recovered slightly in 1939–41, and then nearly expired.[19] It is still unclear whether or not Japanese-controlled firms performed any better.

Meanwhile Manchurian industry under Japanese control grew rapidly from 1936 to at least 1941. Prior to the mid 1930s Manchuria's economic growth was based mainly on the extension of the agricultural frontier. Small-scale Chinese-owned factories were in evidence, but the principal modern industries were a network of Japanese-controlled producers' goods enterprises intended to furnish raw and semi-finished materials to the Japanese economy. The Anshan and Pen-ch'i ironworks and the Fushun coal mines, large vertically integrated installations, were the most prominent among these units. Subsequent to the consolidation of the Manchukuo puppet state, Japanese interests sponsored a major effort to establish an integrated producers' goods sector. The rate of gross investment in fixed capital, financed largely by capital imports from Japan, which had been 9 per cent in 1924, reached 17 per cent in 1934 and 23 per cent in 1939. (The corresponding rate for China as a whole in 1933 was 5 per cent, a figure probably not exceeded before 1949.) Industry broadly defined (mining, manufacturing, public utilities, small-scale industry and construction) expanded at an annual rate of 9.9 per cent between 1936 and 1941 compared to 4.4 per cent in the years 1924–36. Factory industry grew even more rapidly, with the result that Manchuria, containing 8 to 9 per cent of China's total population, contributed almost a third of the total pre-1949 Chinese factory product. The rapid development of manufacturing came apparently at the expense of small-scale industry, that is, was accompanied by a "modernization" of the industrial sector which as a whole expanded at the same rate as the Manchuria gross domestic product and did not gain in relative importance. This appears to be an important contrast with China proper. After 1941, as a consequence of the dwindling flow of equipment, financing, and some critical raw materials from Japan, both the growth and the diversification of Manchurian industry ground to a halt. Heavy wartime damage and the removal of the most modern plants and equipment by the Soviet armies in 1945–46 (losses amounting to U.S.$ one billion or more) seriously reduced the industrial capacity in Manchuria available to post-war China.[20]

The years 1946–49 were chaotic and soon dominated by spreading civil war and rampant inflation. Consumers' goods output had probably returned to pre-war levels by 1947, but the combination of crippled productive capacity in Manchurian heavy industry and mining, and the virtual abandonment of the "hothouse" producers' goods factories of the wartime interior (which had depended on military and other government orders) after the Nationalist government returned to Nanking, resulted in a substantial decline in the volume of output and the relative importance of this sector. There was briefly, in other words, a return to the pre-war pattern of a heavily consumers' goods oriented industrial structure.

The Japanese surrender was accompanied by a partial breakdown in industrial output throughout China. In the formerly occupied areas Japanese technicians and managers were withdrawn and production came to a temporary standstill. There was no adequate planning for the takeover of Japanese industry and the restoration of industrial output. The recovered factories were treated like war booty as each civilian and military faction struggled to acquire a share of the loot. In the interior the plants established during the war were left to decay. The formerly Japanese-controlled plants and mines provided the basis for an expanding state-owned industrial sector. Through the auspices of the National Resources Commission significant parts of producers' goods output, electric power and mining came under government control.[21] At the end of 1947 the Commission supervised 291 plants and mines with a total of 223,770 employees. In the consumers' goods sector, 69 Japanese and "puppet" textile plants (38 cotton mills, six woolen mills and 25 related enterprises) were confiscated in 1945 and turned over to a newly established China Textile Corporation (CTC), a joint-stock company dominated by government investment and operated under the direction of the Ministry of Economic Affairs. In 1947 CTC controlled 36.1 per cent of the cotton spindles in China and 59.4 per cent of the looms. Its plants produced 43.7 per cent of the yarn and 72.6 of the cotton cloth. Supplied with ample working capital by the Chinese government and receiving preferential treatment in the allocation of foreign exchange for the purchase of raw cotton, the CTC mills had a definite advantage over the private mills—a position analogous to that of the Japanese cotton mills in China whose heirs they were; except that the Japanese were more efficient. The CTC managements looked primarily for short-term profits, for themselves and for the Kuomintang government.[22]

From late 1948 both government and private factories and mines succumbed to the ravages of runaway inflation, communist sabotage of transport and the supply of raw materials, power shortages, labor unrest, and human frailty.

The critical measure of industrial development is the growth of production over time. John K. Chang's recent construction of an index of industrial production (excluding handicrafts) in mainland China, 1912–49, which supersedes all previous output estimates, provides a quantitative thread which ties together and confirms the scattered observations offered above. Based on 15 manufacturing and mining products, covering perhaps 50 per cent of industrial output and employing 1933 price weights, Chang's index is presented in table 28. Chinese- and foreign-owned firms, China proper and Manchuria are all included in his estimate. Starting from a very low base, to 1936 there was a steady rise in industrial production. Manufacturing and mining as a whole were apparently not adversely affected by the world depression, in spite of the substantial temporary difficulties experienced by many individual factories. Some upward bias is introduced for the depression years by combining China proper and Manchuria, in that Shanghai industry was more severely affected than was industrial enterprise in Manchuria. The outbreak of war brought a sharp decline in 1937–38, followed by a rise in output in both unoccupied China and Manchuria to a 1942 peak. From 1942 the picture is less clear: a fall in output through 1946, succeeded by a slight recovery in 1947–48, but not to the 1936 level.

Average annual growth rates for selected sub-periods (in net value-added) reflect substantial industrial expansion during and after the Firast World War (1912–20, 13.4 per cent) followed by a post-war recession in 1921–22. From 1923 to 1936 the average rate was 8.7 per cent; for 1912–42, 8.4 per cent; and for the whole period from 1912 to 1949—because 1949 was a low year—5.6 per cent. In a typical pre-war year, therefore, the output of China's modern industry and mining as measured in 1933 prices was growing at an impressive rate of 8 to 9 per cent.[23]

Yet, as the Liu-Yeh national income estimate in table 24 indicates, industry, including traditional industry, occupied a small place in the Chinese economy, and within the broadly defined industrial sector, modern factory production was overshadowed by handicraft manufacturing. In 1933 the combined output of factories, handicrafts, mining and utilities in China constituted only 10.5 per cent of net domestic product. The output of handicrafts accounted for 67.8 per cent of the industrial share; factories 20.9 per cent; mining, 7.0 per cent; and utilities, 4.3 per cent. Of a total non-agricultural working population estimated at 46.91 million, 12-13 million (25.9 per cent) were employed in handicraft industry, 1.13 million (2.4 per cent) in factories, 0.77 million (1.6 per cent) in mining, and 0.04 million (0.09 per cent) in utilities. In spite of the 8 to 9 per cent annual rate of growth estimated by Chang, the base from which this growth began was a very low one, with the consequence that the overall sectoral distribution of domestic product was not radically changed during the four decades of the republican era. China's modern industrial sector in the 1930s was small, however, only in relation to contemporary developed economies. As compared, for example, with Japan in 1895 it was neither inconsiderable nor without potential for further development.

There is no doubt that the relative share of handicrafts in the industrial sector as a whole was less in the 1930s than it had been in 1850 or 1912 (see table 25). In the mid-nineteenth century, of course, there was no modern industry at all in China, and even in 1912 it was a tender shoot in-

TABLE 28
INDEX OF INDUSTRIAL PRODUCTION OF MAINLAND CHINA, 1912–49
(15 commodities; 1933 = 100)

| | Gross value of output | Net value-added |
|---|---|---|
| 1912 | 11.9 | 15.7 |
| 1913 | 15.6 | 19.2 |
| 1914 | 10.1 | 24.0 |
| 1915 | 22.5 | 26.1 |
| 1916 | 24.0 | 27.7 |
| 1917 | 26.9 | 32.0 |
| 1918 | 27.8 | 32.2 |
| 1919 | 34.1 | 36.9 |
| 1920 | 40.2 | 42.9 |
| 1921 | 42.4 | 42.4 |
| 1922 | 34.7 | 39.0 |
| 1923 | 41.6 | 45.6 |
| 1924 | 46.9 | 50.5 |
| 1925 | 55.7 | 60.1 |
| 1926 | 59.0 | 61.0 |
| 1927 | 66.6 | 66.3 |
| 1928 | 72.1 | 70.5 |
| 1929 | 76.9 | 75.2 |
| 1930 | 81.6 | 80.1 |
| 1931 | 88.1 | 86.5 |
| 1932 | 91.6 | 90.3 |
| 1933 | 100.0 | 100.0 |
| 1934 | 103.6 | 106.8 |
| 1935 | 109.7 | 119.5 |
| 1936 | 122.0 | 135.0 |
| 1937 | 96.0 | 112.3 |
| 1938 | 76.2 | 104.1 |
| 1939 | 88.2 | 120.7 |
| 1940 | 94.1 | 137.6 |
| 1941 | 109.2 | 161.2 |
| 1942 | 115.7 | 176.1 |
| 1943 | 105.6 | 157.1 |
| 1944 | 91.8 | 140.9 |
| 1945 | 62.0 | 94.1 |
| 1946 | 90.7 | 93.6 |
| 1947 | 115.1 | 116.8 |
| 1948 | 96.7 | 101.1 |
| 1949 | 105.6 | 119.2 |

*Source*: John K. Chang, *Industrial development in pre-Communist China: a quantitative analysis*, pp. 60-61.

deed. Table 29 summarizes the Liu-Yeh estimates of the identified handicraft share in the total output of various industries in 1933. Given the incomplete coverage of handicraft production in the available sources as compared to factory output, the average of 64.5 per cent for all industries is certainly too low.[24] Supplementary estimates by Liu and Yeh based on employment and value-added per handicraft worker suggest in fact that the handicraft share of gross value-added was close to 75 per cent in 1933.

Here the relatively hard data end. It has frequently been asserted that traditional handicraft manufacture in the century following the Opium War suffered a continuing decline as a result of competition from both imported foreign goods and the output of Chinese- and foreign-owned modern industry in China.[25] In Manchuria, as indicated above, it may have been the case that factory industry grew at the expense of "small-scale" (that is, handicraft) industry. But was this equally true of China as a whole? The fragmentary information relating to this matter lends itself better to the conclusion that, in *absolute* terms, handicraft output as a whole held its own or even increased than it does to the melancholy view just noted.

TABLE 29
HANDICRAFT PRODUCTION AS PERCENTAGE OF GROSS VALUE-ADDED IN 14 PRODUCT GROUPS, 1933

| Product | % |
|---|---|
| Lumber and wood products | 95.5 |
| Machinery, except electrical | 31.3 |
| Metal products | 12.1 |
| Electrical appliances | 0.5 |
| Transport equipment | 69.4 |
| Stone, clay, and glass products | 67.8 |
| Chemical products | 22.5 |
| Textile goods | 46.1 |
| Clothing and knitted goods | 66.5 |
| Leather and allied products | 56.2 |
| Food products | 90.1 |
| Tobacco, wine, and liquor | 30.2 |
| Paper and printing | 55.9 |
| Miscellaneous | 63.7 |
| All industries | 64.5 |

*Source*: Liu Ta-chung and Yeh Kung-chia, *The economy of the Chinese mainland*, pp. 142-43, table 38; and pp. 512 -13, table G- 1.

The matter is complicated by which definition of "handicraft" is used, the substantially different experiences among handicraft industries, and the timing of the several field surveys relied upon by most commentators to make their observations. Urban or semi-urban handicraft workshops or "manufactories" *(shou-kung-yeh kung-ch'ang)* removed from the household unit have been present in the Chinese economy since at least the T'ang dynasty. Their importance, however, as measured both by employment and by output, before 1912 at least and to a lesser but unknown extent in the following four decades, was overshadowed by the handicraft production of individual rural and urban households.[26] Thus, for example, it is conceivable that the twentieth-century decline in the absolute output of handspun cotton yarn, which had been primarily a peasant household handicraft, was matched, wholly or in part, by new employment opportunities in the numerous handicraft workshops which sprang up under the impetus of growing foreign trade and factory production.

These small-scale factories, typically employing a handful of workers and without mechanical power, processed agricultural products for export (for example, cotton ginning and re-reeling of raw silk), or as subcontractors supplied modern factories with simple parts and assemblies, or ventured to produce coarser and cheaper versions of factory-made goods (for example, textiles, cigarettes, matches and flour).[27] A significant part of China's early industrialization, therefore, like that of Japan, took the form not of a full-scale duplication of the foreign model but of adaptations to China's factor endowment which were characterized by a high labor-capital ratio.

TABLE 30
SOURCES OF COTTON CLOTH SUPPLY, 1875–1931

| | | | | | | | | |
|---|---|---|---|---|---|---|---|---|
| | (million square yards) | | | | | | | |
| | 1875 | | 1905 | | 1919 | | 1931 | |
| | | (%) | | (%) | | (%) | | |
| Manufactures | — | — | 27 | 1.1 | 158 | 5.8 | 831 | 28.2 |
| Imports | 457 | 21.8 | 509 | 20.2 | 787 | 28.7 | 300 | 10.2 |
| Handicrafts | 1637 | 78.2 | 1981 | 78.7 | 1798 | 65.5 | 1815 | 61.6 |
| Total | 2094 | 100.00 | 2517 | 100.00 | 2743 | 100.00 | 2946 | 100.00 |
| | (million pounds) | | | | | | | |
| | 1875 | | 1905 | | 1919 | | 1931 | |
| Manufactures | — | — | 90.2 | 11.5 | 297.6 | 36.8 | 966.9 | 90.9 |
| Imports | 12.4 | 1.9 | 304.3 | 38.6 | 178.5 | 22.0 | –76.0 | –7.1 |
| Handicrafts | 632.3 | 98.1 | 393.2 | 49.9 | 333.6 | 41.2 | 173.3 | 16.3 |
| Total | 644.7 | 100.0 | 787.7 | 100.0 | 809.7 | 100.0 | 1064.2 | 100.0 |

*Source*: Bruce Lloyd Reynolds, "The impact of trade and foreign investment on industrialization: Chinese textiles, 1875–1931," p. 31, table 2.4.

Some handicrafts did not survive the competition. Imported kerosene (paraffin) very nearly replaced vegetable oils for lighting purposes. Silk weaving, which had prospered in the first quarter of the century, declined from the late 1920s as a consequence of Japanese competition, the loss of such markets as Manchuria after 1931, the advent of rayon, and the general depression of the international market.[28] The fall in tea exports in the 1920s and 1930s probably indicates that that industry was in difficulty although we know little about changes in domestic demand. In neither the case of silk or tea, however, was there a simple linear decline from the nineteenth century onwards attributable to the displacement of handicrafts by factory products.

In the case of cotton textile handicrafts one can be more specific. Bruce Reynolds finds that the absolute output of handicraft yarn as well as the handicraft share in total yarn supply fell precipitously between 1875 and 1905, then more slowly to 1919, followed by another sharp drop to 1931 (table 30).[29] Handicraft weaving, in contrast, while its relative share dropped over the period 1875–1931, actually increased its total production in square yards during this half century. On the side of demand, this strong showing was due to the existence of partially discrete markets both for the handicraft cloth—typically woven with imported and domestic machine-spun warp threads and, until the enormous growth of domestic spinning mills in the 1920s, handspun woofs—and for machine-loomed cloths of a finer quality. From the side of supply, the survival and growth of handicraft weaving is attributable to its integral role in the family farm production system of pre-1949 China. The key was the availability of "surplus" labor, specifically household labor which had a claim to subsistence in any case and, unlike factory labor, would be employed in handicraft activities even if its marginal product was below the cost of subsistence. Household handicrafts, that is, could meet the competition of factory industry at almost any price so long as the modern firm had to pay subsistence wages to its workers while the craft workers had no income-earning alternatives. Rural families seeking to maximize income moved into and out of various activities supplementary to farming depending on their estimates of the relative advantages of each, which accounts in part for the variable fates of individual handicrafts. The technology of handicraft weaving improved significantly in the twentieth century with the diffusion of improved wooden looms, iron-gear looms, and jacquard looms, and this made possible a much higher labor productivity as compared to handicraft spinning. Inexpensive imported and domestic machine-spun yarn made handicraft spinning increasingly disadvantageous in relation to other side-line occupations. The combination of the availability and low cost of machine-spun yarn, the example of machine-loomed products, and the comparative advantage of weaving over spinning led to a shift into weaving by rural families. In such handicraft weaving centers as Ting-hsien, Pao-ti, and Kao-yang in Hopei and Wei-hsien in Shantung, which experienced "booms" at various time in the 1920s and 1930s, large numbers of peasant households were supplied with yarn from Tientsin, Tsingtao, and Shanghai mills and sometimes with looms by textile merchants who contracted for their output and distributed it throughout North China and Manchuria.[30]

It is of considerable importance to our received picture of the fate of handicrafts in the twentieth century that many of the better quality field surveys of rural China date from the 1930s, that is, from the brief hey-day of pre-war academic scholarship. After almost two decades of political disruption, this was seen as a hopeful time when China could at last embark on the journey to modern economic growth which had brought wealth and power to the West and Japan. To an impressively unanimous degree, China's economists and rural sociologists, even the majority who were not Marxist in outlook, tended to be as much concerned with the welfare implications of the functioning of the economic system as with analyzing its interrelationships and measuring its performance. That agricultural production roughly kept up with population growth, or that the absolute output of handicrafts at least held its own, in no way compensated for the observable facts that: China's economy was "backward', most Chinese were poor while a very few were rich, and even the low standard of living of the poor was subject to severe uncertainties and fluctuations. Prosperity, moreover, since the "demonstration effect" was powerful, seemed achievable only through large-scale modern industrialization. In this context, there occurred both a disproportionate attention to the small modern sector and, even though the empirical data which were honestly presented frequently contradicted it, a tendency to draw conclusions from the declining phases of a cyclically fluctuating handicraft performance while ignoring the rising phases.[31] It was almost as if the more bankrupt the traditional sector could be shown to be, the more likely it was that a national effort to modernize and industrialize would be undertaken. The early 1930s were in all likelihood a relatively depressed period for the handicraft textile industry among others, but this does not appear to have been caused so much by the competition from modern mills as by the loss of the market in Manchuria and Jehol after 1931. To suggest that there was no recovery by 1936–37 as a result of the development of alternative markets goes beyond what we presently know and contradicts the upward trend of the Chinese economy as a whole in the two years before the outbreak of war in mid-1937. And for the long and bitter years of war and civil war between 1937 and 1949, is it believable that modern and urban consumers goods factories suffered less destruction and curtailment of output than the vast and decentralized handicraft sector?

Given the growth of imports and of the output of domestic factories, the fate of handicraft production in absolute terms depended on two factors: the structure of imports and of factory production, and the size and composition of aggregate demand. In 1925, for example (see table 50), at most 50.5 per cent of imports were competitive with handicrafts (cotton goods, cotton yarn, wheat flour, sugar, tobacco, paper, chemicals, dyes, and pigments). Apart from cotton goods and kerosene whose effects have already been noted, the largest remaining categories are sugar (whose importation was exceptionally high in 1925 and which includes unprocessed sugar not competitive with handicrafts), chemicals, dyes, and pigments (only a small part of which replaced indigenous dyestuffs), and tobacco (the domestic processing of which increased in the 1920s and thus clearly was not swamped by imports). Other potentially competitive imports were minute and could not have seriously affected domestic handicrafts.

With respect to the impact of factory production, again excluding the case of cotton yarn in which handicraft output was sharply curtailed, the situation is similar. The most important handicraft products in 1933 were milled rice and wheat flour, which together accounted for 67 per cent of the identified gross output value of all handicrafts. Of the total production of milled rice and wheat flour plus wheat flour imports, 95 per cent came from the handicraft sector. If there had been any decline since the beginning of the century as a result of competition from modern food product factories or imports, it could not have been a very significant one.[32]

Knowing as little as we do about the domestic market for handicrafts, it is difficult to speak directly about the pattern of aggregate demand in the republican era. Three indirect indicators, however, may be useful. China's population increased at an average annual rate of almost 1 per cent between 1911 and 1949, while the growth rate of the urban population may have been as much as 2 per cent. Population increase alone, and especially the growth of the coastal commercial and manufacturing centers, was adequate to account for a large part of the consumption of imported or domestic factory-made commodities. A significant portion of modern manufactures consisted of urban consumption goods which had little value in rural China. Even for items in universal use such as cotton textiles, product differentiation based on quality and cost was important. With respect to traditional demand, factory goods might be "inferior" goods. And if this was not the case, the rural population continued to use the products of handicraft industry when, given low wage rates and the high price of capital, these were produced at a lower unit cost than by modern industry.

A second indicator is the persistence of external demand until the 1930s. One study reports that the value of handicraft exports in constant 1913 prices increased at a rate of about 2.6 per cent a year between 1875 and 1928. Another estimate suggests an annual increase of 1.1 per cent a year from 1912 to 1931 for a somewhat broader group of handicraft products.[33] Without more knowledge of domestic consumption, figures reporting increased exports are, of course, inconclusive. In the case of silk, however, which was China's largest single export in the 1920s, there are strong indications that in absolute terms the domestic market grew along with exports until 1930 while their relative shares were more or less constant.[34]

Finally, farm output, especially cash crops many of which required processing, increased at about the same rate as population—slightly below 1 per cent a year—between 1912 and 1949. Perkins estimates the annual gross value of farm output in 1914–18 at Ch.$16.01-17.03 billion, and in 1931–37 at Ch.$19.14-19.79 billion, a total increase of perhaps 16 to 19 per cent over two decades.[35] He also argues that "no more than 5 or 6 percent of farm output could have been processed in modern factories in the 1930's, or less than half the percentage of *increase* in farm output between the 1910's and 1930's."[36] At worst, in other words, handicraft processing of agricultural products held its own.

With respect to factory industry, in addition to its relatively small quantitative importance, several other general characteristics are worthy of attention:

1. Modern manufacturing industry, as already noted, was concentrated in the coastal provinces, in particular in the treaty-port cities, and after 1931 in Manchuria. (In the all-important cotton textile industry, 87.0 per cent of all spindles in China and 91.1 per cent of all looms in 1924 were located in the provinces of Hopei, Liaoning, Shantung, Kiangsu,

Chekiang, Fukien, and Kwangtung; the three cities of Shanghai, Tientsin, and Tsingtao accounted for 67.7 per cent and 71.9 per cent of spindles and looms respectively.) While there was some geographical dispersion of, for example, cotton spindles in the 1930s (in 1918, 61.8 per cent of the total spindles were located in Shanghai; 55.4 per cent in 1932; and 51.1 per cent in 1935), modern factory industry remained almost totally unknown in the interior provinces of China before the outbreak of the war with Japan.

TABLE 31
OUTPUT AND NUMBER OF WORKERS IN CHINESE- AND FOREIGN-OWNED FACTORIES, 1933

| | Gross value of output (millions Chinese $) | % | Number of workers (1,000s) | % |
|---|---|---|---|---|
| China proper | | | | |
| Chinese-owned | 1,771.4 | 66.9 | 783.2 | 72.8 |
| Foreign-owned | 497.4 | 18.8 | 161.3 | 15.2 |
| Manchuria | 376.7 | 14.3 | 129.5 | 12.0 |
| Total | 2,645.5 | 100.0 | 1,075.8 | 100.0 |

*Source:* table 26.

2. One reason for this geographical concentration was the very large share which foreign-owned factories occupied within the manufacturing sector. Foreign plants were restricted to the treaty ports. Between 1931 and 1945 the Manchurian economy was not linked to the rest of the Chinese economy, but it was precisely in Manchuria, if anywhere, that modern China experienced a degree of "economic development," including the construction of a substantial base of heavy industry. While the prominence of foreign-owned factories in China's pre-war manufacturing industry is acknowledged by all sources, estimates of exactly how important they were in terms of their share of total output vary quite widely. Combining D. K. Lieu's survey data with other sources, Liu and Yeh have proposed the following figures for the gross value of output and number of workers in Chinese- and foreign-owned factories in China proper and Manchuria in 1933 (table 31).

For China proper, 78 per cent of the output of factory industry was accounted for by Chinese-owned firms. This is a substantially higher proportion than the Chinese-owned share of the capitalization of manufacturing industry in China which, according to one rather crude estimate, was only 37 per cent of the total in the 1930s.[37] The question arises as to whether the significance of foreign-owned industry in China is better measured by its share of output, or by the relative size of foreign capital investment as compared with Chinese. Excessive attention to capitalization tends to exaggerate the importance of foreign-owned industry. Capitalization is notoriously difficult to measure, and it slights the fact that Chinese-owned industry was primarily light manufacturing in which the problem of capital indivisibility was minimal and the degree to which labor could be substituted for capital was quite large. In other words, it implicitly assumes the same capital-output ratio in Chinese- and foreign-owned factories. Table 32 gives some indication of the output share of foreign enterprises in several branches of manufacturing industry in the 1920s and 1930s. (See also table 25, for 1933.) Data on coal mining are included here; in general, apart from the matter of concentration in the treaty ports, what is being said about factories applies as well to mining.

3. Factory industry in China exclusive of Manchuria was predominantly consumers' goods industry. In 1933 producers' goods accounted for 25 per cent of net value added by factories. The largest industries, as measured by the value of their output, were cotton textiles, flour milling, cigarettes, and oil pressing. Among the 2,435 Chinese-owned factories investigated by D. K. Lieu, 50 per cent were engaged in the manufacture of textiles and foodstuffs. These 1,211 plants as a group accounted for 76 per cent of the value of output, 71 per cent of the employment, 60 per cent of the power installed, and 58 per cent of the capital investment of all Chinese-owned factories.

4. The average size of factories was small, and generally smaller for Chinese than foreign-owned firms in the same industry, but not very small as compared, for example, with Japanese plants in the Meiji era or with the early industrial experience of other countries. The 2,435 factories surveyed by D. K. Lieu had a total capitalization of Ch.$406 million, giving an average of Ch.$166,000 or about U.S.$50,000 at the prevailing exchange rate. These plants had a total motive power capacity of 507,300 horse-power or about 200 horse-power per factory. The average number of workers per factory was 202.

5. Of the Chinese-owned factories, even those located in the treaty ports, it may be said that the social context in which they existed and which impinged importantly on the "modern" fact that they employed mechanical

power and complex machinery, remained to a remarkable extent "traditional." Only 617 of D. K. Lieu's 2,435 factories were organized as joint-stock companies. The absence of a well-developed market for the transfer of equity shares contributed to a particular relationship between shareholders and management in which the demands of the former for short-term profits often adversely affected long-term expansion and modernization through reinvestment. Such practices as guaranteed dividends frequently forced firms to borrow at high rates in order to obtain working capital. Financing for modern industry was never adequate in republican China. Investment in agricultural land and urban real estate continued to be attractive; to these were added in more recent times speculation in commodities, foreign exchange and government bonds. We shall see below how government fiscal policy tended to divert funds from productive investment.

Competent management was in short supply. Only 500 of some 4,000 technicians in 82 spinning mills in 1931 had received formal training. Higher management was not greatly different from what it had been, in the *kuan-tu shang-pan* period. Such techniques as cost accounting were sparsely employed: two-story factory buildings on cheap land were not uncommon, and the inadequacy of allowances for depreciation and the repair of equipment is noted by almost all observers. Such circumstances, however, have been characteristic of the early stages of industrialization throughout the world, and were not particularly worse in China than, say, in the American textile industry 50 years earlier.

Foremen in Chinese factories tended to retain a "long-gown" attitude, disdained to engage in menial tasks, and left the actual supervision of workers to technically incompetent overseers who frequently were also "contractors" who had recruited the workers by, for example, making arrangements with the parents of child operatives. While there were over a million factory workers by 1933, this was overall not a skilled, stable, disciplined labor force. Sectoral variations were probably significant, as in Japan. Where experience counted, it was rewarded. Highly skilled male workers were well-paid, well-trained and tended to stay with one employer. In the dominant textile industry, however, experience was not critically important, except for mechanics. Many workers retained their ties with the rural villages which, under force of necessity, they had left in order to supplement a meager farming income with factory wages. This was especially true of the young women and children who formed a very high proportion of the labor force. The 493,257 workers in D. K. Lieu's 2,435 factories included

TABLE 32

PERCENTAGE OF TOTAL OUTPUT BY CHINESE AND FOREIGN † FIRMS IN SELECTED INDUSTRIES

| | Coal* | | Cotton yarn | | Cotton cloth | | Cigarettes | | Electric power | | Matches | |
|---|---|---|---|---|---|---|---|---|---|---|---|---|
| | Chinese | Foreign | Chinese | Foreign | Chinese | Foreign | Chinese | Foreign | Chinese | Foreign | Chinese | Foreign |
| 1913 | 7.0 | 93.0 | | | | | | | | | | |
| 1919 | 24.4 | 75.6 | 57 | 43 | 41 | 59 | | | | | | |
| 1923 | 21.1 | 78.9 | 67 | 33 | 50 | 50 | | | 23 | 77 | | |
| 1928 | 22.0 | 78.0 | 62 | 38 | 44 | 56 | | | | | | |
| 1933 | 16.7 | 83.3 | 71 | 29 | 39 | 61 | 43 | 57 | 37 | 63 | 89 | 11 |
| 1936 | 34.3 | 65.7 | 71 | 29 | 36 | 64 | 42 ‡ | 58 ‡ | 45 | 55 | 89 ‡ | 11 ‡ |

* "Modern" mines only.

† Foreign-owned or foreign-investment/control.

‡ 1935

*Sources*: Yen Chung-p'ing, *Chung-kuo chin-tai ching-chi shih t'ung-chi tzu-liao hsuan-chi* (Selected statistical materials on modern Chinese economic history), pp. 124, 130-31; Reynolds, "The impact of trade and foreign investment on industrialization," pp. 216, 221; Ch'en Chen, *et al.*, comps., *Chung-kuo chin-tai kung-yeh shih tzu-liao* (Source materials on the history of modern industry in China), II. 971.

202,762 men, 243,435 women, and 47,060 children under 16 years of age; for the textile industry, the comparable figures were 84,767, 187,847, and 29,758. With a labor force not fully committed to a lifetime in a factory, and with a potentially plentiful supply of workers available from the peasantry, industrial wages were low by international standards and hours were long. Chinese textile mills before 1937 typically operated on two 12-hour shifts; 11-hour shifts were general in Japanese-owned mills. The real income of the urban worker, however, was high by rural Chinese standards, a factor which sustained migration to the cities. In circumstances where capital was expensive and labor cheap, "rationalization" of production in some Chinese firms took the form of more intensive use of labor by lowering wages and extending hours. The prevalence of low wage rates perpetuated a high labor turnover and made the worker reluctant to sever ties with his village, which continued to offer him a refuge in times of industrial slowdown. This then confirmed the employer's belief that the worker could live on a "handful of rice." The convention of low wages, moreover, partly justified itself by preventing a rise in labor efficiency.[38]

Probably it could not have been otherwise. One fundamental problem faced by Chinese industry was the weakness of demand. So long as outside of the treaty ports and their immediate environs the traditional society and impoverished peasant economy continued basically unchanged, what market could there be for new or improved (and costlier) goods produced with well-paid labor?

6. The concentration of modern industry in coastal cities, the large foreign-owned component, the predominance of consumers' goods, and the small size and technical backwardness of most factories—all of these are correlates of the very small share of modern industry in China's national product before 1949. But to estimate that the modern share of M+ (factory output, mining, utilities, and modern transport) accounted for only 5 per cent (table 24) or 7 per cent (table 25) of total domestic product in the 1930s—that is, that China's economy was clearly an "underdeveloped" one—should not lead to the conclusion that the modern industrial and transport sector was of no consequence for China's post-1949 economic development. If what the People's Republic of China inherited was quantitatively small, nevertheless over two-thirds of the increase in industrial production during 1953–57 was to come from the expanded output of existing factories.[39] In spite of the Soviet removal of industrial machinery and equipment from Manchuria, the new investment necessary to restore out-

put in this major producers' goods base was less than would have been required for entirely new plant. If, taken as a whole, pre-1949 China was not industrialized, nevertheless its cotton textile industry grew rapidly and steadily and was not monopolized by foreign-owned firms. Even in the 1930s China's cotton textile output was one of the largest in the world. After 1949, although new investment in consumers' goods industry lagged far behind producers' goods, the export of textile fabrics and clothing was—next to raw and processed agricultural products—a major source of the foreign exchange which paid for China's imports.[40]

Equally important, the small pre-1949 modern sector provided the People's Republic with skilled workers and technicians, experienced managers, and patterns of organized activity which, supplemented by Soviet advisers and training, made it possible to provide training and experience to the vastly expanded number of new managers and workers who were to staff the many new factories that began production in the late 1950s. And in the producers' goods sector, in particular, the dozens of relatively small Shanghai machine-building firms—many of which were inherited from the pre-1949 period—retained a qualitative flexibility to develop new products and techniques that allowed them to play a large role in overcoming the difficulties in the early 1960s stemming from the Great Leap Forward and the withdrawal of Soviet advisers and their blueprints.[41] "Without this base, China's industrial development in the 1950's and 1960's would have been significantly slower or would have had to rely more heavily on foreign technicians, or both."[42]

## 5. Agriculture

China's economy in the republican era, as in the past, was overwhelmingly agricultural. Net value added by agriculture in 1933 was estimated at Ch.$18.76 billion or 65 per cent of the total net domestic product. This output was produced by 205 million agricultural workers, 79 per cent of the labor force. Only small changes in these percentages occurred between 1912 and 1933, although after 1933 the rapid industrial growth in Manchuria made the share of agriculture decline somewhat more rapidly than in earlier years (table 25). Plant products dominated, and within this category, food crops. Estimates shown in table 33 have been offered for 1933. By weight, certainly a rough measure, food crops (rice, wheat and

TABLE 33
OUTPUT OF THE SEVERAL SECTORS OF AGRICULTURE, 1933

| | Gross value-added (billion Chinese $) |
|---|---|
| Plant products | 15.73 |
| Animal products | 1.37 |
| Forest products | 0.60 |
| Fishery products | 0.41 |
| Miscellaneous products | 1.07 |
| Total | 19.18 |
| Less depreciation | 0.42 |
| Net value-added | 18.76 |

*Source:* Liu Ta-chung and Yeh Kung-chia, *The economy of the Chinese mainland*, p. 140, table 36.

TABLE 34
GROSS VALUE OF FARM OUTPUT, 1914-57 (BILLIONS 1933 CHINESE $)

| | 1914-18 (average year) | 1931-37 (average year) | 1957 |
|---|---|---|---|
| Grain | 9.15-10.17 | 10.31-10.96 | 12.32 |
| Soy-beans | 0.43 | 0.66 | 0.78 |
| Oil-bearing crops | 0.51 | 1.13 | 0.77 |
| Cotton and other fibers | 0.78 | 0.86 | 1.28 |
| Tobacco, tea, and silk | 0.49 | 0.52 | 0.32 |
| Sugar-cane and Sugar-beet | 0.11 | 0.11 | 0.14 |
| Animals | 1.14 | 1.40 | 2.74 |
| Sub-total | 13.63 | 15.65 | 19.36 |
| Other products | 3.40 | 4.14 | 4.91 |
| Total gross value | 16.01-17.03 | 19.14-19.79 | 24.27 |
| Per capita (Ch.$) | 36.10-38.40 | 38.10-39.40 | 37.50 |

*Source*. Perkins, *Agricultural development in China*, p. 30, table II.8.

other grains, potatoes, vegetables, fruits) accounted for 80 per cent of the plant products.

Until 1937 the total output of agriculture approximately kept pace with the growth of population (from 430 million in 1912, to 500 million in the mid 1930s). The per capita value in constant prices of farm output in 1931–37 was about the same as it had been in 1914–18 (table 34), reflecting an output increase of slightly less than 1 per cent a year. In part this increment resulted from an expansion of cultivated land area which Perkins estimates at 1,356 million *shih mou* in 1918 and 1,471 million *shih mou* in 1933.[43] The balance came from increased output of grains and of cash crops on existing land. Grain output per capita remained unchanged at about

Ch.$21 during this whole period while the per capita output of other products, including cash crops, increased from Ch.$15 to Ch.$17. Table 35 shows the changes in quantities of plant products 1914–57. From 1914–18 to 1931–37 all grains (in catties = 1.1 pounds) increased by 12.9 per cent. But rice output fell 5.8 per cent, while the production of potatoes and corn grew by 16.4 per cent and 39.2 per cent, respectively.

TABLE 35
PHYSICAL OUTPUT OF PLANT PRODUCTS, 1914–57 (1,000,000 catties)

| | 1914–19 (average year) | 1931–37 (average year) | 1957 |
|---|---|---|---|
| Rice | 147,610 | 139,110 | 173,600 |
| Wheat | 39,570 | 46,200 | 47,100 |
| Corn | 14,680 | 20,440 | 37,470 |
| Potatoes (grain equivalent) | 7,060 | 15,280 | 43,800 |
| Kaoling | 23,750 | 24,680 | 20,030 |
| Millet | 22,180 | 27,680 | 23,330 |
| Barley | 18,090 | 19,440 | 9,300 |
| Other grain | 10,370 | 10,940 | 15,170 |
| Total grain | 283,300 | 319,960 | 370,000 |
| Soy-beans | 10,970 | 16,860 | 20,100 |
| Peanuts | 4,540 | 5,250 | 5,142 |
| Rapeseed | 3,800 | 5,080 | 1,775 |
| Sesame | 670 | 1,810 | 625 |
| Cotton | 1,606 | 1,888 | 3,280 |
| Fibers | 1,410 | 1,350 | 1,290 |
| Tobacco | 1,590 | 1,830 | 1,220 |
| Sugar-cane | 18,720 | 18,720 | 20,785 |
| Sugar-beet | — | — | 3,002 |
| Tea | 445 | 399 | 223 |
| Silk | 406 | 420 | 225 |

*Source:* Perkins, *Agricultural development in China*, pp. 66-89.

These changes reflect a shift of cropping patterns to the production of plant products which yielded more calories per unit of land, thus releasing land for the increased cultivation of cash crops. Wheat, which grew by 16.8 per cent, was a cash crop in some areas of North China where it was marketed to buy rougher grains such as kaoliang and millet for farm consumption. In North and Central China wheat and cotton impinged on rice acreage, while in Central China oil seed-bearing crops were also augmented. Cash crop output accounted for approximately 14 per cent of farm output by value in 1914–18 and 17 per cent in 1931–37, while the physical output of individual crops increased more rapidly than grains: sesame, 70.1 per cent; soy-beans, 53.7; rapeseed, 33.7; cotton, 17.6; peanuts, 15.6; and tobacco, 15.1.[44]

In addition to supporting a slowly growing rural population, in "normal" times China's pre-war agriculture supplied part of the food and raw material needs of the urban areas which were growing somewhat more rapidly. Transport difficulties and other disruptions resulting from civil war in the 1920s required the increasing supplementation of urban consumption with imported grains. Imports then dropped off somewhat in the 1930s before rising again with the advent of war.[45] Agricultural commodities, moreover, accounted for the bulk of China's exports (see table 50). As a whole exports grew in value 3.5 per cent a year and in quantity terms 1.7 per cent a year during the period 1912–31.[46]

All told, this was a creditable performance for an agricultural sector which experienced no significant technological improvements before 1949. For individual farm families or particular localities and regions, of course, the annual outcome was not so uniform during the four decades of the republican era. Output and income could fluctuate greatly due to weather, natural disasters, destructive warfare or unfavorable price trends.[47] Barely adequate overall production left no margin of protection against such all too frequent contingencies, nor against the frightening year-to-year uncertainty as to whether one's family would be fed. Even this "creditable performance" requires some explanation.

Amano Motonosuke's magistral history of Chinese agriculture, which carefully examines the technology associated with each major crop as well as the development of farming implements, impressively demonstrates that the agricultural technology of the republican era was a continuation, with few improvements, of the farming practices of the Ch'ing period.[48] Sporadic efforts to improve seeds and develop better farm practices can be noted throughout the republican years. For example, 251 agricultural experimental stations were established in the provinces between 1912 and 1927.[49] The Nanking government's Bureau of Commerce and Industry, and later the Bureau of Agriculture and Mining and the National Economic Council, also encouraged agricultural research and the diffusion of agronomic knowledge.[50] These efforts, however, were small in scale and lacked the support of local government.

The slow growth of total farm production in the early decades of the twentieth century shown in tables 33 and 34 was not principally the result of improved seeds, and fertilizer, or increased irrigation and water control.

Seventy per cent of the expansion in cultivated acreage between 1913 and the 1930s occurred in Manchuria, in particular through the growth of the soy-bean acreage as well as that for kaoliang and other grains consumed by a population which rose from about 18 million in 1910 to 38 million in 1940–51. Thus, the extensive development of Manchurian agriculture employing "traditional" technology, accounted for a large share of the increase in total farm output. There were also small acreage increases in Kiangsu, Hupei, Yunnan, and Szechwan, but for the most part other increments to output were the result of the adoption of the best traditional farming practices in areas that had hitherto failed to use them. Part (perhaps most) of the increased yields on existing cropland came from the application of more labor.

Both the opening of the Manchurian frontier and the more intensive use of traditional practices were facilitated by the responsiveness of the Chinese farm family to rising export demand, favorable price trends, and the availability of urban off-farm employment opportunities, all of which persisted until the depression of the early 1930s. The increased agricultural output which resulted was adequate statistically to feed China's population because the rate of population growth was a very modest one—on the average less than 1 per cent a year. The slow growth rate, resulting from a relatively high birth rate in combination with a high but fluctuating death rate, reflected the generally low standard of living, poor public health conditions, and high susceptibility to the effects of natural and man-made disasters. Agricultural output was deemed adequate only because the average Chinese remained poor and population growth was subject to Malthusian controls. Within these dire limits, the demand for cash crops for export and by industries in the urban sector permitted some degree of shifting to the production of crops yielding a higher income per unit of land, especially on smaller farms.

Prices were favorable to the farmer until 1931 (see table 36). The general trend was upwards during the first three decades of the century—prices of agricultural products, goods purchased by the farmer for both production and consumption, land values, farm wages, and taxes all increased. While the terms of trade between agriculture and manufactured goods fluctuated in the 1910s, they were increasingly favorable to agriculture in the 1920s, indicating that prices received by the farmer rose even more rapidly than the prices he paid. Agricultural prices increased by 116 per cent (if one uses Buck's index in table 36) between 1913 and 1931,

TABLE 36
INDEX NUMBERS OF AGRICULTURAL PRICES, TERMS OF TRADE, LAND VALUES, FARM WAGES, LAND TAX, 1913-37 (1926=100)

| | (1) Agricultural products, wholesale prices | | | (2) Terms of Trade: (1) / Wholesale prices of all manufactured goods | | (2) Terms of Trade: (1) / Wholesale prices of consumers' goods | | (2) Terms of Trade: (1) / prices paid by farmers | (3) Land Values | | (4) Farm Wages | (5) Land Tax |
|---|---|---|---|---|---|---|---|---|---|---|---|---|
| Year | Tientsin | Shanghai | China* | Tientsin | Shanghai | Tientsin | Shanghai | China* | Buck | NARB | | |
| 1913 | 61 | | 58 | 82 | | 86 | | 89 | 63 | | 72 | 79 |
| 1914 | 58 | | 59 | 78 | | 83 | | 92 | 66 | | 74 | 80 |
| 1915 | 58 | | 61 | 74 | | 81 | | 90 | 68 | | 77 | 84 |
| 1916 | 61 | | 65 | 72 | | 81 | | 92 | 72 | | 80 | 86 |
| 1917 | 70 | | 69 | 77 | | 88 | | 91 | 75 | | 83 | 83 |
| 1918 | 64 | | 69 | 67 | | 74 | | 87 | 77 | | 86 | 84 |
| 1919 | 59 | | 69 | 61 | | 63 | | 84 | 81 | | 88 | 86 |
| 1920 | 77 | | 80 | 76 | | 79 | | 94 | 83 | | 89 | 87 |
| 1921 | 78 | 75 | 90 | 77 | 66 | 80 | 76 | 102 | 87 | | 91 | 86 |
| 1922 | 75 | 86 | 92 | 78 | 83 | 78 | 90 | 101 | 89 | | 93 | 86 |
| 1923 | 82 | 92 | 98 | 84 | 86 | 83 | 91 | 103 | 92 | | 95 | 88 |
| 1924 | 89 | 92 | 97 | 90 | 92 | 90 | 94 | 96 | 95 | | 95 | 89 |
| 1925 | 100 | 95 | 102 | 101 | 94 | 102 | 95 | 101 | 100 | | 97 | 92 |
| 1926 | 100 | 100 | 100 | 100 | 100 | 100 | 100 | 100 | 100 | | 100 | 100 |
| 1927 | 103 | 103 | 95 | 101 | 98 | 98 | 98 | 92 | 100 | | 105 | 109 |
| 1928 | 103 | 95 | 106 | 97 | 92 | 94 | 92 | 97 | 96 | | 112 | 118 |
| 1929 | 107 | 99 | 127 | 96 | 94 | 94 | 96 | 108 | 100 | | 118 | 119 |
| 1930 | 107 | 113 | 125 | 90 | 98 | 81 | 101 | 99 | 99 | (1931=100) | 124 | 140 |
| 1931 | 96 | 106 | 116 | 72 | 80 | 70 | 82 | 86 | 103 | 100 | 126 | 132 |
| 1932 | 90 | 95 | 103 | 73 | 79 | 69 | 80 | 81 | 93 | 95 | | |
| 1933 | 73 | 94 | | 64 | 84 | 61 | 86 | | | 89 | | |
| 1934 | 64 | 86 | | 60 | 83 | 59 | 84 | | | 82 | | |
| 1935 | 82 | 83 | | 79 | 83 | 75 | 82 | | | 81 | | |

| | | | | | | | | | |
|---|---|---|---|---|---|---|---|---|---|
| 1936 | 102 | 102 | | 87 | 91 | 82 | 91 | | 84 |
| 1937 | | 140 | | | 106 | | 108 | | |

* 37 localities in 36 hsien in 15 provinces.

*Sources:* (1) and (2), Nan-k'ai ta hsueh ching-chi yen-chiu so (Nankai Institute of Economics), comp., *1913 nien-1952 nien Nan-k'ai chih-shu tzu-liao hui-pien* (Nankai price indexes 1913-52), pp. 12-13; *Shanghai chieh-fang ch'ien hou wu-chia tzu-liao hui-pien* (Shanghai prices before and after Liberation), p. 135; John Lossing Buck, *Land utilization in China: a study of 16,786 farms in 168 localities, and 38,256 farm families in twenty-two provinces in China, 1929-1933*, pp. 149-50.

(3) Buck, *Land utilization in China, Statistics*, pp. 168-69; *Nung-ch'ing pao-kao*, 7.4 (April 1939), p. 47, in Li Wen-chih and Chang Yu-i, comps., *Chung-kuo chin-tai nung-yeh shih tzu-liao* (Source materials on China's modern agricultural history), III, pp. 708-10.

(4) Buck, *Land utilization in China, Statistics*, p. 151.

(5) Buck, *Land utilization in China, Statistics*, p. 167.

while prices paid by farmers rose by 108 per cent. In the same period land values increased by 63 per cent, farm wages by 75 per cent, and land taxes by 67 per cent. Wages tended to lag behind prices in North China but more nearly kept up with prices in the southern rice region, indicating a greater demand for labor and relatively more non-farm employment opportunities in South China. Where prices stayed ahead of wages, the farmer employing hired labor clearly profited more from the higher prices he received for his crops. Land values and land taxes increased least of all in these two decades. It appears that the real as opposed to the monetary burden of land taxes declined during these decades of generally rising prices.

From 1931 until the beginning of the recovery, in 1935 and continuing into 1936, however, Chinese farmers experienced a sharp fall in income and a striking reversal in the terms of trade. These consequences were brought about by both the contraction of export markets resulting from the world depression (the effects were delayed in China as silver prices continued to fall until 1931), and by the outflow of silver from China as the gold price of silver rose from 1931, pushed upwards first by the abandonment of the gold standard in England, Japan, and the United States, and then by the U.S. Silver Purchase Act of 1934. In this period of steeply failing prices, the farmer's fixed costs and the prices of manufactured goods tended to decline less than prices received for agricultural commodities which fell the first and most rapidly. There was a clear tendency for farmers to cut back on cash crop production and return to the cultivation of traditional grain crops in response to the depression.[52] Opportunities for off-farm employment, which had been essential to the family incomes of small farmers in particular, may also have declined temporarily after 1931, resulting in a flow of urban labor back to the rural areas.[53] Data on farm wages are sporadic, but wages probably fell less than agricultural prices. Land taxes on the average increased by 8 to 10 per cent during 1931–34 (and then declined in 1935 and 1936), while land values fell from 1931, indicating an increase in the farmer's real tax burden during the depression.[54] The outflow of silver from rural areas to Shanghai and other cities made it more difficult for farmers to obtain loans. In short, some of the gains made by the agricultural sector during the previous long inflationary phase were lost between 1931 and 1935. Recovery of both agricultural prices and cash crop output was underway by 1936, but very soon the Japanese invasion and full-scale war in mid 1937 introduced new problems.

The extent to which many farm families were affected, first, by the favorable rise in prices to 1931 and second, by their precipitous decline of almost 25 per cent between 1931 and 1936, depends on how far agriculture was commercialized and involved in market transactions. Perkins has estimated that in the 1920s and 1930s 20 to 30 per cent of farm output was sold locally, another 10 per cent shipped to urban areas, and 3 per cent exported. There was an increase in the last two categories mentioned, from 5 to 7 per cent and from 1 to 2 per cent, respectively, when compared with before 1910. Increasing commercialization in the twentieth century is attested also by qualitative data compiled by Chang Yu-i, even though his primary purpose is to illustrate the deleterious consequences for China's peasants of the activities of both indigenous and foreign imperialist merchants.[55] Yet outside of more commercialized regions like the Yangtze provinces and apart from commercially minded rich peasants, most farmers were still only marginally involved with markets. If we recall that cash crops (most of which were marketed) accounted for 17 per cent of farm output in the 1930s, Perkins' estimate of the extent of commercialization implies that less than a quarter of food crop output was sold by farmers and most of that in local markets little affected by international price trends. Even in Changsha, the major rice market in Hunan and one of the largest in China, prices in the 1930s fluctuated mainly with the provincial harvest and local political conditions. In the majority of farming communities a national average decline of prices by 25 per cent would have meant a much smaller drop in real income, maybe only by 5 per cent. That is, the effect of the depression—and other price changes, up and down—in the interior provinces of China may have been no more calamitous than the inevitable fluctuations in the weather.

China's agriculture supported the Chinese people, even producing a small "surplus" above minimum consumption levels. Over all, food consumption represented 60 per cent of domestic expenditure by end use, and total personal consumption accounted for more than 90 per cent, leaving almost insignificant amounts for communal services, government consumption, and investment.[56] As the average per capita farm output of Ch.$38-39 shown in table 34 indicates, this plainly remained a "poor" economy with minimal living standards for the mass of the population. China's grain yields per *mou* in the 1920s and 1930s were no means low by international standards. Rice yields, for example, were slightly higher than those of early Meiji Japan—although 30 per cent lower than Japan in the

1930s—and double or triple those of India and Thailand. Wheat yields were about the same as the United States. The average output of grain-equivalent per man-equivalent (one farmer working a full year) in China in the 1920s, however, was only 1,400 kilograms; the comparable figure for the United States was 20,000 kilograms—14 times as large.[57] Here was the essential reason for China's poverty: four-fifths of the labor force was employed in agriculture, and the technical and organizational characteristics of this industry were such that the value added per worker was strikingly low both in comparison with developed economies and with the modern sector of China's economy.

The principal obstacle, probably, to overcoming China's economic "backwardness" was the failure of either the private sector or the Peking and Nanking governments to marshal and allocate the funds, resources, and technology required for significant and continued new investment. Annual gross investment in China proper probably never exceeded 5 per cent of national product before 1949. Due to the weakness of political leadership, China's continuing disunity, and the exigencies of war and civil war, the agricultural sector was unable to meet any greatly enhanced demands for urban food and raw materials or for exports to exchange for major new imports of industrial plants and machinery. This contributed to the slow rate of structural change. The alternative route of imposing drastic "forced savings" on a slowly growing agricultural sector was not feasible for the weak governments of republican China.

Neither the "distributionist" nor the "technological" analysis of China's failure to industrialize before 1949, and in particular to achieve significant growth in agriculture, is by itself satisfactory. The technological or "eclectic" approach rejects the notion that rural socio-economic relationships were the major problems of the agricultural sector, and concludes as I have done above—that on the whole the performance of agriculture before 1937 was a creditable one. To the extent that growth was inhibited, this is attributed to the unavailability of appropriate inputs—especially technological improvements—and not to institutional rigidities.[58]

The emphasis of the distributionist approach is upon the contributions of unequal land ownership, tenancy, rural indebtedness, inequitable taxation and allegedly monopolistic and monopsonistic markets to supposed agricultural stagnation and increasing impoverishment. It concludes that "lack of security of tenure, high rents and a one-sided relationship between landlord and tenant gave rise to a situation in which both the incentive and the material means to undertake net farm investment were lacking."[59] At a more general level, the distributionist school attributes China's "continuing rural stagnation" to "the siphoning off of income from the tiller of the soil and its unproductive expenditure by a variety of parasitic elements who lived on, but contributed nothing to the rural surplus."[60]

There are at least two potential difficulties with a purely technological analysis. It may ignore the extremely low absolute levels of per capita output and income resulting from the modest expansion of agriculture which it recounts, and thus underestimate the urgency of demands for improvement. More important, it may be ahistorical in seeming to believe that adjustments, say of the agricultural production function by introducing improved technology, could be made within the given equilibrium. But it was problematic indeed in republican China, that within any reasonable time significant new inputs could be made without substantial institutional change.

Likewise, a number of shortcomings weaken a purely distributionist analysis. First, the progressive immiseration which is implied is not supported by any studies of the overall performance of the agricultural sector during several decades. That individual farmers, localities, and even larger regions suffered severe difficulties of varying duration is beyond doubt. This is not, however, evidence that, so long as population growth remained low, the existing agricultural system could not sustain itself at low and constant per capita output and income levels. For how long may be a valid query—as is the ethical question of the desirability that it should do so. But secular breakdown is not proven before the destructive years between 1937 and 1949.

There is a problem, too, about the proportion of the "surplus" produced by agriculture that was potentially available for productive investment. Following Victor Lippit, who identifies the rural surplus with the property income (mainly rents) received by landowners plus taxes paid by owner-cultivators, Carl Riskin finds the actual total rural surplus in 1933 equal to 19 per cent of net domestic product. (The surplus produced by the non-agricultural sectors he estimates at 8.2 per cent of NDP, giving a total actual surplus of 27.2 per cent of NDP.) After deducting the proportion of investment, communal services, and government consumption attributable to the rural surplus (four per cent out of a total of 5.8 per cent of NDP for these purposes in 1933), a further assumption is made that 15 per cent of NDP was utilized for luxury consumption by the rural elite.[61] Indeed some part was, but other parts were hoarded, "invested" in real estate, or reloaned to peasant borrowers. The principal difficulty with assuming that a rural surplus above mass consumption equivalent to 15 per cent of NDP was available for redistribution is that neither Lippit, nor Riskin, nor I have any useful quantitative data with which to estimate the importance of these various alternative uses of the surplus. If, for example, net landlord purchases of agricultural land and urban real estate, hoarding of gold and silver, and consumption loans to farmers were large, this in effect led to a "recirculation" of part of the landlords' income to peasant consumption. None of these was a direct burden on consumption in a given period, although in the longer run they may possibly have increased individual landlord claims to a share of national income. Only the conspicuous consumption of the wealthy, in particular their spending on imported luxuries, was an "exhaustive" expenditure, a direct drain on the domestic product, because it thereby depleted the foreign exchange resources which might otherwise have been available for the purchase of capital goods.

And then, of course, the experience of China's agriculture in the first decade of the People's Republic should be evidence enough that while substantial social change may have been a necessary condition for sustained increases in output, it was far from being a sufficient one. Even with the post-1958 increased emphasis on investment in agriculture, China's farm output still lags behind. The problems of supplying better seed stock, adequate fertilizer and water, optimum cropping patterns, and mechanization at critical points of labor shortage have not been easily met. In sum, the whole experience of the first three-quarters of the twentieth century suggests that only with institutional reorganization and large doses of advanced technological inputs could China's agrarian problem be solved.

If the agrarian organization of the republican period cushioned rural China from the forced savings of an authoritarian regime, it did so by abandoning any hope that the lot of a farmer would ever be any better than that which his father, and his father before him, had experienced. In other words, if the redistributive effects of peasant-landlord-government relations in rural China before 1949 were perhaps not so onerous for the peasantry as is generally believed, their long-term output effects were debilitating for the economy as a whole. Land tenure, rural usury, and regressive taxation were the natural issues around which sentiment could be mobilized for the overthrow of a social system which offered little prospect for betterment.

The estimates we have used for population (430 million in 1912, 500 million in the mid 1930s) and for cultivated acreage (1,356 million *mou* and 1,471 million *mou*), suggest that the area of cultivated land per capita decreased from 3.15 *mou* to 2.94 *mou* in the first decades of the twentieth century. Responses collected by Buck's investigators also indicate a decline from 1870 to 1933 in the size of the average farm operated.[62] Although derived from different sources and by different methods, the two estimates (1 *mou* = 0.167 acre) are very close—Buck: 1910, 2.62 acres (crop area) per farm family; 1933, 2.27 acres. Perkins (assuming an average household of five persons): 1913, 2.6 acres; 1930s, 2.4 acres. The size distribution of farms operated as of 1934-35 is shown in table 38(3). In the southern provinces (Buck's "rice region"), the average unit of cultivation tended to be substantially smaller than in the north (the "wheat region"). In all regions there was a significant correlation between size of household and farm size, an indication that high population density had forced the price of land so high that peasants could afford to fill it only in a lavishly labor-using fashion. Therefore, farm size was small when household members were few.

The uneconomic aspects of miniature cultivation were aggravated by the fact that farms tended to be broken up into several non-adjacent parcels, a product in large part of the absence of primogeniture in the Chinese inheritance system. Considerable land was wasted in boundary strips, excessive labor time was used in travel from parcel to parcel, and irrigation was made more difficult. Buck's average was six parcels per farm; other writers mention from five to 40 parcels.

While the Chinese farmer had skillfully exploited the traditional agricultural technology to the very limits of possibility, few of the nineteenth and twentieth-century advances in seeds, implements, fertilizers, insecticides and the like had found their way into rural China. Investment in agriculture was overwhelmingly investment in land. Human-power was more important than animal-power, and the farmer's implements—little changed over the centuries—were adapted to human-power. The utilization of human labor per acre of land was probably more intensive than in any other country of the world, while paradoxically the individual laborer was not intensively used except at peak periods such as planting or harvesting. Only 35 per cent of rural men aged between 16 and 60 were engaged in full-time agricultural work, while 58 per cent worked only part-time. Part of the surplus labor power was devoted to subsidiary occupations, usually home industry, which provided 14 per cent of the income of farm families so engaged.[65]

The kind and quantity of agricultural output summarized at the beginning of this section were the results of the decisions as to the allocation of their human and material resources and the application of their farming skills by millions of peasant households. Nearly half of these family farms were less than 10 *mou* (1.6 acres) in size, and 80 per cent were smaller than 30 *mou* (5 acres). It is necessary, however, to distinguish between unit of cultivation and unit of ownership, and inquire into the effects of substantial tenancy upon agricultural output and the individual farm family.

How much land was rented in the 1930s? Buck, for example, estimated that 28.7 per cent of privately-owned farm land was rented to tenants [table 38(2)]. If the 6.7 per cent of farm land that was publicly owned (*kung-t'ien*, government land, school land, temple land, ancestral land, soldiers' land and charity land) and which was almost entirely rented out is added to this figure, it appears that a total of 35.5 per cent of agricultural land was rented to tenants.[64] This estimate is confirmed by data on the quantity of land that was redistributed in the course of land reform in the first years of the People's Republic—from 42 to 44 per cent of the cultivated area in 1952.[65] The proportion beyond 35.5 per cent is perhaps an indication of the zeal with which land owned by "rich peasants" as well as landlords was confiscated during the land reform.

Land ownership in China was very unequal, but probably less so than in many other "underdeveloped" countries. The best data for the 1930s were obtained by a land survey in 16 provinces excluding Manchuria conducted by the National Land Commission of the National Economic Council and the Ministries of Finance and Interior (shown in table 37). Some downward bias is present in these figures as a consequence of including information only about landlords actually resident in the areas surveyed. The average holding of the 1,295,001 owners covered by this 1934–35 survey was 15.17 *mou* (2.5 acres). But the 73 percent of the families surveyed who owned 15 *mou* or less held only 28 per cent of the total land, while the 5 per cent of families owning 50 *mou* or more held 34 per cent the total land.

Few of the large holdings were farmed as such by their owners; commercial farming with hired labor was a rarity. In general the land was leased to tenants, or part was farmed by the landlord (using the labor of his family and/or hired labor depending on the size of his holding and his social status) with the balance being leased. In the twentieth century, with the breakdown of civil order in many parts of the interior there was an increase of absentee landlords who abandoned the rural town for the protection of city walls. They ordinarily retained only a financial interest in their property, and entrusted the supervision of tenants and rent collection to local agents (*tsu-chan* or "landlord bursaries" in the Yangtze valley, for example) who often stood to profit the more they were able to "squeeze" their charges.[66] Particularly in the southern and eastern coastal provinces, this introduced an increasing harshness into rural class relations—never the subject for a pastoral idyll even under the best Confucian landlord, but possibly a little more personal and human than under the inexorable pressure of the market.

Perkins suggests that in the 1930s three-quarters of rented-out land was owned by absentee landlords, most of whom attained their initial wealth from sources other than farming. Land, in other words, was an investment for rich merchants and others in those parts of China where rates of return were reasonable because well-established markets for grain were served by inexpensive water transport, namely in the more urbanized and commercialized Yangtze valley and in the south.[67] The data in table 28(5) show a rough correlation between rents as a percentage of land value and the incidence of tenancy in the several provinces. Kweichow is something of an anomaly in the south-west, as is Shantung in the north. In the former case, as perhaps in other relatively poor and backward areas, the basis for high rates of tenancy may have lain in the persistence of "feudal" landlord-tenant relations (labor services, miscellaneous exactions, tighter controls) rather than in the strictly commercial return on the land.[68] High returns to land ownership in Shantung where the overall tenancy rate was low may result from the figure chosen by the National Agricultural Research Bureau's investigators for the "average" value of a *mou* of land in Shantung.[69]

Estimates of the extent of tenancy in republican China vary considerably, and of course local differences were enormous, but overall about 50 per cent of the peasantry were involved in the landlord-tenant relationship—about 30 per cent as tenants who rented all of the land that they farmed, and 20 per cent more as owner-tenants who rented part of their land. Table 38(1) presents two estimates of the rates of tenancy by province in the 1930s, which, although they differ in detail, clearly indicate the much greater incidence of pure tenancy in the rice-growing province of the Yangtze valley and the southern coast than in the wheat-growing north.[70]

TABLE 37
DISTRIBUTION OF RURAL LAND OWNERSHIP, 1934-35* (16 PROVINCES)

| Size classes of land owned (*mou*) | Number of families (*hu*) surveyed | % of families surveyed | Land owned (1,000 *mou*) | % of land owned | Average land per family (*mou*) |
|---|---|---|---|---|---|
| < 5 | 461,128 | 35.61 | 1,217 | 6.21 | 2.64 |
| 5-9.9 | 310,616 | 23.99 | 2,245 | 11.42 | 7.23 |
| 10-14.9 | 170,604 | 13.17 | 2,090 | 10.63 | 12.25 |
| 15-19.9 | 103,468 | 7.99 | 1,802 | 9.17 | 17.42 |
| 20-29.9 | 106,399 | 8.22 | 2,589 | 13.17 | 24.33 |
| 30-49.9 | 80,333 | 6.20 | 3,053 | 15.54 | 38.01 |
| 50-69.9 | 28,094 | 2.17 | 1,646 | 8.38 | 58.59 |
| 70-99.9 | 17,029 | 1.31 | 1,408 | 7.16 | 82.61 |
| 100-149.9 | 9,349 | 0.72 | 1,124 | 5.71 | 120.21 |
| 150-199.9 | 3,146 | 0.24 | 514 | 2.76 | 171.97 |
| 200-299.9 | 2,587 | 0.20 | 623 | 3.17 | 240.95 |
| 300-499.9 | 1,368 | 0.11 | 518 | 2.63 | 378.40 |
| 500-999.9 | 674 | 0.05 | 453 | 2.30 | 671.87 |
| > 1,000 | 196 | 0.02 | 344 | 1.75 | 1,752.60 |
| Total | 1,295,001 | 100.00 | 19,650 | 100.00 | 15.17 |

* Provinces included: Chahar, Suiyuan, Shensi, Shansi, Hopei, Shantung, Honan, Kiangsu, Anhwei, Chekiang, Hupei, Hunan, Kiangsi, Fukien, Kwangtung, Kwangsi.

*Source:* National Land Commission, *Ch'üan-kuo t'u-ti tiao-ch'a pao-kao kang-yao* (Preliminary report of the national land survey), p. 33.

These provincial data often obscure very considerable local variations within any province resulting from location, land quality, degree of commercialization and historical accretions.[71] It should also be noted that the categories owner, owner-tenant, and tenant do not necessarily represent a descending order of economic well-being. The somewhat more complex categorization of the National Land Commission's 1934 survey shown in table 39, for example, is a warning that the rubric "owner tenant" in table 38(1) subsumes every case from a landlord who rents 1 per cent of his land to a poor peasant who rents 95 per cent. And the farmers of Shansi, Shantung, Hopei, and Honan with less population pressure and larger farms, who were predominantly owner-cultivators, were not better off with respect to family income than their tenant brethren in Kwangtung. Nor is tenancy incompatible with economic progress: note that in the United States the percentage of farm operators who were tenants increased from 25.6 per cent in 1879 to 34.5 per cent in 1945.

Reliable historical data on the changing incidence of tenancy are nearly non-existent. A comparison of the estimates compiled by local observer missionaries and others in the 1880s with those for the 1930s suggest considerable variation by locality but no significant change in the overall tenancy rate.[72] National Agricultural Bureau estimates show only a slight change (farmers who rented all of their land increased from 28 per cent in 1919 to 30 per cent of farm families in 1931–36), which is probably not significant since the 1931–36 data were obtained from regular mail questionnaires completed by thousands of volunteer crop reporters, many of whom were rural school teachers, while those for 1912 are only conjecture.[73] Ramon Myers' comparison of 22 counties in Shantung in the 1890s and 1930s discloses that the percentage of tenant households fell in 13 and rose in nine counties.[74] Comparative data from Honan, Anhwei, Kiangsi, and Hupei for 1913, 1923, and 1934 show no significant changes: tenants increased from 39 to 41 per cent and owner-tenants from 27 to 28 per cent, while owner-cultivators declined from 34 to 31 per cent.[75]

The relatively slow rise of land values as compared with other prices shown in table 36 may imply that the demand for land was comparatively weak in the relatively unsettled circumstances of the 1920s when, as Buck observed, "agitation against landlords ... reduced the demand for land and even encouraged owners to sell their property."[76] Finally, as indicated above, the amount of cultivated land distributed during land reform in the first years of the People's Republic was—even after a dozen very bad years of

TABLE 38
TENANCY, RENTED LAND, FARM SIZE, RENT SYSTEMS, AND RENTAL RATES IN THE 1930S (22 PROVINCES, EXCLUDING MANCHURIA)

| | (1) Per cent farming families (*hu*) who are owners, owner-tenants, tenants | | | | | | | |
|---|---|---|---|---|---|---|---|---|
| | NARB, 1931–36 average | | | | Buck, 1929–33 | | | |
| Province | No. hsien reporting 1936 | Owner | Owner-tenant | Tenant | No. localities surveyed | Owner | Owner-tenant | Tenant |
| *NW* | | | | | | | | |
| Chahar | (10) | 39 | 26 | 35 | — | — | — | — |
| Suiyuan | (13) | 56 | 18 | 26 | — | — | — | — |
| Ninghsia | (5) | 62 | 11 | 27 | (1) | 96 | 1 | 3 |
| Tsinghai | (8) | 55 | 24 | 21 | (2) | 20 | 8 | 72 |
| Kansu | (29) | 59 | 19 | 22 | (6) | 58 | 16 | 26 |
| Shensi | (49) | 55 | 22 | 23 | (20) | 68 | 15 | 17 |
| *N* | | | | | | | | |
| Shansi | (90) | 62 | 21 | 17 | (4) | 38 | 38 | 24 |
| Hopei | (126) | 68 | 20 | 12 | (6) | 71 | 17 | 12 |
| Shantung | (100) | 71 | 17 | 12 | (15) | 72 | 18 | 10 |
| Honan | (89) | 56 | 22 | 22 | (8) | 58 | 23 | 19 |
| *E* | | | | | | | | |
| Kiangsu | (56) | 41 | 26 | 33 | (6) | 31 | 23 | 46 |
| Anhwei | (41) | 34 | 22 | 44 | (2) | 35 | 13 | 52 |
| Chekiang | (62) | 21 | 32 | 47 | (14) | 29 | 20 | 51 |
| *C* | | | | | | | | |
| Hupei | (48) | 31 | 29 | 40 | (5) | 35 | 31 | 34 |
| Hunan | (41) | 25 | 27 | 48 | (13) | 16 | 27 | 57 |
| Kiangsi | (57) | 28 | 31 | 41 | (7) | 33 | 35 | 32 |
| SE | | | | | | | | |
| Fukien | (42) | 26 | 32 | 42 | (1) | 30 | 55 | 15 |
| Kwangtung | (55) | 21 | 27 | 52 | (13) | 16 | 35 | 49 |
| Kwangsi | (50) | 33 | 27 | 40 | — | — | — | — |
| *SW* | | | | | | | | |
| Kweichow | (23) | 32 | 25 | 43 | (6) | 25 | 22 | 53 |
| Yunnan | (39) | 34 | 28 | 38 | (8) | 49 | 27 | 24 |
| Szechwan | (87) | 24 | 20 | 56 | (3) | 27 | 15 | 58 |
| National average (excluding Manchuria) | (1,120) | 46 | 24 | 30 | (140) | 44 | 23 | 33 |

TABLE 38 (continued)

| Province | (2) Rented land as per cent farm area: National Land Commission | Buck | (3) Percentage distribution of size of farms operated, 1934–35 (*mou*) < 10 | 10-29.9 | 30-49.9 | 50-99.9 | > 100 |
|---|---|---|---|---|---|---|---|
| *NW* | | | | | | | |
| Chahar | 10.2 | — | 1.4 | 7.9 | 2.2 | 8.9 | 79.6 |
| Suiyuan | 8.7 | 5.0 | 9.3 | 33.3 | 16.2 | 18.4 | 22.8 |
| Ninghsia | — | 0.5 | — | — | — | — | — |
| Tsinghai | — | 9.5 | — | — | — | — | — |
| Kansu | — | 9.1 | — | — | — | — | — |
| Shensi | 16.6 | 17.4 | 38.7 | 35.9 | 12.8 | 10.1 | 2.5 |
| *N* | | | | | | | |
| Shansi | — | 15.8 | 16.9 | 41.0 | 20.3 | 16.1 | 5.7 |
| Hopei | 12.9 | 9.8 | 40.0 | 41.4 | 10.8 | 6.1 | 1.7 |
| Shantung | 12.6 | 9.8 | 49.7 | 38.5 | 7.9 | 3.3 | 0.6 |
| Honan | 27.3 | 19.7 | 47.9 | 34.6 | 9.5 | 6.2 | 1.8 |
| *E* | | | | | | | |
| Kiangsu | 42.3 | 33.3 | 52.3 | 38.1 | 5.8 | 2.5 | 1.3 |
| Anhwei | 52.6 | 51.0 | 47.0 | 38.2 | 9.6 | 4.5 | 0.7 |
| Chekiang | 51.3 | 31.0 | 67.0 | 27.8 | 3.5 | 1.4 | 0.3 |
| *C* | | | | | | | |
| Hupei | 27.9 | 31.2 | 60.4 | 32.0 | 5.5 | 1.8 | 0.2 |
| Hunan | 47.8 | 36.6 | 56.5 | 33.4 | 6.3 | 3.1 | 0.8 |
| Kiangsi | 45.1 | 51.4 | 54.2 | 41.6 | 3.7 | 0.5 | * |
| SE | | | | | | | |
| Fukien | 39.3 | 55.7 | 71.8 | 24.8 | 2.5 | 0.8 | 0.1 |
| Kwangtung | 76.9 | 59.6 | 87.4 | 12.3 | 0.3 | * | — |
| Kwangsi | 21.2 | 26.0 | 51.1 | 37.7 | 7.2 | 3.0 | 0.9 |
| *SW* | | | | | | | |
| Kweichow | — | 25.8 | — | — | — | — | — |
| Yunnan | — | 27.6 | — | — | — | — | — |
| Szechwan | — | 52.4 | — | — | — | — | — |
| National average (excluding Manchuria) | 30.7 | 28.7 | 47.0 | 32.4 | 7.8 | 5.4 | 7.4 |

TABLE 38 (continued)

| | (4) Percentage distribution of types of rent, 1934 | | | (5) Rents as per cent of land values, 1934 | | | |
|---|---|---|---|---|---|---|---|
| Province | Cash | Fixed kind (crop) | Share | Cash | Fixed kind (crop) | Share | Fixed kind and share rents as per cent of value of crop, 1934 |
| *NW* | | | | | | | |
| Chahar | 19 | 51 | 30 | 2.9 | 4.4 | 6.9 | 37.5 |
| Suiyuan | 31 | 23 | 46 | 6.4 | 14.4 | 12.0 | — |
| Ninghsia | 46 | 19 | 35 | — | — | — | } |
| Tsinghai | 11 | 54 | 35 | — | — | — | } 30.9 |
| Kansu | 14 | 51 | 35 | 11.4 | 12.0 | 13.7 | } |
| Shensi | 15 | 9 | 26 | 10.1 | 13.0 | 12.6 | 41.1 |
| *N* | | | | | | | |
| Shansi | 27 | 45 | 27 | 6.2 | 5.9 | 6.2 | 50.1 |
| Hopei | 52 | 22 | 26 | 7.3 | 7.6 | 8.1 | 49.1 |
| Shantung | 30 | 31 | 39 | 16.0 | 18.8 | 20.8 | 46.5 |
| Honan | 17 | 39 | 44 | — | — | — | 49.5 |
| *E* | | | | | | | |
| Kiangsu | 28 | 53 | 19 | 8.7 | 7.8 | 12.8 | 40.3 |
| Anhwei | 14 | 53 | 33 | 9.4 | 9.4 | 16.4 | 40.4 |
| Chekiang | 27 | 66 | 7 | 9.6 | 10.3 | 13.2 | 42.4 |
| *C* | | | | | | | |
| Hupei | 20 | 58 | 22 | 8.3 | 6.8 | 13.6 | 38.6 |
| Hunan | 8 | 74 | 18 | 17.4 | 17.4 | 28.5 | 44.2 |
| Kiangsi | 7 | 80 | 13 | 19.2 | 18.1 | 36.8 | 42.6 |
| SE | | | | | | | |
| Fukien | 19 | 56 | 25 | 17.8 | 19.9 | 21.0 | 44.7 |
| Kwangtung | 24 | 58 | 18 | 17.0 | 19.0 | 15.4 | 42.5 |
| Kwangsi | 6 | 65 | 29 | — | — | — | 43.1 |
| *SW* | | | | | | | |
| Kweichow | 10 | 40 | 50 | 6.2 | 13.4 | 12.1 | 51.4 |
| Yunnan | 14 | 61 | 25 | 13.9 | 16.6 | 16.8 | 43.4 |
| Szechwan | 26 | 58 | 16 | 11.4 | 14.5 | 16.9 | 49.1 |
| National average (excluding Manchuria) | 21 | 51 | 28 | 11.0 | 12.9 | 14.1 | 43.3 |

* less than 0.05%

*Sources:* (1) *Nung-ch'ing pao-kao,* 5.12. (December 1957): 330, in Li Wen-chih and Chang Yu-i, comps., *Chung-kuo chin-tai nung-yeh shih tzu-liao,* III. 728-30. Buck, *Land utilization in China, Statistics,* pp. 57-59.

(2) Buck, *Land utilization in China, Statistics,* pp. 55-56. National Land Commission, *Ch'üan-kuo t'u-ti tiao-ch'a pao-kao kang-yao,* p. 37.

(3) *Ch'üan-kuo t'u-ti tiao-ch'a pao-kao kang-yao,* pp. 26-27.

(4) *Nung-ch'ing pao-kao,* 3.4 (April 1935): 90, in National Government, Directorate of Statistics, *Chung-kuo tsu-tien chih-tu chih t'ung-chi fen-hsi* (Statistical analysis of China's land rent system), p. 43.

(5) *Nung-ch'ing pao-kao,* pp. 5-6 (June 1935), in *Chung-kuo tsu-tien chih-tu chih t'ung-chi fen-hsi,* p. 79. Ch'en Cheng-mo, *Chung-kuo ko-sheng ti ti-tsu* (Land rents in China by province), pp. 94-95

TABLE 39
PERCENTAGE OF FARM FAMILIES IN VARIOUS OWNERSHIP CATEGORIES
(1,745,344 FAMILIES IN 16 PROVINCES, 1934–35)

| | |
|---|---|
| Landlord | 2.05 |
| Landlord-owner | 3.15 |
| Landlord-owner-tenant | 0.47 |
| Landlord-tenant | 0.11 |
| Owner | 47.61 |
| Owner-tenant | 20.81 |
| Tenant | 15.78 |
| Tenant-laborer | 0.02 |
| Laborer | 1.57 |
| Other | 8.43 |

*Source: Ch'üan-kuo t'u-ti tiao-ch'a pao-kao kang-yao,* p. 31.

war and civil war—approximately the same as that controlled by landlords in the mid 1930s. One may perhaps conclude that while land was regularly bought and sold, the basic pattern of high tenancy in some areas and low tenancy in others—based primarily on the differential economic return to landlords, but also in the most backward areas on the persistence of "extra-economic" labor service and other exactions—was not significantly altered in the republican era.

Was the tenant's position secure? Overall, it may have become slightly less so in the course of the twentieth century. A rough comparison of 93 counties in eight provinces between 1924 and 1934 shows a small increase in the percentage of annual rentals, no change in three- to 10-year contracts, and slight decreases in 10- to 20-year and permanent rentals.[77] That the 1930 Land Law, for example, contained a provision to the effect that the tenant had the right to extend his lease indefinitely unless the landlord took the land back at the expiration of the contract and farmed it himself, indicates recognition of the problem of insecure peasant holdings. No effort was made to enforce the law; hence insecurity of tenure undoubtedly continued to be a problem. As part of the process of modernization of property concepts in rural China the system of "permanent tenancy" (*yung-tien*) which had sharply differentiated the tenant's ownership of a "surface right" from the landlord's "bottom right," was gradually disappearing. Permanent tenure was replaced by less permanent contracts. The insecurity of the annual contract put the peasant at considerable disadvantage and allowed the landlord to impose additional burdens in the form of land deposits (as security against non-payment of rents) and higher rents.

But these trends were occurring only very slowly. Of greater immediate significance for the productivity of China's agriculture is the continuing positive correlation in the eight provinces referred to above between the incidence of longer rent contracts, including permanent tenure, and the percentage of tenancy. The National Land Commission's 1934–35 survey also found "permanent tenancy" to be most prevalent in Kiangsu, Anhwei, and Chekiang—three provinces with high tenancy rates.[78] While tenants would have had an even greater incentive to improve their land if they had owned it outright, the long-run economic interests of both tenant and landlord appear to have resulted in sufficiently long rental contracts in areas of high tenancy so that tenant incentives to increase productivity by investing in the land they farmed were not completely discouraged.

A 1932 survey of 849 counties by the Ministry of Interior found that the rent deposit system (*ya-tsu*) was prevalent in 220 counties (26 per cent) and present in 60 others.[79] Land rents were paid in three principal forms: cash, crop, and share rent. The National Agricultural Research Bureau's 1934 survey reported that 50.7 per cent of tenants paid a fixed amount of their principal crops, 28.1 per cent were share-croppers, and 21.2 per cent paid a fixed cash rent; see table 38(4). Comparable data in the 1934–35 land survey were: crop rent, 60.01 per cent; cash rent, 24.62 per cent; share rent, 14.99 per cent; labor rent, 0.24 per cent; and others, 0.14 per cent.[80] The incidence of cash rent was perhaps increasing very slowly in the twentieth century.[81]

In general, as shown in table 38(5), the burden of share rent (which depended upon the extent to which the landlord provided seeds, tools, and draught animals, and which on average equaled 14.1 per cent of land value) was slightly greater than crop rent (12.9 per cent), and crop rent greater than cash rent (11.0 per cent). Rents in kind, fixed and share, averaged 43.3 per cent of the value of the crop when the tenant supplied seeds, fertilizer, and draught animals. The failure of the Kuomintang policy of limiting rents to 37.5 per cent of the main crops is evident.

In whatever form they were paid, rents were considerably higher, in absolute terms and in relation to the value of the land, in South China than they were in the north—but so too was the output per *mou* of land. A fixed rent in kind was the dominant system except for North China and Kweichow in the south-west, accounting for 62 per cent of rental arrangements in the five provinces with the highest incidence of tenancy (Anhwei, Chekiang, Hunan, Kwangtung, and Szechwan) but only 39 per cent in the five provinces with the lowest tenancy rates (Shensi, Shansi, Hopei, Shantung, and Honan). Under this arrangement, a tenant paid his landlord a fixed amount of grain whether he had a good harvest or bad (with possibly a reduction or postponement in catastrophically bad years). When combined with longer-term contracts, which were also more common in the high tenancy rice-growing provinces, a fixed rent in kind permitted the tenant to benefit from improvements in productivity resulting from his labor and investment, and thus provided a greater incentive for increased output than did share-cropping. Share rents were more common (32 per cent) in the five low tenancy North China provinces, where security of tenure was also less, than they were in the five high tenancy provinces (18 per cent). Contract terms were thus less encouraging to peasant investment in land improvements in the north than in the south, but tenancy was also less prevalent in the north.

The province-level quantitative treatment offered above does not deal adequately with the fate of individual tenant families, or the rich variety of local practices, or the limits within which increased output could be furthered by these apparently rational aspects of the tenancy system. To what degree real peasant tenants in specific areas at specific times realized sufficient family income to make improvements which increased their total output can only be determined by detailed local studies such as those by Ramon Myers of Hopei and Shantung and by Robert Ash of Kiangsu; the former's finding is positive and the latter's negative.

The patterns of land tenure and cultivation described above were intimately connected with the structure of credit, marketing, and taxation related to agriculture. Agriculture being an industry of slow turn-over, the small peasant in China, as in other countries, was often unable to survive the interval between sowing and harvesting without borrowing. Indebtedness was a major source of rural discontent. Buck reports that 39 per cent of the farms surveyed in 1929–33 were in debt. The National Agricultural Research Bureau estimated that, in 1933, 56 per cent of farms had borrowed cash and 48 per cent had borrowed grain for food. A third national estimate noted that 43.87 per cent of farm families were in debt in 1935.[82] All observers agree overwhelmingly that the rural debt had been incurred to meet household consumption needs rather than for investment in production, and that for the poorer peasants indebtedness was the rule.[83] Interest rates were high. This was a reflection of the desperate need of the peasant, the shortage of capital in rural China, the risk of default, and the absence of alternative modern lending facilities either government or cooperative. On small loans in kind, an annual rate of 100 to 200 per cent might be charged. The bulk of peasant loans, perhaps two-thirds, paid annual rates of 20 to 40 per cent; about one-tenth paid less than 20 per cent; and the rest, more than 40 per cent. About two-thirds of all loans were for periods of six months to one year.[84] Agricultural credit came largely from individuals—landlords, wealthier farmers, merchants—as the 1934 data in table 40 indicate.

There were few modern banks (government or private) in rural areas, and in any case such banks did not invest in consumption loans. The seven modern banks in Kiangsi, to give an example, had only 0.078 per cent of their outstanding loan funds in 1932 invested in farm loans.[85] Considerable attention has been directed to the rural cooperative movement which began in the 1920s, but the cooperatives even at their peak never involved more than a tiny fraction of Chinese farmers.[86] The money-lender, who was often the landlord or the grain merchant, performed the function of transferring part of the surplus of agriculture back to the peasant, thus allowing him to live beyond his means, but at the ultimate cost of preserving intact a landlord dominated rural society.

TABLE 40
SOURCES OF FARM CREDIT, 1934

| Source of farm credit | % of total number of loans |
|---|---|
| Banks | 2.4 |
| Cooperatives | 2.6 |
| Pawnshops | 8.8 |
| Native banks | 5.5 |
| Village stores and shops | 13.1 |
| Landlords | 24.2 |
| Well-to-do farmers | 18.4 |
| Merchants | 25.0 |

*Source:* National Agricultural Research Bureau, *Crop reporting in China, 1934*, p. 70.

The Chinese village was not economically self-sufficient, although a larger unit, Skinner's "standard marketing area," for many purposes can be considered so. To meet cash obligations such as rent and taxes, and to purchase many necessities, some part of the farmer's crop had to be disposed of on the market. About 15 per cent of the rice crop and 29 per cent of the wheat crop were sold by the peasants covered in Buck's survey, while the proportion for cash crops such as tobacco, opium, peanuts, rapeseed, and cotton was, of course, considerably higher.[87] In many cases the peasant had no choice but to sell in the local market. He was separated from more distant markets not only by inadequate and thus costly transport, but perhaps also by an information barrier—although the burden of rural illiteracy has probably been exaggerated. The market was subject to considerable price fluctuations, which might be unfavorable to the peasant as a result of the fact that supply would naturally be larger at harvest time when he wanted to sell and smaller in the spring when he wanted to buy. Moreover, in those areas near the major cities in eastern and southern coastal China where the commercialization of agriculture had made some headway, exploitative collection systems (such as that operated by the British and American Tobacco Company) put the farmer at the mercy of the buyer.

While as a small individual buyer and seller the peasant was unable to influence the markets in which he had to trade, to imply in crude Marxist (and Confucian) terms that all merchants were parasites who contributed nothing to the economy or to suggest that increased commercialization of agriculture in the twentieth century had a negative effect on rural production and income is absurd. In the atomistic rural sector there were no barriers to entry (other than the often exaggerated information barrier), virtually no government intervention, and low capital requirements for all businesses, so that most types of commerce were quite competitive. High profits quickly lured new entrants into existing markets. The richest merchants, in China as elsewhere, were those who did business in the more commercialized areas where almost everyone was informed, mobile and experienced in dealing with markets. They made their profits not by fleecing their customers, but by specialization, division of labor, and offering critical services at low unit prices. The local market has frequently been described as tending to monopsony for what the peasant sold and to monopoly for what he bought, but in fact there have been few studies to document this common assumption. If more than two-thirds of marketed crops were sold locally (as Perkins suggests; see page 129 above), then this trade may have involved few merchants at all; periodic markets were places where farmers bought and sold from and to each other. And if Perkins is also right that most rice marketings were by landlords (see page 136 above), who did not have to sell at harvest time and who had the information and connections which made it difficult to fleece them, then there is little support for monopsony.

I have noted above that the terms of trade between agriculture and industry were generally favorable to the farmer before 1931. The ability to grow and market cash crops was a major factor supporting the modest increase in total agricultural output that occurred between 1912 and the 1930s and which kept per capita rural incomes roughly constant over this period. Indeed, the agricultural market was fragmented, sometimes appeared to be stacked against the small peasant producer, and perhaps was burdened with excessive middlemen, all of which prevented greater increases in output and clearly detracted from rural welfare. But it did function well enough before 1937 to help keep the traditional economic system afloat.

Under both the Peking government until 1927 and the Nanking government which followed, agricultural taxation was probably inequitable in incidence, but the matter has never been carefully studied. The land tax was largely a provincial or local levy. Collusion between the local elite and the tax collector was common, with the result that a disproportionate share of the burden fell upon the small owner-farmer. Land taxes were also shifted onto tenants in the form of higher rents. And such additional abuses as forced collections in advance, the manipulation of exchange rates, and multiple surcharges were reported.[88] In the last decade of Kuomintang rule, the tax burden on the small owner and the tenant was increased by wartime tax collection in kind and compulsory grain purchases by the Chungking government.

If the incidence were inequitable, the most important economic characteristic of the pre-1949 land tax was its failure to recover a major share of the agricultural surplus appropriated by the landlord for redistribution to productive investment. The level of taxation in fact was low, reflecting the superficial penetration of the state into local society (see page 155 below). As in the cases of credit and marketing, the system of agricultural taxation reinforced a pattern of income distribution which allowed only a very modest overall growth of output with no increase at all in individual income and welfare.

Quantitative treatment of China's agriculture between 1937 and 1949 is nearly impossible. War and civil war put an end to even the modest collection of rural statistical data of the Nanking government decade. The principal scene of fighting was North China, and it is certain that physical damage to agricultural land, transport disruptions, conscription of manpower, and draught animals, requisitions of grain for the armies, and mounting political conflict affected farmers in the north much more severely than in South and West China.[89] The pre-war process of increasing commercialization was reversed, agricultural productivity and output declined, and commodity trade between rural and urban areas was disrupted. Even by 1950, according to rural surveys made in the first two years of the People's Republic, some areas in North China had not returned to their peak pre-war output levels due to manpower and draught animal losses.[90] Both the harsh Japanese occupation and the great battles of 1948–49 left the south and west relatively unscathed, but here too manpower and grain requisitions by the military took their toll, and runaway inflation from 1947 undermined the supply of foodstuffs and industrial crops to the urban areas. The collapse of both the rural and the urban economy of China was a fact by mid 1948.

## 6. Transport

Poorly developed transport continued to be a major shortcoming of the Chinese economy throughout the republican period. This is apparent at both the microscopic and macroscopic levels. In 1919 the cost of production of a ton of pig iron at the Hanyang Ironworks in Hupei, China's major producer, was Ch.$48.50 while in 1915 the Japanese ironworks Pen-ch'i in Manchuria produced pig iron at Ch.$22.00 per ton. Coke produced locally at Pen-ch'i cost Ch.$5.74 a ton, but high transport charges attributable to slow progress in building the Canton-Hankow railway and to inefficient handling by native boats for the river trip to P'inghsiang in Kiangsi 300 miles away, forced up the cost of coke at Hanyang to Ch.$24.54 a ton.[91] Since both firms obtained their raw materials from their own "captive" mines, it is unlikely that the difference was due to market fluctuations between the two dates.

The wages of coolie labor were incredibly low, but the economic efficiency of the human carriers who dominated transport at the local level was even lower. One observer reported:

> On the road from the Wei Basin to the Chengtu Plain, in Szechuan Province, one may meet coolies carrying on their backs loads of cotton weighing 160 pounds. They will carry these loads fifteen miles a day for 750 miles at a rate of seventeen cents (Mexican) a day, which is the equivalent of fourteen cents a

> ton mile. At this rate it costs $106.25 to transport one ton 750 miles. The railways should be able to haul this for $15, or one seventh the amount. The Peking-Mukden Railway carries coal for the Kailan Mining Company at less than 1½ cents a ton mile. With the coolie carriers the cotton spends fifty days on the road, whereas the railway would make the haul in two days, thereby saving forty-eight days interest on the money and landing the cotton in better condition.[92]

Comparative costs of transport in China by the principal modes of conveyance have been estimated (in Ch. cents per ton-kilometer) as follows: junks, 2 to 12; steamers and launches, 1 to 15; railways, 3.2 to 17; carts, 5 to 16.5; wheelbarrows, 10 to 14; camels, 10 to 20; motor trucks, 10 to 56; donkeys, mules, and horses, 13.3 to 25; human porterage, 14 to 50; and rickshaw, 20 to 35.[93] Throughout the republican era, the bulk of goods continued to be carried by traditional modes of transport. The data for 1933, for example, which was not an atypical year, show that old-fashioned forms of transport contributed three times as much (Ch.$ 1.2 billion) to national income as did modern transport methods (Ch.$ 430 million).

An adequate railway network would have greatly reduced transport costs and facilitated the development of the interior. Among other things, goods carried by rail more often escaped likin (*li-chin*) and other local transit duties. And the presence of a railway tends to standardize weights, measures and currency along the line. But the example of British India should make it evident that a great railway network can coexist with a backward agricultural economy, that mere length does not lead automatically to economic development. In any case, the railways of republican China were inadequate in length, distribution, and operation. At the end of the Second World War, China, including Manchuria and Taiwan, had a total of 24,845 kilometers of main and branch railway lines.[94] The amount built in each of the periods into which we may conventionally divide the republican era was as follows:

| | | |
|---|---|---|
| Before 1912 | 9618.10 | km |
| 1912–27 | 3,422.38 | |
| 1928–37 | 7,895.66 | |
| 1938–45 | 3,909.38 | |
| Total | 24,845.52 | km |

Map 5. Railways as of 1949

TABLE 41
INDEX NUMBERS OF PASSENGER MILES AND FREIGHT TON MILES CARRIED ON THE CHINESE GOVERNMENT RAILWAYS, 1912-47

| (1912=100) | | | (1917=100) | | | | | |
|---|---|---|---|---|---|---|---|---|
| Year | Passenger miles | Freight ton miles | Total freight ton miles | Manufactures | Mineral products | Agricultural products | Forest products | Animal products |
| 1912 | 100.0 | 100.0 | | | | | | |
| 1915 | 61.1 | 92.5 | | | | | | |
| 1916 | 127.2 | 107.7 | 94.7 | 94.8 | 93.8 | 91.3 | 81.0 | 126.9 |
| 1917 | 131.1 | 113.8 | 100.0 | 100.0 | 100.0 | 100.0 | 100.0 | 100.0 |
| 1918 | 143.0 | 140.8 | 123.8 | 124.6 | 127.6 | 123.5 | 120.9 | 97.8 |
| 1919 | 155.2 | 158.8 | 139.6 | 132.6 | 159.0 | 114.3 | 147.3 | 104.1 |
| 1920 | 194.8 | 186.7 | 164.1 | 138.2 | 165.0 | 186.2 | 171.6 | 102.3 |
| 1921 | 194.8 | 193.6 | 170.2 | 138.9 | 175.7 | 168.8 | 198.2 | 92.1 |
| 1922 | 204.6 | 163.7 | 143.9 | 155.7 | 151.4 | 127.8 | 188.8 | 127.7 |
| 1923 | 210.3 | 211.2 | 185.7 | 183.3 | 240.8 | 135.6 | 264.8 | 144.1 |
| 1924 | 220.7 | 187.9 | 165.2 | 157.5 | 199.4 | 102.7 | 226.1 | 121.5 |
| 1925 | 231.7 | 169.0 | 148.6 | 152.5 | 132.6 | 97.0 | 220.6 | 105.9 |
| 1926 | 159.9 | 99.6 | | | | | | |
| 1927 | 164.1 | 109.4 | | | | | | |
| 1928 | 144.8 | 96.0 | | | | | | |
| 1929 | 196.1 | 102.7 | | | | | | |
| 1931 | 267.4 | 183.3 | 161.1 | 217.0 | 165.3 | 101.2 | 151.6 | 113.9 |
| 1932 | 212.6 | 183.2 | 161.1 | 197.3 | 189.2 | 89.2 | 150.6 | 82.9 |
| 1933 | 248.3 | 196.1 | 172.4 | 200.9 | 192.4 | 94.6 | 146.3 | 89.3 |
| 1934-35 | 250.0 | 257.7 | 226.5 | 237.9 | 273.4 | 149.4 | 169.7 | 110.4 |
| 1935-36 | 267.9 | 266.8 | 234.5 | 268.3 | 282.6 | 132.9 | 152.0 | 122.3 |
| 1936-37 | 128.5 | 94.9 | 83.4 | 79.0 | 111.9 | 37.5 | 34.1 | 37.4 |
| 1937-38 | 56.3 | 51.4 | 45.2 | 22.0 | 22.9 | 27.1 | 44.3 | 18.2 |
| 1938-39 | 69.7 | 24.9 | 21.9 | 10.7 | 11.1 | 13.1 | 21.5 | 8.8 |
| 1939-40 | 88.6 | 20.5 | 18.0 | 9.9 | 8.8 | 10.7 | 9.7 | 7.3 |
| 1940-41 | 95.7 | 21.3 | 18.7 | 10.2 | 10.6 | 8.4 | 16.0 | 8.8 |
| 1941-42 | 90.7 | 19.1 | 16.8 | 8.7 | 10.0 | 6.1 | 14.2 | 4.9 |
| 1942-43 | 129.9 | 22.4 | 19.7 | 7.8 | 12.0 | 5.8 | 15.3 | 4.6 |
| 1943-44 | 62.1 | 9.4 | 8.5 | 3.1 | 5.7 | 1.8 | 10.5 | 1.6 |
| 1944-45 | 112.1 | 15.1 | 13.2 | 8.0 | 10.4 | 4.1 | 32.1 | 10.8 |
| 1945-46 | 765.1 | 154.4 | 135.8 | 83.2 | 80.0 | 54.3 | 249.1 | 89.5 |
| 1946-47 | 524.7 | 112.5 | | | | | | |

*Source:* Yen Chung-p'ing, *Chung-kuo chin-tai ching-chi shih t'ung-chi tzu-liao hsuan-chi*, pp. 207-08, 217.

The first railway in China was an unauthorized 15-kilometer line running from Woosung to Shanghai built by Jardine, Matheson and Company and other foreigners. It was opened in 1876, but official and local antipathy was so violent that this line was purchased and scrapped by the Chinese government. Continued opposition from both the local population and conservative officials prevented any progress with railway construction until China's defeat by Japan in 1894–95. On the one hand, the "self-strengtheners" were able to convince the imperial court of the necessity to build railways as a means of bolstering the dynasty against further foreign incursions. On the other hand, the exposure of China's weakness attracted foreign capital which saw the financing of railway construction as a means to promote foreign political influence and economic penetration. Only 364 kilometers of track had been laid by 1894. In the first great wave of railway building, between 1895 and 1911, 9,253 kilometers of line were completed, for the most part with funds borrowed from foreign creditors. Of this total the Russian-built Chinese Eastern Railway across Manchuria and its southern extension from Harbin to Dairen accounted for 2,425 kilometers.

The failure of private railway projects undertaken by provincial gentry and merchants in the last decade of the Manchu dynasty inspired Peking's railway nationalization program, an immediate cause of the overthrow of the dynasty. In the era of Yuan Shih-k'ai and the warlord regimes which followed until 1927, railway construction perceptibly slowed down. The several private lines were nationalized without the violent opposition which had been fatal to the Ch'ing dynasty, and for the most part in exchange for government bonds that were soon in default. While new loans were arranged with foreign lenders and some pre-1912 loans renegotiated, the First World War halted European investment in Chinese railways. When a new four-power consortium was assembled in 1920, the Peking government, contrary to American expectations, refused to transact business with it. Construction within China proper was limited to the completion of the Peking-Suiyuan line, and of sections of the Canton-Hankow and Lunghai railways, altogether totaling about 1,700 kilometers. An equal amount of new track was built in Manchuria, consisting on the one hand of Japanese financed feeder lines to the South Manchurian Railway and, on the other hand, of rival lines built by Chang Tso-lin in part with funds obtained from the revenue of the Peking-Mukden railway. Both the Chinese construction in North China and the new Manchurian lines were motivated as much by strategic as by economic considerations.

Between 1928 and 1937 approximately 3,400 kilometers of railway were constructed within China proper, including the completion of the Canton-Hankow line, the Chekiang-Kiangsi railway, and the T'ung-p'u line in Shansi. This was achieved without major foreign borrowing. The Chekiang-Kiangsi railway, for example, was financed mainly by loans from the Bank of China, and the Shansi railway out of provincial revenues. As in other areas, however, the demands of military spending and debt service left very few funds for the economic "reconstruction" extensively discussed by the Nanking government. In the same period, some 4,500 kilometers were built in Manchuria, consisting mainly of new Japanese construction after 1931 as part of the planned development of Manchukuo into an industrial base. In spite of formidable obstacles during the Sino-Japanese war, the Chinese government claimed to have completed some 1,500 kilometers in unoccupied China which played an important part in supporting the economy and military effort. The Japanese, on their part, constructed a number of additional lines in Manchuria.

Of the railways built in these 50 years, approximately 40 percent of the total track was located in Manchuria, 32 per cent in China proper north of the Yangtze River, 22 per cent in South China, and 4 per cent in Taiwan. The relatively small railway mileage in densely populated South China testifies to the persistence of an elaborate pre-modern (junk and sampan) and modern (steamboat and steam launch) network of water transport which continued to compete effectively with the steam train. In proportion to area and population, Manchuria was far better served than any other region in China, a circumstance underlying and reflecting Manchuria's more extensive industrialization. No railway had penetrated to the rich province of Szechwan or to such western areas as Kansu, Sinkiang, and Tibet. In addition to the notoriously small total mileage in relation to the size of the country, the development of China's railways had been quite haphazard, and the distribution of lines was often uneconomic. For China proper a more desirable system might have been a radial network centering perhaps around Hankow. The actual system was a parallel network heavily concentrated in Northern and Eastern China. In Manchuria, a combined radial-parallel network had developed which was marred by the uneconomic duplication of lines resulting from Chinese-Japanese competition in the northeast in the 1920s.

The construction of the Chinese railway system had involved considerable borrowing from Great Britain, Belgium, Japan, Germany, France, the United States, and the Netherlands, listed in the order of the total amount of railway loans extended by each country from 1898 to 1937. These loans (the terms of which often involved *de facto* foreign control of the lines constructed) were concentrated in the last years of the Ch'ing dynasty and first decade of the republic, and reflect the scramble for railway concessions and loan contracts by foreign syndicates whose rivalry and intrigues were as much political as financial. Repayment of the railway debt was to come from the operating revenue of the lines, but from about 1925 to 1935 most of the foreign railway loans were in default. On 31 December 1935 the total outstanding indebtedness, including principal and interest in arrears, amounted to approximately £53,827,443 or Ch.$891,920,730.[95] Railway bonds had fallen to as little as 11 per cent of their face value in the case of the Lunghai railway.

The earning power of the Chinese Government Railways was potentially just sufficient to pay the interest due to bondholders. Annual net operating revenue during 1916–39 averaged 7.4 per cent of the cost of track and equipment while interest rates on railway loans ranged from 5 to 9 per cent. That is, while their operation was apparently less efficient than that of the South Manchurian Railway, the government railways were economically viable enterprises which both contributed to such economic growth as the republican years saw and generally produced a small profit. On the average, however, only 35 per cent of the net operating revenue in these two decades was allocated to interest payments. Large portions of the net operating revenue—more than 50 per cent for example in the years 1926, 1927, and 1930–34—were remitted to the Chinese government which utilized these funds for its general expenditures.[91] Remittances to the government during 1921–36 were double the amount appropriated for additions to railway equipment.

A principal cause of the low profitability of the Chinese Government Railways was the prolonged civil strife throughout the republic. Rival warlords not only commandeered railway lines for the movement of troops but at times diverted passenger and freight revenues to the maintenance of their armies. Of the passenger traffic (in passenger miles) carried on the Peking-Hankow railway between 1912 and 1925, for example, 21 per cent was military traffic; on the Peking-Mukden line between 1920 and 1931, 17 per cent of the passenger traffic was military.[97] Apart from direct war damage, which was perhaps minimal, repairs to the track and rolling stock were neglected. For more than two decades the Ministry of Railways could rely regularly only on the income of a few smaller lines: and the system as a whole became increasingly obsolescent and inefficient.

During the period 1912 to 1947, both passenger and freight traffic increased annually on the Chinese Government Railways until the mid 1920s (see table 41). The Northern Expedition and civil wars attendant upon the establishment of the Nanking regime affected both adversely, but in the relative calm of the 1930s railway traffic revived and exceeded previous levels. Japanese seizure of the bulk of China's railways as the Nationalist government was forced into the interior between 1937 and 1945 is reflected in the figures for that period.

About 40 per cent of the operating revenues of the Chinese Government Railways was realized from passenger service, of which a considerable part was troop movements. Minerals made up more than half of the freight carried; second in importance were agricultural products. The general pattern of freight traffic was one in which agricultural products and minerals were carried from inland points to the coastal treaty ports, while manufactured goods flowed into the interior. Increased transport of agricultural products in the first decade of the republic reflects the growth of cash crop output suggested in my discussion of agricultural trends above. The railways in Manchuria in particular but also in North China facilitated the slow expansion of agricultural production shown in tables 34 and 35. Similarly both the adverse effects of the depression on cash crop output and the recovery just prior to the outbreak of war in 1937 are evident in table 41.

Little need be said about road mileage apart from indicating that no improved roads suitable for motor vehicles existed in 1912; before July 1937, about 116,000 kilometers had been completed, of which 40,000 kilometers were surfaced.[98] Most of this construction occurred after 1928, in which year there were perhaps 32,000 kilometers, and was undertaken for military as much as for commercial reasons by the Bureau of Public Roads of the National Economic Council. The Seven Provinces Project, for example, in which Honan, Hupei, Anhwei, Kiangsi, Kiangsu, Chekiang, and Hunan cooperated, was conceived of as a means of tying together by a system of roads those provinces in which the Kuomintang government had its greatest strength. Sparse and primitive though they were, roads in 1937 tended to be better distributed within China proper than was the railway network.

The war led to additional road construction in the interior provinces including, of course, the famous Yunnan-Burma highway. But in 1949 as in 1912, inland China continued to depend much more on traditional means of transport, by water and land, for local and regional carriage than it did on motor vehicles or trains. By September 1941, for example, in the three provinces of Kiangsu, Chekiang, and Anhwei, 118,292 native boats (*min-ch'uan*), totaling 850,705 tons and with crews totaling 459,178, had registered with the boatmen's associations established by the Wang Ching-wei government.[99] This was the principal means of short- and medium-distance bulk carriage in the lower Yangtze valley and elsewhere in South and Central China where a combination of rivers, lakes, and centuries' accumulation of man-made canals had produced a complex and extensive network of water transport. Inter-port trade, in contrast to local carriage, even by the 1890s was already primarily carried by steamships, mainly foreign-owned. But the tonnage of Chinese junks entered and cleared by the Maritime Customs at the several treaty ports remained more or less constant from 1912 to 1922, and began to drop sharply only in the 1920s.[100] On China's major rivers steam shipping increased steadily in the first decades of the twentieth century as evidenced by the growth of registered tonnage of vessels under 1,000 tons from 42,577 in 1913 to 246,988 in 1933. But the river junk held its own in many places for a considerable period. Up-river from Ichang on the Yangtze, for example, junk tonnage increased slightly from the 1890s to 1917 before plunging downward in the 1920s. Between Nanning and Wuchow on the West River, junk traffic similarly gave way to steam ships only in the 1920s.[101]

In the transport sector as in others, the commonplace fact that China's economy changed only a little in the first half of the twentieth century has tended to be obscured, pushed out of sight by the disproportionate attention devoted to the small modern sector of the economy in official word and deed, in the writings of China's economists, in the yearbooks and reports intended for foreign consumption, and in the research which non-Chinese scholars have conducted on China's pre-1949 economy— apart from the Japanese, who in this matter, at least, had a more "realistic" view of China. For the Nanking government, which had abandoned the land and drew its revenues overwhelmingly from the modern sector, this amounted to building paper castles.

## 7. Government and the Economy

Both the Peking warlords and the Nanking regime which followed financed their governments primarily from the urban sector of the economy. Central government in republican China neither collected substantial revenue from the rural sector nor had very much influence over its collection and disbursal by semi-autonomous provincial and local interests. In other words, no national government before 1949 was able to channel a significant share of total national income through the central government treasury. And, as a result, government policies, while not without far-reaching consequences for the economy, were never realistically capable of pushing the Chinese economy forward on the path of modern economic growth.

During the years 1931-36, for example, total national expenditures of the central government varied between a low of 2.1 per cent and a high of 4.9 per cent of the gross national product, and averaged 3.5 per cent. (If the expenditures of all levels of local government were included, the percentage would perhaps be doubled.) Tax revenues were considerably less than this and reflected, on the one hand, the failure of the national government to mobilize the resources of the rural sector and, on the other, its inability or unwillingness to levy income taxes on society in general. Even this limited government revenue, moreover, was largely dissipated in maintaining a hypertrophic military establishment and financing continued civil war, or hypothecated to service the foreign and domestic debt. Neither the Peking nor the Nanking regime was able to finance any significant developmental investment out of its revenues, and the policies of neither were conducive to capital formation in the private sector of the economy.

Following the Revolution of 1911, the new republican government at first struggled along with the Ch'ing fiscal system. While nomenclature and bureaucratic structure were soon changed, the republican government was even less able to control the revenue sources of China than its predecessor had been. In 1913 an effort was made to demarcate the sources of central, provincial and local revenue, but the central government even under Yuan Shih-k'ai was too weak to enforce these regulations. After 1914, except for the maritime customs and the salt gabelle, the major taxes were administered by the provinces. Technically, the land tax (and several consumption taxes) still belonged to the central government, but in fact it was under provincial control and the proceeds were spent in and by the provinces albeit under the accounting rubric "national expenditures of X province." Yuan

Shih-k'ai, until his death in 1916, was able to extract some land tax remittances from the provinces, and these continued fitfully and minimally until 1921 when the political situation dramatically worsened and civil warfare became so widespread that Peking's financial control all but evaporated.[102]

Maritime customs revenue was almost entirely committed to the service of foreign loans and indemnities. From 1912 through 1927 only 142,341,000 haikwan taels, or 20 per cent out of a total revenue net of first charges of 717,672,000 haikwan taels, was available to the Peking government for administrative and other expenditures.[103] In spite of the revision of specific duties in 1902 and 1918, due to rising prices the actual rate of duty collected on imports varied between 2.5 and 3.5 per cent until 1923, when a further revision brought the effective duty to 5 per cent. But no major increase of revenue under this heading was possible until China regained tariff autonomy in 1930.

From 1913 through 1922, gross revenue from the salt gabelle exceeded gross maritime customs revenue. After 1922, however, only a part of the income from salt was available to the central government. In order to furnish security for the Reorganization Loan of 1913, without which the government of Yuan Shih-k'ai might not have survived, a foreign chief inspector was appointed to supervise and in effect control the Salt Administration. While national pride might be hurt, this measure resulted in an immediate jump in the revenues collected on the account of the central government. Actual payments on foreign loans secured on the salt revenues were small—from 1917 the Reorganization Loan, for example, was paid from the customs revenue. But this relatively happy situation was swept away by the continuous civil warfare. Provincial interference in the salt tax collection grew to serious proportions, salt funds were misappropriated, and smuggling increased. Total revenue fell markedly after 1922, as did the proportion of the collection that was actually remitted to Peking. Net collections, which had hit a peak of Ch.$86 million in 1922, fell to Ch.$71 million in 1924, Ch.$64 million in 1926, and down to Ch.$58 million in 1927. Even in 1922 only Ch.$47 million (or 55 per cent of the net collection) was actually remitted to Peking; Ch.$12 million was retained by the provinces with the central government's consent; but Ch.$20 million (23 per cent) was appropriated locally without consent. The total amount retained by provincial authorities and military commanders climbed to Ch.$37 million in 1926 while the amount actually remitted to Peking in that year was barely Ch.$9 million.[104]

Faced with a chronic state of financial embarrassment, the Peking government was forced to depend heavily on domestic and foreign borrowing. Between 1912 and 1926, 27 domestic bond issues were floated by the Ministry of Finance with a combined face value of Ch.$ 614,000,000.[105] Actual receipts to the government, however, were considerably smaller, for the bonds were always sold at a discount—in an extreme case as low as 20 per cent of the face value. Much is obscure about the details of domestic loan flotations in this period, and on into the period of the Nanking government as well. There seems to have been a close relationship between the establishment of new banks with the right of note issue and government domestic borrowing. A large part of these domestic bonds was taken up by the Chinese "modern" banks who held government securities as investment and as reserves against note issue, while also making direct advances to the government.

The Peking government transmitted a domestic indebtedness of only Ch.$241,000,000 to its successor, which would seem to indicate that its creditors, in spite of defaults, did not fare too badly with the discounted Peking government bonds. And Peking's domestic borrowing permitted warlord coffers to be replenished time and again. But the proceeds of these loans brought little benefit to the economy of the country. Debt service on domestic and foreign loans was the largest single expenditure of the Peking government; together with military expenditure it made up at least four-fifths of the total annual outlay.[106] After general administrative costs were met, there was nothing left for developmental investment. Provincial and local revenues, too, were drained by military and police outlays.[107] Nor were the foreign loans of the Peking regime usually undertaken with a view to furthering economic development.

New foreign loan obligations incurred in the period 1912-26 were smaller in amount than the indemnity and railway obligations of the last years of the Manchu dynasty. Total foreign holdings of Chinese government obligations (excluding the Boxer indemnity) increased from approximately U.S.$526,000,000 in 1913 to U.S.$696,000,000 in 1931.[108] The 1913 Reorganization Loan of £25,000,000 was the largest single new foreign debt. A further significant part of this foreign borrowing was represented by the so-called "Nishihara loans" of 1918—unsecured advances by Japanese interests to the Anfu warlord clique then in power in Peking, and to several provincial governments, the proceeds of which were used largely for civil war and political intrigue. Some of these advances were subsequently converted into legitimate railway or telegraph loans, but the largest part, perhaps Ch.$150,000,000, was never recognized by the Nanking government. Like the Japanese indemnity loans of the 1890s, Yuan Shih-k'ai's Reorganization Loan, and the domestic debt, this desperate borrowing by the Peking warlords, except for the several railway loans, contributed nothing to the development of the Chinese economy. In fact, there is reason to believe that China annually made greater out-payments on account of government debt (including the Boxer indemnity) than she received in new loans. C. F. Remer, for example, estimates that annual out-payments averaged Ch.$89.2 million during 1902–13, and Ch.$70.9 million during 1913–30, while average in-payments in the two periods were Ch.$61.0 million and Ch.$23.8 million respectively. So large a "drain" of capital must be counted as net withdrawal from China's economic resources, the effect of which was probably to handicap economic growth.[109]

The establishment of the Nanking government in 1928 nominally brought political unity after a decade of civil war. In the nine years 1928-37, the central government probably achieved a greater degree of fiscal control over China proper than had existed at any time since the Ch'ing dynasty. Both revenues and the revenue system showed a remarkable improvement as compared with the warlord years of 1916–27. Tariff autonomy was recovered in 1929–30, and a new tariff with substantially higher rates gave a boost to the government finances. The shifting of import duties from a silver to a gold basis in 1930 through the instrumentality of customs gold units both preserved the real value of custom revenue and provided increased yields in terms of falling silver, thus facilitating service of the large foreign and domestic debt. Salt revenue, which before 1928 was largely appropriated locally, was integrated into the national fiscal system. Transfers to the provinces continued, but a substantial part of the salt tax became effectively available to the central government. Many, although not all, of the numerous central and local excises were combined into a nationwide consolidated tax collected for the central government in exchange for provincial appropriation of the land tax revenue. Likin was substantially although not completely abolished. The currency system was unified with the virtual elimination of the tael (the old silver unit of account) in 1933, and then the adoption in 1935 of a modern paper money system backed by foreign exchange reserves. This last was unintentionally facilitated by American silver purchases which drove up the price of silver and provided a substantial part of the required foreign currency reserves. In November 1935 silver was na-

TABLE 42

REPORTED RECEIPTS AND EXPENDITURES OF THE NANKING GOVERNMENT, 1928-37 (MILLIONS CHINESE $ AND %)

| | 1928-29 Ch$ | % | 1929-30 Ch$ | % | 1930-31 Ch$ | % | 1931-32 Ch$ | % | 1932-33 Ch$ | % |
|---|---|---|---|---|---|---|---|---|---|---|
| *Receipts** | 434 | 100.0 | 585 | 100.0 | 774 | 100.0 | 749 | 100.0 | 699 | 100.0 |
| a. Revenue* | 334 | 77.0 | 484 | 82.7 | 557 | 72.0 | 619 | 82.6 | 614 | 87.8 |
| i. Customs duty | 179 | 41.2 | 276 | 47.2 | 313 | 40.4 | 357 | 47.7 | 326 | 46.6 |
| ii. Salt tax | 30 | 6.9 | 122 | 20.8 | 150 | 19.4 | 144 | 19.2 | 158 | 22.6 |
| iii. Commodity taxes | 33 | 7.6 | 47 | 8.0 | 62 | 8.0 | 96 | 12.8 | 89 | 12.7 |
| iv. Other† | 92‡ | 21.2 | 39 | 6.7 | 32 | 4.1 | 22 | 2.9 | 41 | 5.9 |
| b. Deficit covered by borrowing | 100 | 23.0 | 101 | 17.3 | 217 | 28.0 | 130 | 17.4 | 85 | 12.2 |
| *Expenditures** | 434 | 100.0 | 585 | 100.0 | 774 | 100.0 | 749 | 100.0 | 699 | 100.0 |
| a. Party | 4 | 0.9 | 5 | 0.9 | 5 | 0.6 | 4 | 0.5 | 5 | 0.7 |
| b. Civil* | 28 | 6.4 | 97 | 16.6 | 120 | 15.5 | 122 | 16.3 | 131 | 18.7 |
| c. Military | 210 | 48.4 | 245 | 41.9 | 312 | 40.3 | 304 | 40.6 | 321 | 45.9 |
| d. Loan and indemnity service | 160 | 36.9 | 200 | 34.2 | 290 | 37.5 | 270 | 36.0 | 210 | 30.0 |
| e. Other§ | 32‖ | 7.4 | 38 | 6.5 | 47 | 6.1 | 49 | 6.5 | 32 | 4.6 |

| | 1933-34 Ch$ | % | 1934-35 Ch$ | % | 1935-36 Ch$ | % | 1936-37 Ch$ | % |
|---|---|---|---|---|---|---|---|---|
| *Receipts** | 836 | 100.0 | 941 | 100.0 | 1,072 | 100.0 | 1,168 | 100.0 |
| a. Revenue* | 689 | 82.4 | 745 | 79.2 | 817 | 76.2 | 870 | 74.5 |
| i. Customs duty | 352 | 42.1 | 353 | 37.5 | 272 | 25.4 | 379 | 32.4 |
| ii. Salt tax | 177 | 21.2 | 167 | 17.7 | 184 | 17.2 | 197 | 16.9 |
| iii. Commodity taxes | 118 | 14.1 | 116 | 12.3 | 150 | 14.0 | 173 | 14.8 |
| iv. Other† | 42 | 5.0 | 109¶ | 11.6 | 211¶** | 19.7 | 121 | 10.4 |

| | | | | | | | | |
|---|---|---|---|---|---|---|---|---|
| b. Deficit covered by borrowing | 147 | 17.6 | 196 | 20.8 | 255 | 23.8 | 298 | 25.5 |
| *Expenditures** | 836 | 100.0 | 941 | 100.0 | 1,072 | 100.0 | 1,168 | 100.0 |
| a. Party | 6 | 0.7 | 6 | 0.6 | 8 | 0.7 | 7 | 0.6 |
| b. Civil* | 160 | 19.1 | 151 | 16.1 | 163 | 15.2 | 160 | 13.7 |
| c. Military | 373 | 44.6 | 388 | 41.8 | 390 | 36.4 | 521 | 44.6 |
| d. Loan and indemnity service | 244 | 29.2 | 238 | 25.3 | 294 | 27.4 | 302 | 25.9 |
| e. Other | 53†† | 6.3 | 158‖†† | 16.8 | 217†† | 20.2 | 178†† | 15.2 |

* Includes cost of revenue collection, except 1928-29; excludes cash balances.

† Stamp tax, provincial remittances, profits of government enterprises, miscellaneous.

‡ Ch.$ 62.4 million = national revenue collected by provinces and directly disbursed for military expenses.

§ Largely transfers to provinces from salt revenue.

‖ Capital of Central Bank, Ch.$ 20 million, 1928-29; Ch.$ 74 million, 1934-35.

¶ Government enterprises receipts, 1934-35; Ch.$ 61 million; 1935-36, Ch.$ 67 million, mainly from railways, including value of transport services for military.

** Includes Ch.$ 78 million of various internal transfers.

†† Includes "Reconstruction," 1933-34, Ch.$ 7 million; 1934-35, Ch.$ 26 million; 1935-36, Ch.$ 88 million; 1936-37, Ch.$ 54 million; in part this may have been investment in military-related industry.

*Sources*: Annual reports of the minister of finance, in P. T. Chen, "Public finance," *The Chinese yearbook, 1935-36*, pp. 1192-237; *The Chinese yearbook, 1936-37*, pp. 587-88; Arthur N. Young, *China's nation-building effort, 1927-1937: the financial and economic record*, pp. 433-40.

tionalized; the use of silver as currency forbidden; and the notes of the Central Bank of China, the Bank of China, and the Bank of Communications made full legal tender. The government experimented with an annual budget, and greatly improved its collection and fiscal reporting services. Conferences were held and commissions appointed for the purpose of formulating and enforcing programs of fiscal reform and economic development. A National Economic Council was established in 1931 to direct the economic "reconstruction" of the country.

But however impressive these accomplishments appeared at the time in contrast to what had gone before, they were still largely superficial. Based as it was on indirect taxation applied to the modern sectors of the economy, national government revenue was severely limited by the slow growth of output. The inability to tax agriculture placed a formidable constraint on potential tax revenues—and thus on government programs. Customs, salt, and excise taxes probably bore heaviest on the small consumer, although the matter of the real incidence of taxation is a notably difficult one to trace; the well-to-do were not significantly taxed. The land tax in the hands of the provinces was neither reformed nor developed; it likewise burdened the small peasant farmer disproportionately. The economic policies of the Kuomintang government did not cope with the fundamental problems of agriculture, did not promote industrial growth, and did not effectively harness the political and psychological support of the populace in an attempt to raise the Chinese economy out of its stagnation.[110] Whatever small gains had been made by 1937 were swept away by the war and civil war which filled the next 12 years; and by the absence of governmental action to equalize in some measure the sacrifices which these years demanded of the Chinese people.

Table 42 shows the principal receipts and payments of the Nanking government for the nine fiscal years 1928-37. Provincial and local government expenditure remained important until 1938, after which in wartime it rapidly declined in relation to central expenditure. But even when provincial and local government expenditures are added to those of the central government, the total constituted a very small proportion of China's gross national product, only 3.2 to 6 per cent during 1931-36. Comparable figures for the United States are 8.2 per cent in 1929, 14.3 per cent in 1933, and 19.7 per cent in 1941.[111] The smallness of China's central government expenditures in relation to national income reflect both the narrowness of the national tax base and the limited size of the modern sector of the economy that in fact was called upon to shoulder the largest burden of national government taxation.

In early 1929 the Kuomintang government exercised some degree of fiscal control, apart from the Maritime Customs revenue, only in the five provinces of Chekiang, Kiangsu, Anhwei, Kiangsi, and Honan. This situation later improved, but complete central government dominance over north, north-west, and south-west China was never achieved before 1937. And soon after the outbreak of full-scale war, of course, the coastal and

Yangtze provinces on which the government had principally based itself, were lost to the Japanese.

The demarcation of central and provincial-local revenues at a National Economic Conference in June 1928, by which the central government formally ceded the land tax to the provinces, was then less a policy aimed at improving the admittedly chaotic financial administration inherited from the Peking regime than it was a recognition of political reality by the Nanking government. It meant, however, that in return for tenuous political support, the central government of China abandoned any fiscal claim on that part of the economy which produced 65 per cent of the national product. Abandoned too was any effort to overhaul an inequitable land tax system under which faulty land records and corrupt officials permitted the wealthy to escape a fair share of the burden. In consequence, a large part of the potential revenue of agriculture was withheld from community disposal for the general welfare.

In 1941, under the stress of war, the land-tax administration in unoccupied China was reclaimed from the provinces by the central government, which granted cash subsidies to the local governments to compensate for their loss of revenue. Collection of the land tax in kind and the forced borrowing of grains which accompanied it provided 11.8 per cent and 4.2 per cent of total central government receipts respectively in 1942–43 and 1943–44, but when the war with Japan ended central government taxation of agricultural land was quickly dropped. Wartime collection of the land tax in kind did provide the central government with the greater measure of control over food supplies which it sought, and at the same time it considerably dampened the wartime rate of increase in note issue by reducing the government's direct outlay on foodstuffs needed to supply the army, civil servants and city workers. It was carried out, however, without correcting any of the injustices of the antiquated land tax system, and individual small farmers were burdened with new inequities while other groups in the nation for the most part were exempted from or could avoid comparable direct taxation.[112]

Like almost all "underdeveloped" countries—Meiji Japan and post--1949 China are the major exceptions—the pre-war Nanking government relied principally upon indirect taxation for its revenue. The three most important levies were customs duties (receipts from which rose rapidly after tariff autonomy was regained), the salt tax and commodity taxes. As table 42 indicates, revenue under these three headings provided 55.7 per cent of total receipts/expenditures in the still unsettled 1928–29 fiscal year. During the next eight years this proportion varied between a high of 81.9 per cent in 1932–33 and a low of 56.6 per cent in 1935–36, and averaged 71.4 per cent. The balance came from various miscellaneous taxes, income from government enterprises, and above all from borrowing. Only in October 1936 were the first steps taken to introduce an income tax. The outbreak of the war in 1937 obstructed this program; taxation on incomes, the inheritance tax and the wartime excess profits tax together never brought in more than 1 or 2 per cent of total government receipts. Speculative commercial and financial transactions which brought enormous profits to a few, including government "insiders," during the war and civil war were never effectively taxed. Kuomintang fiscal policy depended on essentially regressive indirect taxation before the war, and although 1937–49 receipts were derived less and less from taxation, indirect taxes continued to dominate.

Foreign borrowing did not figure very largely in the finances of the Kuomintang government before the outbreak of the war. Several relatively small loans were made in the 1930s, including two American commodity loans totaling U.S.$2.6 million that was utilized and some borrowing for railway construction. Post-war United Nations (UNRRA) and American (ECA) aid funds (not loans of course) were used largely to meet China's large trade deficits, but without adequate plan or control and with little benefit to the economy. Wartime credits and Lend-Lease actually utilized between 1937 and 1945 amounted to approximately U.S.$2.15 billion (from the United States, $1.854 billion; Soviet Union, $173 million; Great Britain, $111 million; and France, $12 million). These were received in part in the form of military supplies and services, and in part were dissipated during and after the war along with accumulated government foreign-exchange holdings (obtained largely through American wartime purchases of local currency at an inflated exchange rate) in a vain effort to maintain the external value of the Chinese dollar.[113] In sum, foreign credits and aid helped the Kuomintang government survive the war; they contributed nothing to pre-war or post-war economic development.

The annual deficit between revenue and expenditures shown in table 42 was met principally by domestic borrowing, which in fact after 1931–32 annually exceeded the amount of the deficit itself, since some of the proceeds were held as cash balances in various accounts. Between 1927 and 1935, the Finance Ministry of the Nanking government floated 38 internal loan issues with a face value of Ch.$1,634 million.[114] This "general purpose" borrowing was made necessary principally by the government's heavy military costs. These grew out of its political inability to "break rice bowls" by reducing the swollen central and provincial armies, the mounting expenses of the campaigns against the communist-held Soviet areas, and after 1931 the modernization of Chiang Kai-shek's forces in the face of quickening Japanese aggression.

The troubled political and economic situation in 1931 and 1932 severely depressed the Shanghai bond market. Treasury issues secured on customs revenue fell, for example, from Ch.$62.90 in January 1931 to Ch.$26.60 in December. Scheduled payments on the domestic debt in January 1932 were about Ch.$200 million, a third of the revenue anticipated in the fiscal year 1931–32, and most of the internal debt was due to be repaid within five years. With further borrowing impossible and faced with the prospect of default, the banks and bondholders were reluctantly forced to accept a reorganization of the debt which reduced interest payments to a fixed 6 per cent and extended amortization periods to roughly double their former length. Beginning in 1933, as the effects of the world depression reached China, the pressure of deficits grew again. As table 42 shows, the amount of borrowing rose each year from fiscal 1933 to fiscal 1935 as military expenditures increased. In February 1936 a second reorganization of the internal debt was carried out by the issue of a consolidated loan of Ch.$1,460 million. This replaced 33 older issues of varying maturities and interest rates with five issues secured on the customs revenue which paid 6 per cent and matured in 12, 15, 18, 21, and 24 years. In addition a new loan of Ch.$340 million was floated, bringing the total of domestic bond issues through 1936 to nearly Ch.$2 billion.

The floating of this sizable internal debt and its treatment reveals the interesting symbiotic relationship between the Kuomintang government and the Shanghai banking community, including the four large official banks. (The Farmers' Bank had been set up in 1933.) A very large part of the bond issues was absorbed by the banks. In February 1936, for example, they held two-thirds of the total outstanding issues. With few exceptions, at least before 1932, the practice of the Nanking government was to deposit bonds with the banks as collateral for cash advances of perhaps 50 to 60 per cent of face value. After the issue was publicly offered and a market price established, the banks purchased the bonds from the government for the difference between the original advances and the market price. While the issuing price of most bonds might be 98, maximum quotations on the market never exceeded 80 and at times fell to as low as 30 or 40. One informed estimate is that the cash yield to the Nanking government between 1927 and 1934 from loan issues with a face value of Ch.$1.2 billion was probably in the range of 60 to 75 per cent.[115] Nominal interest rates of 8.4 to 9.6 per cent, therefore, actually cost the Ministry of Finance 12 to 16 per cent, and if interest and amortization were duly paid bondholders might realize a 20 to 30 per cent return per annum. The burden of domestic borrowing improved somewhat after the loan reorganization of 1932. Average yields on domestic bonds ranged from 15 to 24 per cent through 1932, dropped to 16.8 per cent in 1933, and to 11.6 per cent in 1936.[116] Bonds were also purchased by the banks as reserves against note issues, which grew rapidly after the currency reform of 1935. Public demand for government bonds on the Shanghai market was largely for speculation rather than investment. The reorganization of the domestic debt in 1932 and 1936, which was forced upon the government by ever-mounting loan service costs, shook the market somewhat by reducing nominal interest rates and extending amortization schedules. Until wartime inflation in effect canceled the domestic public debt—the only really "progressive taxation" during the republican era—this providing of credit to the government remained highly profitable to the lenders.

Resort to this high-cost credit was linked to the fact that the principal creditors, the four government banks which dominated the modern banking system, were under the influence of individuals prominent in the government who utilized these institutions both in the political intrigues of the capital and to profit personally in the private sector of the economy. It was widely believed in the 1930s that the Central Bank of China was the preserve of K'ung Hsiang-hsi (H. H. Kung), the Bank of Communications of the "C-C Clique," the Bank of China of Sung Tzu-wen (T. V. Soong), and the Farmers' Bank of China of the highest officers of the Chinese army. Personal corruption, however, is not easy to document. In any case it was probably less important in its economic consequences than the diversion of scarce capital resources, which might have been used for industrial or commercial investment, to the financing of current government military expenditures or to speculation in the bond market.

The Chinese banking system in the twentieth century failed lamentably to carry out the function of credit creation for the development of the economy as a whole. First, modern banking in China was undeveloped. While 128 new banks were established from 1928 to 1937, and in 1937 China had 164 modern banks with 1,597 branches, these were overwhelmingly concentrated in the major cities of the coastal provinces (Shanghai alone had 58 head offices and 130 branch offices in 1936). Modern banking facilities were meager in the agricultural interior and never adapted themselves to the credit needs of a peasant economy. The cooperative societies which grew up in the 1920s and 1930s and which might have served as intermediaries between the banking system and the peasant farmer were in fact insignificant in number and tended to provide the bulk of their credit to those richer farmers who in any case could obtain loans at relatively low rates from other sources. The "native" banks (*ch'ien-chuang*, etc.), which survived and sometimes thrived into the 1930s, tended to limit themselves to financing local trade. While the foreign banks in the treaty ports were amply supplied with funds, including large deposits by wealthy Chinese, their principal operations were the short-term financing of foreign trade and speculation in foreign exchange.

But beyond these considerations, the Chinese modern banking system that did develop in the decade before the war was distorted into an instrument primarily involved in financing a government which was continuously in debt. The capital and reserves of the principal modern banks increased from Ch.$186 million in 1928 to Ch.$447 million in 1935. Deposits during the same period increased from Ch.$1,123 million to Ch.$3,779 million. Much of the increment was accounted for by the growth of the "big four" government banks. In 1928 the Central Bank of China, Bank of China, Bank of Communications, and Farmers' Bank of China had capital and reserves of Ch.$64 million or 34 per cent of the total; by 1935 the figure was Ch.$183 million or 41 per cent. Deposits of the four banks totaled Ch.$ 554 million or 49 per cent of all deposits in 1928; by 1935 they were Ch.$2,106 million or 56 per cent. At the end of 1935 the government held Ch.$146 million, or four-fifths, of the capital of 10 banks (including the four government banks). This represented 49 per cent of the total capital and 61 per cent of the combined resources of all modern banks. Other leading private banks were under the control or influence of the "big four," and numerous interlocking directorates tied together the principal regional banking cliques, the government banks, native banking syndicates, and the insurance, commercial, and industrial enterprises in which they invested. The largest provincial bank, that of Kwangtung which had 40 per cent of the total resources of all provincial and municipal banks, was closely linked with the Bank of China. Collaboration between the government and private banks facilitated meeting the needs of the Ministry of Finance for borrowed funds, but also diverted capital from private production and trade. The Central Bank of China, created in 1928, moreover did not become a true central bank with respect to the supply of money and credit; it was primarily a vehicle for the short-term financing of the government debt.[117]

In sum, this was a centralized banking structure dominated by the four government banks, and the concentration of banking resources which it represented was in line with the general goal of "economic control" which characterized the economic thinking of the Kuomintang government. The purposes to which this control was directed, however, were not primarily economic reform and development. Credit made available by the banks to the government in the 1930s was devoted to financing the unification of China by force—the overriding priority in the eyes of the Nanking regime. Little was left for developmental expenditure despite the plan-making that kept numerous central and provincial government offices busy.

Even according to the published data for 1928-37, which may not reveal the full amount of government military allocations, from 40 to 48 per cent of annual expenditures were devoted to military purposes. Military appropriations together with loan and indemnity service—most of the borrowing was for army needs—annually accounted for 67 to 85 per cent of total outlays. An unduly large part of "civil" expenditures represented the costs of tax collection—Ch.$60 million out of Ch.$120 million in 1930-31 and Ch.$66 million out of Ch.$122 million in 1931-32, for example. Appropriations for public works were small and welfare expenditures almost non-existent.

While total government spending was a relatively small part of national income, the pattern of income and expenditure described above tended to have a negative effect on both economic development and the stability of the Kuomintang government. It is of course true that military outlays in the 1930s probably never exceeded 2 per cent of China's gross domestic product—the 1933 ratio was 1.2 per cent of the gross domestic product. And the looming Japanese threat was a real one. Furthermore military expenditures may have had substantial economic side-effects: roads being built, peasant soldiers learning how to operate and repair simple machines, some industrial development (for example, chemicals for munitions), etc. The phrase "hypertrophic military establishment (page 156 above) may therefore in part reflect the bad press that the Nationalist government fully earned on other counts. But in terms of effectively available rather than potential financial resources, it remains true that Nanking's large military expenditures withdrew from the economy resources that alternatively could have been used for investment or consumption in the private sector of the economy, and yet did not conclusively provide either an end to internal disorder or protection against Japanese encroachment. Service of the domestic debt, given the prevalence of regressive indirect taxes, tended to transfer real purchasing power from lower income groups to a small number of wealthy speculators. Since the proceeds of the loans were spent largely for military purpose and debt service, and the bond-holding classes preferred speculation to productive investment, domestic borrowing produced neither public nor private expenditure aimed at increasing the output of goods in a way to offset the burden on the Chinese population of the regressive national tax structure. In addition, for the private industrial entrepreneur credit was always short. A situation in which the banks in the 1930s paid 8 to 9 per cent on fixed deposits which were used to purchase government bonds, necessitated an interest rate on bank loans too high to permit extensive financing of private industry, commerce, and agriculture.

In the last two years before the war a mild inflationary trend had already appeared, traceable in part to the ease with which the supply of money could be expanded following the currency reform of 1935. This was as nothing, however, compared with the inflation that began with the outbreak of hostilities in 1937 and ended in the complete collapse of the monetary system and of the Kuomintang government in 1948–49. China's runaway inflation was due principally to the continued fiscal deficit which was financed by ever-growing note issues. That ultimately it was caused by the Japanese seizure of China's richest provinces in the first year of the war and that it fed on eight years of war and three of civil war is undeniable. But it is equally of consequence that in the face of peril the Kuomintang government did little that was significant to stem the inflation, that the years 1937–49 saw a remarkable continuity of economic policies which had already been defective before 1937.[118]

Table 43 shows the growth of note issue and the soaring index of prices from 1937 to 1948. Until 1940 the inflation was still moderate and for the most part confined to the more sensitive urban sector of the economy. But the poor harvest of that year, the continued decline of food production through 1941, and the outbreak of the general Pacific war unleashed new inflationary pressures. From 1940 to 1946 annual price increases in unoccupied China averaged more than 300 per cent. Prices broke briefly after the Japanese surrender in the autumn of 1945, but from November to December 1945 the price index began to climb at an unprecedented rate. There was a momentary halt in August 1948, when new gold yuan notes were issued, and then onwards to catastrophe.

TABLE 43
NOTE ISSUE AND PRICE INDEX, 1937-48

| Year* | Note Issue Outstanding† (million Ch.$) | Price Index‡ (January-June 1937=100) |
|---|---|---|
| 1937 | 2,060 | 100 |
| 1938 | 2,740 | 176 |
| 1939 | 4,770 | 323 |
| 1940 | 8,440 | 724 |
| 1941 | 15,810 | 1,980 |
| 1942 | 35,100 | 6,620 |
| 1943 | 75,400 | 22,800 |
| 1944 | 189,500 | 75,500 |
| 1945 | 1,031,900 | 249,100 |
| 1946 | 3,726,100 | 627,210 |
| 1947 | 33,188,500 | 10,340,000 |
| 1948 | 374,762,200 | 287,700,000 |

* At the end of each calendar year, except 1948 where the data are for June and July respectively.

† 1937–44: Arthur N. Young, *China and the helping hand, 1937–1945*, pp. 435–36.
1946–48: Chang Kia-ngau, *The inflationary spiral: The experience of China, 1939–1950*, p. 374.

‡ At the end of each year, except 1937 (January-June average) and 1948 (July). 1937–45: Index of average retail prices in main cities of unoccupied China (Young, *China and the helping hand*, pp. 435–36); 1946-47: all China; 1948: Shanghai (Chang, *The inflationary spiral*, pp. 372-33).

Real government revenue and expenditure both decreased drastically during the war, the former considerably more than the latter, however. The largest single source of pre-war revenue, the customs duty, was lost to the Chinese government as the Japanese quickly occupied China's coastal provinces. As the size of the territory under Kuomintang control contracted, receipts from commodity taxes and other revenues naturally fell too. On the expenditure side, the real cost of servicing the domestic debt was reduced radically by the inflation, while by early 1939 payments on foreign loans secured on the customs and salt revenue were suspended. Military expenditure, as before 1937, dominated government outlays. Especially from 1940 a massive expansion of the army occurred as Chiang Kai-shek prepared both for a protracted resistance against Japan and a post-war denouement with the Communists. At the end of the war the Nationalist army was five million men strong, had consumed 70 to 80 per cent of government wartime expenditures, was inadequately equipped and poorly officered, and by its excessive recruitment of rural labor had probably contributed to a decline of agricultural production, while by its concentration near the larger towns of unoccupied China it was adding enormously to the inflationary pressure. There is little to suggest, any more than before the war, that the size and cost of the military establishment contributed proportionately either to the defense of China or to the stability of the Kuomintang government. As the civil war grew in ferocity in 1947 and 1948, the demands of the military, supported by the leaders of the government, shattered all checks to runaway expenditure.

Again, following a pre-war pattern, insofar as the wartime Kuomintang government was financed by tax revenues, these were predominantly regressive indirect taxes. (One exception was the wartime land tax in kind discussed above; this, however, hit the poor farmer more heavily than it did the rich). In particular, no effort was made to tax the windfall gains of entrepreneurs and speculators who profited immensely by the inflation. The interlude, however brief, between war and civil war in 1945-46, as the government returned to formerly Japanese-occupied China, presented an opportunity to institute sweeping and equitable tax reforms to offset the expansion of money supply, but it was not taken.

Wartime and post-war government expenditures, however, were financed not by taxation but primarily by bank advances which generated continuous increases in the note issue. The sale of bonds, even with compulsory allocation, amounted to only 5 per cent of the cumulative deficit for the years 1937–45 and even less during 1946–48. After the exclusive right to note issue was given to the Central Bank of China in 1942, even the formality of depositing bonds with the banks as collateral for advances was dropped. Efforts to offset the inflationary effects of the note issue and to maintain the international value of the Chinese dollar by the sale of foreign exchange or gold and the post-war importation of commodities, served only to drain the country of accumulated foreign assets which might have been devoted to economic development after the defeat of Japan.

The inflation, of course, resulted from excessive monetary demand generated by the government deficit in circumstances of inadequate supply. To a limited extent the output of industrial consumer commodities in unoccupied China increased during the war, but the absolute magnitude was inconsequential in relieving the inflationary pressure. These commodities tended to be produced by small-scale private firms. In contrast, investments in producer goods industries were mainly by government or semi-official organs. In general, as in pre-war China, there was no effective policy channeling scarce resources to the most essential needs. In any case, the small industrial base which was developed in the interior in wartime was virtually abandoned as the government returned to coastal China.

Whatever hopes were held that the recovery of the industrially more developed provinces of China would solve the supply problem were rudely shattered by events: the Soviet removal of major industrial equipment from Manchuria; the communist control of important parts of the North China countryside which, for example, denied raw cotton supplies to the Shanghai mills; the incompetence and corruption of the National Resources Commission and China Textile Development Corporation which took over the operation of former Japanese and puppet firms; the absence of a rational and equitable plan to allocate the foreign exchange resources available at the war's end; and the same inability as in the pre-1937 period on the part of the Kuomintang government to control speculation, reform the tax structure, and give sufficient priority to developmental economic investment.

## 8. Foreign Trade and Investment

Foreign trade and investment played a relatively small role in the Chinese economy—even in the twentieth century. The effects of the Western and Japanese economic impact must be taken into account in a consideration of various distinct sectors, but most of the Chinese economy remained beyond the reach of the foreigner.

According to estimates by C. F. Remer and the Japanese East Asia Research Institute (Tōa Kenkyūjo), foreign investment in China had reached a total of U.S.$3,483 million by 1936, growing from U.S.$733 million in

1902., U.S.$1,610 million in 1914, and U.S.$3,243 million in 1931 (table 44). On a per capita basis—taking the Chinese population in 1914 as 430 million and in 1936 as 500 million—the figures for these two years are approximately U.S.$3.75 and U.S.$6.97 respectively. These per capita amounts are notably smaller than foreign investment in other "underdeveloped" countries: for example, in 1938, India, U.S.$20; Latin America, U.S.$86; and Africa excluding the Union of South Africa, U.S.$23. Per capita foreign investment as of a given year may not be the most significant measure of the significance of that investment. Available data do not, however, permit any precise estimate of annual capital inflow figures which might be compared with national income and domestic capital formation. Very roughly, net private foreign investment in the early 1930s accounted for slightly less than one per cent of China's gross national product, and about 20 per cent of total investments.[119] That is, the aggregate was small, but not insignificant.

TABLE 44
FOREIGN INVESTMENTS IN CHINA, 1902–36
(U.S.$ millions; % in parentheses)

| Type of Investment | 1902 | 1914 | 1931 | 1936 |
|---|---|---|---|---|
| Direct investments | 503.2 (64) | 1,067.0 (66) | 1,493.2 (77) | 2,681.7 (77) |
| Obligations of Chinese Government | 284.7 (36) | 525.8 (33) | 710.6 (22) | 766.7 (22) |
| Loans to private parties | 0.0 | 17.5 (1) | 38.7 (1) | 34.8 (1) |
| Total | 787.9 (100) | 1,610.3 (100) | 3,242.5 (100) | 3,483.2 (100) |

*Source:* Chi-ming Hou, *Foreign investment and economic development in China, 1840–1937,* p. 13, which in turn is based on C. F. Remer, *Foreign investments in China,* and Tōa Kenkyūjo, *Rekkoku tai-Shi tōshi to Shina kokusai shūshi* (Foreign investments in China and China's balance of payments).

Remer's data indicate that, when the annual inflow of new investment capital is balanced against outpayments of interest and amortization on government loans and profits on foreign business investments, there was a substantial net outflow of capital in these accounts in the years 1902--31.[120] As table 49 indicates, however, overseas Chinese remittances to China more than balanced this outflow, so that overall there was an inflow of capital which, together with out-payments of specie, financed China's continued excess of imports over exports. The growth in the total value of foreign investment in these circumstances, apart from the effect of the upward movement of prices, seems to have been due to reinvestment of their profits by foreigners in China. Indeed, some of the "foreign" remittances never left China, but were paid directly to foreign creditors in Shanghai or Hong Kong who ploughed a substantial portion back into enterprises located in the several treaty ports. The growth of Jardine, Matheson and Company over the course of a century from a small agency house in the 1830s to the largest trading company in China with many industrial and financial interests illustrates. this process quite well.

TABLE 45
FOREIGN INVESTMENT IN CHINA, 1902–36, BY CREDITOR COUNTRY
(U.S.$ millions; % in parentheses)

| | 1902 | | 1914 | | 1931 | | 1936 | |
|---|---|---|---|---|---|---|---|---|
| Great Britain | 260.3 | (33.0) | 607.5 | (37.7) | 1,189.2 | (36.7) | 1,220.8 | (35.0) |
| Japan | 1.0 | (0.1) | 219.6 | (13.6) | 1,136.9 | (35.1) | 1,394.0 | (40.0) |
| Russia | 246.5 | (31.3) | 269.3 | (16.7) | 273.2 | (8.4) | 0.0 | |
| United States | 19.7 | (2.5) | 49.3 | (3.1) | 196.8 | (6.1) | 298.8 | (8.6) |
| France | 91.1 | (11.6) | 171.4 | (10.7) | 192.4 | (5.9) | 234.1 | (6.7) |
| Germany | 164.3 | (20.9) | 263.6 | (16.4) | 87.0 | (2.7) | 148.5 | (4.3) |
| Belgium | 4.4 | (0.6) | 22.9 | (1.4) | 89.0 | (2.7) | 58.4 | (1.7) |
| Netherlands | 0.0 | | 0.0 | | 28.7 | (0.9) | 0.0 | |
| Italy | 0.0 | | 0.0 | | 46.4 | (1.4) | 72.3 | (2.1) |
| Scandinavia | 0.0 | | 0.0 | | 2.9 | (0.1) | 0.0 | |
| Others | 0.6 | (0.1) | 6.7 | (0.4) | 0.0 | | 56.3 | (1.6) |
| Total | 787.9 | (100.00) | 1,610.3 | (100.00) | 3,242.5 | (100.00) | 3,483.2 | (100.00) |

*Source:* Chi-ming Hou, *Foreign investment and economic development in China,* p. 17.

TABLE 46
FOREIGN DIRECT INVESTMENTS IN CHINA BY INDUSTRY
(U.S.$ millions, % in parentheses)

| | 1914 | | 1931 | | 1936 | |
|---|---|---|---|---|---|---|
| Import-export trade | 142.6 | (13.4) | 483.7 | (19.4) | 450.2 | (16.8) |
| Banking and finance | 6.3 | (0.6) | 214.7 | (8.6) | 548.7 | (20.5) |
| Transport (railways and shipping) | 336.3 | (31.5) | 592.4 | (23.8) | 669.5 | (25.0) |
| Manufacturing | 110.6 | (10.4) | 372.4 | (14.9) | 526.6 | (19.6) |
| Mining | 34.1 | (3.2) | 108.9 | (4.4) | 41.9 | (1.6) |
| Communications and public utilities | 23.4 | (2.2) | 99.0 | (4.0) | 138.4 | (5.1) |
| Property | 105.5 | (9.9) | 339.2 | (13.6) | 241.1 | (9.0) |
| Miscellaneous | 308.2 | (28.9) | 282.9 | (11.3) | 65.3 | (2.4) |
| Total | 1,067.0 | (100.0) | 2,493.2 | (100.0) | 2,681.7 | (100.0) |

*Source*: Ch-ming Hou, *Foreign investment and economic development in China,* p. 16.

The largest foreign interest until 1931, when the Japanese seized Manchuria and began to invest heavily in its development, was that of Great Britain (see table 45). Of British direct investment, which accounted for 66 per cent and 81 per cent respectively of total British investments in 1914 and 1931, about half in 1931 was in fields directly associated with foreign trade, 21 per cent in real estate, 18 per cent in manufacturing, 5 per cent in public utilities, 2 per cent in mining, and 3 per cent miscellaneous. Japanese capital in China increased rapidly after 1905 when Japan became firmly entrenched in South Manchuria. Japanese direct investments, 77 per cent of the total in 1931, were mainly in transport (the South Manchurian Railway), import and export trade, manufacturing (chiefly cotton textiles) and mining. Russia's investment is accounted for almost entirely by the Chinese Eastern Railway which was sold to Japan in 1935.[121]

Direct business investment formed 66 per cent, 77 per cent, and 77 per cent of total foreign investments in the years 1914, 1931, and 1936 respectively. The balance represented principally the borrowing of the Chinese government. Chi-ming Hou's recalculation of Remer's data and those of the East Asia Research Institute (table 46) indicates that in 1931 this direct investment was distributed as follows: import and export trade, 19.4 percent; railways, 16.0 percent; manufacturing, 14.9 per cent; property, 13.6 per cent; banking and finance, 8.6 per cent; shipping, 7.8 per cent; mining, 4.4 per cent; communications and public utilities, 4.0 per cent; and miscellaneous, 11.3 per cent. It is immediately evident from these figures that, in contrast to the typical pattern of foreign investment in many "underdeveloped" countries, very little foreign capital in China had gone into export-oriented industries such as mining or plantation agriculture. Even in Manchuria, Japanese investment in agriculture was negligible.

TABLE 47
GEOGRAPHICAL DISTRIBUTION OF FOREIGN INVESTMENTS IN CHINA, 1902, 1914, 1931
(U.S.$ millions; % in parentheses)

| | 1902 | | 1914 | | 1931 | |
|---|---|---|---|---|---|---|
| Shanghai | 110.0 | (14.0) | 291.0 | (18.1) | 1,112.2 | (34.3) |
| Manchuria | 216.0 | (27.4) | 361.6 | (22.4) | 880.0 | (27.1) |
| Rest of China | 177.2 | (22.5) | 433.1 | (26.9) | 607.8 | (18.8) |
| Undistributed | 284.7 | (36.1) | 524.6 | (32.6) | 642.5 | (19.8) |
| Total | 787.9 | (100.0) | 1,610.3 | (100.0) | 3,242.5 | (100.0) |

*Source*: Remer, *Foreign investments in China*, p. 73.

In those countries—much of Latin America, for example, or Indonesia under the Dutch—where foreign capital was in fact concentrated in export industries, the result had been lop-sided development of the recipient economies which had come to specialize in one or more agricultural or mineral exports, the market for which was extremely sensitive to foreign business cycles. Foreign investment on this "colonial" pattern, moreover, had allegedly reinforced the position of the native landowning class who were the chief beneficiaries of the commercialization of agriculture. Their increased income, however, was not invested in industrial development but was utilized in much the same way as in the past: in hoarding at home (land concentration, port real estate) and now also more safely abroad (in foreign banks and securities); and in luxury consumption (import surplus). The growth of export industries also had the further consequence of attracting native capital into intermediary tertiary activities, such as petty trade ancillary to the business of foreign firms, and as a consequence is alleged to have drawn off talent and the capital that might have been employed more productively. In very limited areas, as on the south-east coast and around Canton, some such process as the above may be discerned in China on a small scale. But the Chinese economy in the republican era was not significantly restructured by foreign capital so as to tie its fate to the vagaries of the world market.

Direct investment was heavily concentrated in the treaty ports, Shanghai in particular until 1931 as table 47 indicates. Japanese efforts to develop a Manchurian industrial base in the 1930s were discussed above, and the share of foreign-owned factories in the manufacturing sector which was located mainly in the treaty ports is suggested in tables 31 and 32. To many commentators, foreign-owned enterprises and foreign investment (which is often equated with control) in Chinese enterprises were primarily responsible for obstructing the development of Chinese modern industry. In this view Chinese firms simply could not compete successfully with foreign firms which had larger revenues, better technology and management, enjoyed the privileges of extraterritoriality and exemption from Chinese taxes, and were free from the depredations of Chinese officialdom. To counter this "oppression argument" Chi-ming Hou has shown that, far from being overwhelmed, Chinese-owned modern enterprises maintained a "remarkably stable" share of the modern sector over the years before 1937.[122] Although it might be argued that in the absence of foreign competition Chinese firms might have grown even faster, it is by no means certain that without the "exogenous shock" of foreign trade and investment the pre-modern economy of nineteenth-century China would have been capable of embarking at all on the path of development.[123]

Apart from railway construction and industrial loans, it is doubtful whether Chinese government borrowing abroad was of any advantage to the Chinese economy. The relatively high service costs of these obligations (interest, discounts, commissions) was excessive considering the small benefit derived from them. An analysis of the indebtedness incurred during the period 1912–37 according to the purposes for which the borrowed funds were utilized seems to support the conclusion that foreign borrowing tended to be economically sterile.[124] Approximately 8.9 per cent (in constant 1913 prices) of the total was borrowed for military purposes and indemnity payments to foreigners. Another 43.3 per cent was earmarked for general administrative purposes, which meant largely for interest payments on the foreign debt itself. While the 36.9 per cent accounted for by railway loans was a potentially productive investment, its usefulness was limited by endemic civil wars and disturbances, and by provisions in the loan agreements which prevented efficient central management by establishing boundaries within which the several lines were treated as separate enterprises, and so could not pool their shop resources or gain other benefits of unified management. Telephone and telegraph loans constituted the largest part of the 10.8 per cent accounted for by industrial loans.

In view of the paucity of useful national income data, the ratio of total foreign trade turn-over to national product during the republican era can only be roughly estimated. In 1933, the one year for which an acceptable measure of domestic product is available, imports and exports together were valued at 7 per cent of gross domestic product. This was, however, after the loss of Manchuria whose foreign trade was not insubstantial and after the onset of the great depression. In the late 1920s China's foreign trade was probably equal to somewhat more than 10 per cent of national product. This is a relatively low proportion but not abnormally low in terms of international comparisons given China's size, level of development, distance from major maritime routes, abundant resources, and large domestic market. Values and index numbers of China's foreign trade for the years 1912–36 are given in table 48.

In current prices there was a slow growth of both imports and exports from the 1880s to 1900. Growth was more rapid from 1901 to 1918, and then noticeably accelerated from 1919 to 1931. Measured in terms of quan-

TABLE 48
VALUES AND INDEX NUMBERS OF FOREIGN TRADE, 1912-36

| | Value in current prices* | | | Index of value of total trade 1913=100 | Indices of quantity 1913=100 | | Terms of trade (import price ÷ export price) 1913=100 |
|---|---|---|---|---|---|---|---|
| | Net imports | Net exports | Import surplus | | Imports | Exports | |
| 1912 | 473 | 371 | 102 | 86.7 | 82.8 | 103.8 | 112.9 |
| 1913 | 570 | 403 | 167 | 100.0 | 100.0 | 100.0 | 100.0 |
| 1914 | 569 | 356 | 213 | 95.1 | 91.6 | 83.8 | 103.3 |
| 1915 | 454 | 419 | 35 | 89.7 | 70.3 | 96.5 | 104.8 |
| 1916 | 516 | 482 | 34 | 102.5 | 73.7 | 102.3 | 104.6 |
| 1917 | 550 | 463 | 87 | 104.0 | 73.4 | 108.3 | 123.4 |
| 1918 | 555 | 486 | 69 | 106.9 | 66.1 | 105.5 | 128.4 |
| 1919 | 647 | 631 | 16 | 131.3 | 75.4 | 140.0 | 134.1 |
| 1920 | 762 | 542 | 220 | 133.9 | 75.9 | 119.3 | 155.6 |
| 1921 | 906 | 601 | 305 | 154.8 | 94.7 | 126.9 | 142.3 |
| 1922 | 945 | 655 | 290 | 164.4 | 112.6 | 130.5 | 117.7 |
| 1923 | 923 | 753 | 170 | 172.2 | 108.5 | 137.3 | 109.1 |
| 1924 | 1,018 | 772 | 246 | 183.9 | 119.6 | 136.6 | 105.4 |
| 1925 | 948 | 776 | 172 | 177.1 | 109.9 | 132.9 | 103.5 |
| 1926 | 1,124 | 864 | 260 | 204.2 | 130.5 | 141.1 | 98.6 |
| 1927 | 1,013 | 919 | 94 | 198.4 | 109.8 | 154.1 | 108.6 |
| 1928 | 1,196 | 991 | 205 | 114.6 | 131.5 | 156.1 | 100.4 |
| 1929 | 1,266 | 1,016 | 250 | 234.4 | 139.9 | 149.2 | 93.1 |
| 1930 | 1,310 | 895 | 415 | 226.5 | 131.0 | 131.1 | 102.5 |
| 1931 | 1,433 | 909 | 524 | 240.7 | 129.9 | 136.5 | 116.0 |
| 1932 | 1,049 | 493 | 556 | 158.4 | 106.0 | 100.8 | 128.6 |
| 1933 | 864 (1,346) | 393 (612) | 471 (734) | 129.1 | 97.5 | 124.7 | 142.7 |
| 1934 | 661 (1,030) | 344 (536) | 317 (494) | 103.2 | 85.1 | 118.6 | 136.1 |
| 1935 | 590 (919) | 370 (576) | 220 (343) | 98.6 | 83.6 | 126.7 | 122.9 |
| 1936 | 604 (942) | 453 (707) | 151 (235) | 108.6 | 77.9 | 125.6 | 109.4 |

* in million haikwan taels; from 1933 trade was valued in Ch.$ as shown in parentheses.

*Sources*: Hsiao Liang-lin, *China's foreign trade statistics, 1864-1949*, pp. 23-24, 274-75; Yu-Kwei Cheng, *Foreign trade and industrial development of China*, p. 259.

tity rather than value, trade grew somewhat less rapidly. Imports were fairly steady in the last two decades of the nineteenth century; from 1900 there was a steady upward trend broken only by the disruptions resulting from the First World War which, we have noted, allowed some leeway for the growth of Chinese industry. Exports grew steadily from about 1907. Available data indicate that the trend in the simple terms of trade was against China (see table 48), but this would only be significant to the degree that the Chinese economy was linked to the world market as a result of expanding foreign trade. In the case of China that linkage was of less importance than in many other "underdeveloped" countries.

TABLE 49
BALANCE OF INTERNATIONAL PAYMENTS, 1903, 1930, 1935
(millions Chinese $)

| | 1903 | 1930 | 1935 |
|---|---|---|---|
| *Current out-payments* | | | |
| Merchandise imports | 492 | 1,965 | 1,129 |
| Specie imports | 58 | 101 | — |
| Service of foreign loans | 69 | 111 | 108 |
| Chinese expenditures abroad | 7 | 3 | 55 |
| Remittances of foreign enterprises and other profits | 35 | 227 | 55 |
| Total | 661 | 2,417 | 1,347 |
| *Current in-payments* | | | |
| Merchandise exports | 374 | 1,476 | 662 |
| Specie exports | 51 | 48 | 357 |
| Foreign expenditures in China | 81 | 218 | 150 |
| Overseas remittances | 114 | 316 | 260 |
| Total | 620 | 2,058 | 1,429 |
| *Capital in-payments* | | | |
| New foreign investments in China | 42 | 202 | 140 |
| *Unaccounted for* | –1 | –157 | 222 |

*Source:* Li Choh-ming, "International trade," in H. F. MacNair, ed., *China*, p. 501.

In all the years of the republic, as had been the case since the 1880s, China's foreign trade was marked by an import surplus, and the current account balance was consistently unfavorable. China's ability to sustain merchandise imports in excess of merchandise exports to a large extent appears to have been due to remittances from Overseas Chinese, which year after year flowed back to the homeland, as well as to new foreign investment. All available estimates of China's balance of international payments, however, include a substantial amount "unaccounted for" even after remittances and investment are considered. The estimates in table 49 for 1903, 1930, and 1935 are by H. B. Morse, C. F. Remer, and the Bank of China respectively.

TABLE 50
COMPOSITION OF FOREIGN TRADE (PER CENT CURRENT VALUE)

| | 1913 | 1916 | 1920 | 1925 | 1928 | 1931 | 1936 |
|---|---|---|---|---|---|---|---|
| *Imports* | | | | | | | |
| Cotton goods | 19.3 | 14.1 | 21.8 | 16.3 | 14.2 | 7.6 | 1.5 |
| Cotton yarn | 12.7 | 12.4 | 10.6 | 4.4 | 1.6 | 0.3 | 0.2 |
| Raw cotton | 0.5 | 1.6 | 2.4 | 7.4 | 5.7 | 12.6 | 3.8 |
| Rice and wheat | 3.3 | 6.6 | 0.8 | 6.8 | 5.7 | 10.6 | 4.1 |
| Wheat flour | 1.8 | 0.2 | 0.3 | 1.6 | 2.6 | 2.0 | 0.5 |
| Sugar | 6.4 | 7.1 | 5.2 | 9.5 | 8.3 | 6.0 | 2.2 |
| Tobacco | 2.9 | 5.8 | 4.7 | 4.1 | 5.1 | 4.4 | 1.8 |
| Paper | 1.3 | 1.8 | 1.9 | 2.0 | 2.4 | 3.2 | 4.1 |
| Kerosene | 4.5 | 6.2 | 7.1 | 7.0 | 5.2 | 4.5 | 4.2 |
| Petroleum | — | 0.2 | 0.4 | 0.9 | 1.4 | 1.8 | 4.1 |
| Transport materials | 0.8 | 4.0 | 2.6 | 1.9 | 2.3 | 2.3 | 5.6 |
| Chemicals, dyes, and pigments | 5.6 | 4.1 | 6.4 | 5.6 | 7.5 | 8.0 | 10.8 |
| Iron, steel, and other metals | 5.3 | 5.1 | 8.3 | 4.7 | 5.4 | 6.2 | 13.2 |
| Machinery | 1.4 | 1.3 | 3.2 | 1.8 | 1.8 | 3.1 | 6.4 |
| All others | 34.2 | 29.5 | 24.3 | 26.0 | 30.8 | 27.4 | 37.5 |
| | 100.0 | 100.0 | 100.0 | 100.0 | 100.0 | 100.0 | 100.0 |
| *Exports* | | | | | | | |
| Silk and silk goods | 25.3 | 22.3 | 18.6 | 22.5 | 18.4 | 13.3 | 7.8 |
| Tea | 8.4 | 9.0 | 1.6 | 2.9 | 3.7 | 3.6 | 4.3 |
| Beans and bean cake | 12.0 | 9.3 | 13.0 | 15.9 | 20.5 | 21.4 | 1.3 |
| Seeds and oil | 7.8 | 8.4 | 9.1 | 7.9 | 5.8 | 8.4 | 18.7 |
| Eggs and egg products | 1.4 | 2.6 | 4.0 | 4.3 | 4.4 | 4.1 | 5.9 |
| Hides, leather, and skins | 6.0 | 6.0 | 4.3 | 4.0 | 5.4 | 4.1 | 5.7 |
| Ores and metals | 3.3 | 6.3 | 3.2 | 2.9 | 2.1 | 1.6 | 7.7 |
| Coal | 1.6 | 1.2 | 2.3 | 2.6 | 2.9 | 3.0 | 1.6 |
| Cotton yarn and cotton goods | 0.6 | 0.8 | 1.4 | 2.0 | 3.8 | 4.9 | 3.0 |
| Raw cotton | 4.0 | 3.6 | 1.7 | 3.8 | 3.4 | 2.9 | 4.0 |
| All others | 29.6 | 30.5 | 40.8 | 31.2 | 29.6 | 32.7 | 40.0 |
| | 100.0 | 100.0 | 100.0 | 100.0 | 100.0 | 100.0 | 100.0 |

*Source*: Yu-Kwei Cheng, *Foreign trade and industrial development of China*, pp. 32, 34.

In the mid nineteenth century China's principal exports had been silk and tea. They accounted for 92 per cent of the total in 1871, dropped to about 80 per cent during the 1880s, to approximately 50 per cent in 1898, and thereafter continued to decline as table 50 indicates. While they continued to be predominantly natural resource products, China's exports were considerably diversified in the course of the twentieth century. The principal new export was the soy-bean and its products, grown largely in Manchuria. Of increasing importance, too, were the export of iron ore and coal to Japan, and the shipment of cotton yarn to Japan by Japanese-owned spinning mills in China.

Until the 1890s when it was surpassed by cotton cloth and yarn, opium was the most important import into China. In about 1900 cotton cloth and yarn constituted 40 per cent of total imports. The growth of Chinese- and foreign-owned textile mills in China led to a decline in cotton textile imports. To supply these new mills, however, China became a significant importer of raw cotton. By 1936 domestic cotton output was almost able to meet the demand; but in the post-1945 period raw cotton was again critically short, testifying both to the decline of agricultural production and to the disruption of transport by the civil war. In general, the proportion of industrial raw materials and equipment in total imports grew steadily but very slowly, while such manufactured consumer goods as textiles, cigarettes and matches declined. In the late 1920s and early 1930s, rice, wheat, and wheat flour climbed in importance among imports but then fell again with economic recovery in 1935 and 1936. Rural and especially urban population growth, lagging agricultural output, and poor transport made the task of feeding China's urban population always a difficult one.

Table 51 shows the proportions of China's trade with her leading suppliers and customers. There was a gradual diversification of trade between 1906 and 1936 as the growing percentage attributable to "others" indicates (the apparent sharp drop in imports from Hong Kong is the result of a new invoice system, introduced in 1932, intended to identify the actual national origin of goods shipped to China through Hong Kong). Great Britain, Japan, and the United States were China's principal trading partners. Japanese trade was predominant in Manchuria and North China and smallest in the south. The reverse was true of Great Britain. American trade, which exceeded that of all other countries in the mid 1930s, was concentrated in Central China. The decline in Japan's share after 1931 is to some degree a measure of the effectiveness of Chinese boycotts following the "Mukden incident."

The question remains of the overall consequences for China's economy of the patterns of foreign trade and investment just described. We have been categorical in stating that in aggregate terms they bulked much smaller than in many other "underdeveloped" economies. Yet to many Chinese and foreign observers these were the most critical influences shaping the

TABLE 51
DISTRIBUTION OF FOREIGN TRADE AMONG TRADING PARTNERS
(PER CENT CURRENT VALUE)

| | 1906 | 1913 | 1919 | 1927 | 1931 | 1936 |
|---|---|---|---|---|---|---|
| *Imports from:* | | | | | | |
| Great Britain | 18.4 | 16.5 | 9.5 | 7.3 | 8.3 | 11.7 |
| Hong Kong | 33.8 | 29.3 | 22.6 | 20.6 | 15.3 | 1.9 |
| Japan and Taiwan | 14.3 | 20.4 | 36.3 | 28.4 | 20.0 | 16.3 |
| United States | 10.4 | 6.0 | 16.2 | 16.1 | 22.2 | 19.6 |
| Russia | 0.1 | 3.8 | 2.1 | 2.2 | 1.7 | 0.1 |
| France | 1.0 | 0.9 | 0.5 | 1.4 | 1.5 | 2.0 |
| Germany | 4.0 | 4.8 | — | 3.8 | 5.8 | 15.9 |
| Others | 18.0 | 18.3 | 12.8 | 20.2 | 25.2 | 32.5 |
| | 100.0 | 100.0 | 100.0 | 100.0 | 100.0 | 100.0 |
| *Exports to:* | | | | | | |
| Great Britain | 5.6 | 4.1 | 9.1 | 6.3 | 7.1 | 9.2 |
| Hong Kong | 35.0 | 29.0 | 20.8 | 18.5 | 16.3 | 15.1 |
| Japan and Taiwan | 14.1 | 16.2 | 30.9 | 22.7 | 27.4 | 14.5 |
| United States | 10.9 | 9.3 | 16.0 | 13.3 | 13.2 | 26.4 |
| Russia | 7.9 | 11.1 | 3.4 | 8.4 | 6.0 | 0.6 |
| France | 10.7 | 10.1 | 5.4 | 5.6 | 3.8 | 4.3 |
| Germany | 2.4 | 4.2 | — | 2.2 | 2.5 | 5.5 |
| Others | 13.4 | 16.0 | 14.4 | 23.0 | 23.7 | 24.4 |
| | 100.0 | 100.0 | 100.0 | 100.0 | 100.0 | 100.0 |

*Source*: Yu-Kwei Cheng, *Foreign trade and industrial development of China*, pp. 20, 48-49.

course of modern Chinese history. The difficulty here, we suggest, is one of precipitating out purely economic factors from the complex mixture that was the foreign impact upon twentieth-century China.[125] China was changed by her modern encounter with the West, and it was the hope of economic gain which first brought the foreigner and his ways to the Middle Kingdom. Foreign economic activity was largely responsible for calling forth a small modern sector of Chinese and foreign-owned trading and manufacturing enterprises on the fringe of the Chinese empire. But the Chinese economy as a whole underwent no significant transformation; at best there occurred only a "partial development." The large foreign role in the modern sector of the economy was based on an artificially low tariff and the privileges of extraterritoriality, was supported by highly-developed industrial economies at home, and was abetted by the siphoning off of capital in indemnity and loan payments to foreign creditors. But all this cannot be made to bear more than a part of the obloquy for China's economic stagnation. To assert more than this is to obscure the ideological and political disequilibrium which was the most profound consequence of the impact of the West, and which for decades obstructed the emergence of a new political integration capable of replacing the Confucian imperial pattern of the past and taking advantage of the possibilities of economic development inherent in modern industrial technology.

The Chinese economy, in the years covered by this chapter at least, did not occupy center stage in the unfolding of the drama of Chinese history. It was only one of the supporting cast—with a few choice lines perhaps—waiting on the words of emperors, bureaucrats, diplomats, generals, propagandists, and party organizers.

# Notes

## Notes to Part I

1. The author gratefully acknowledges the support of the Committee on the Chinese Economy of the Social Science Research Council, and of the Center for Chinese Studies at the University of Michigan in the preparation of this essay.

2. Ping-ti Ho, *Studies on the Population of China, 1368-1953*, pp. 47-64.

3. Ibid., p. 97.

4. C. M. Chiao and J. L. Buck, "The composition and growth of rural population groups in China," *Chinese Economic Journal*, 2.22 (March 1928): 219-35.

5. See Muramatsu Yūji, "A documentary study of Chinese landlordism in the late Ch'ing and the early republican Kiangnan," *BSOAS*, 29.5 (1966) 566-99, and Professor Muramatsu's numerous studies of the *tsu-chan* cited therein.

6. There are no survey data describing nineteenth-century land tenure or utilization patterns comparable even to the admittedly inadequate twentieth-century reports. My comments are based in part on the results of an 1888 questionnaire to local informants compiled by George Jamieson for the Royal Asiatic Society: "Tenure of land in China and the condition of the rural population," *Journal of the North China Branch of the Royal Asiatic Society*, NS, 23 (1889): 59-117.

7. See Shigeru Ishikawa, *Economic development in Asian perspective*, p. 69-77.

8. Yen Chung-p'ing, *Chung-kuo mien-fang-chih shih-kao, 1289-1937* (Draft history of the Chinese cotton industry, 1289-1937), p. 311.

9· P'eng Tse-i, comp. *Chung-kuo chin-tai shou-kung-yeh shih tzu-liao, 1840-1949* (Source materials on the history of handicraft industry in modern China, 1840-1949), 2. 382-90, lists 13 references in eighteenth- and early nineteenth-century writings to handicraft workshops; this is, of course, neither a controlled sample nor an exhaustive count.

10. Cheng Kuan-ying, *Sheng-shih wei-yen* (Warnings to a prosperous age), 7.20a-b.

11. Blackburn Chamber of Commerce, *Report of the mission to China of the Blackburn Chamber of Commerce, 1896-7,* Neville and Bell's section, p. 212.

12. *Blackburn report,* F. S. A. Bourne's section, pp. 5-6.

13. *Report on the native cloth in use in the Amoy consular district* (Foreign Office, miscellaneous series, 1886, no. 19), p. 4.

14. *Blackburn report,* F. S. A. Bourne's section, p. 36.

15. See, for example, Fan Pai-ch'uan, "Chung-kuo shou-kung-yeh tsai wai-kuo tzu-pen-chu-i ch'in-ju hou ti tsao-yü ho ming-yun" (The fate of Chinese handicraft industry after the incursion of foreign capitalism), *Li-shih yen-chiu*, 1962, 3.88-115.

16. China. Inspectorate-General of Customs, *Decennial reports ..., 1902-1911*, 2.229-30.

17. P'eng Tse-i, *Chung-kuo chin-tai shou-kung-yeh shih tzu-liao*, 2. 356-66.

18. The currency unit given as Ch. $ in this section is the *yang-yuan* or "foreign dollar," commonly the Mexican silver dollar which had considerable currency in the treaty ports. These were gradually supplemented by Chinese silver dollars. Until 1933, both the dollar and the tael were used as units of account. One dollar was valued at approximately 0.72 taels.

19. Sun Yü-t'ang, comp., *Chung-kuo chin-tai kung-yeh shih tzu-liao, ti-i-chi, 1840-1895 nien* (Source materials on the history of modern industry in China, 1st collection, 1840-1895), 2.1166-69, 1170-73.

20. Wang Ching-yü, "Shih-chiu shih-chi wai-kuo ch'in Hua ch'i-yeh chung ti Hua-shang fu-ku huo-tung" (Investment by Chinese merchants in the foreign firms which invaded China in the nineteenth century), *Li-shih yen-chiu*, 1965. 4, pp. 39-74.

21. Wang Ching-yü, comp., *Chung-kuo chin-tai kung-yeh shih tzu-liao, ti-erh chi, 1895-1914 nien* (Source materials on the history of modern industry in China, 2nd collection, 1895-1914), 2.1065.

22. *Ibid.* 2.1017.

23. G. William Skinner, "Marketing and social structure in rural China, part II," *JAS*, 24.2 (February 1965): 227.

24. China. Inspectorate-Gencral of Customs, *Decennial reports ..., 1882-1891*, 661.

25. Amano Motonosuke, *Chūgoku nōgyō no sho mondai* (Problems of Chinese agriculture), 2.241-7, gives a meticulously detailed account of each item of cost from Anhwei to Shanghai.

26. Chungking was first reached by small steamship in 1898. Regular steamer service began in 1908.

27. The distribution of stations on official routes suggests that most official travel was by horse overland. For the travel of government officials the Ch'ing statutes provided for the maintenance of 1,634 land stations, 92 water stations and 54 land and water stations throughout the empire. At each stage in the journey these stations provided horses, carts, sedan chairs, or boats as needed, as well as lodging and food. Official documents were carried overland among some 15,000 postal stations. See Kono Michihiro, "Shindai Santōshō kansei rikujō kōtsūro" (Official overland communication routes in Shantung in the Ch'ing dynasty), *Shirin*, 33.3 (May 1950): 317-36.

28. The Chinese, of course, were irritated by the fact that foreign goods could, to a degree, escape the likin if covered by "transit passes" obtained by payment of half of the regular import duty. It should be remembered, however, that these passes were valid only so long as the goods remained in their original packaging and

were transported to the destination stated on the pass. In effect, it was possible that the tax on goods under pass was only delayed until they reached the final consumer.

29. *Blackburn report*, F. S. A. Bourne's section, pp. 70-71.

30. Even in the very unlikely case that the average tonnage of the 1,130 inland steamers of 1913 was as high as 100 tons (the 1900 average for Chinese-owned steamers was 35 tons), the total tonnage would be only 113,000. In September 1941, in the three provinces of Kiangsu, Chekiang, and Anhwei, 118,292 junks and sampans of all sizes (*min-ch'uan*), totaling 850,704 tons and with crews of 459,178 persons, had registered with the boatmen's association established by the Wang Ching-wei government. I have no data on the number and tonnage of junks in the late-Ch'ing period, but it is improbable that they could have been smaller than the 1941 figures for three provinces alone. See Mantetsu Chōsabu, *Chū-Shi no minsengyō* (The junk trade of Central China), pp. 134-35.

31. *Decennial reports ..., 1902-1911*, 1.292-93.

32. A substantial decline in the position of the Shansi banks from about 1900 is, however, to be noted. The semiofficial modern banks established after 1896 absorbed much of their transfer business and the deposits of public funds upon which they had depended.

33. Alexander Gerschenkron, *Economic backwardness in historical perspective.*

34. Yeh-chienWang, *Land taxation in imperial China, 1750-1911*, pp. 73-83.

35. Government revenue or expenditure in my estimate includes some part of the share which Chang attributes to gentry services.

36. Simon Kuznets, *Modern economic growtb: rate, structure, spread*, 236-39.

## Notes to Part II

1. This chapter excludes any consideration of communist-controlled China which included areas inhabited by some 90 million people in 1945 and operated in part with different economic assumptions. See Peter Schran, *Guerrilla economy: the development of the Shensi-Kansu-Ninghsia border region, 1937-1945.*

2. G. William Skinner, "Marketing and social structure in rural China," pt. 1, *JAS*, 26.1 (November 1964), pp. 3-44.

3. The characterization is Mark Elvin's, in Mark Elvin and G. William Skinner, eds., *The Chinese city between two worlds*, p. 3.

4. These are surely very rough estimates, but they are consistent with what little hard data are available. See Gilbert Rozman, *Urban networks in Ch'ing China and Tokugawa Japan*, pp. 99-104; Dwight H. Perkins, *Agricultural development in China, 1368-1968*, app. E: Urban population statistics (1900-58), pp. 290-96; and H. O. Kung, "The growth of population in six large Chinese cities," *Chinese Economic Journal*, 20.3 (March 1957): 301-14.

5. Rhoads Murphey, *The outsiders: the Western experience in India and China,* provides a major reexamination of the treaty-port experience.

6. About 470 million seems to be a charmed number for official population estimates in the 1920s and 1930s: the Nanking government Ministry of the Interior attempted a "census" in 1928, which produced an estimate of 474,787,386 based on "reports" from 16 provinces and special municipalities and guesses by the ministry for 17 provinces. The same ministry published a figure of 471,245,763 in 1938 compiled from local "reports" for 1936-37.

7. The largest discrepancy between the Liu-Yeh and Ou estimates is in the figures for net value added by agriculture, and within agriculture for the value of crops. While Ou's figures at probably too low, Perkins has made a plausible case that those of Liu-Yeh are based on too high a grain-yield estimate for 1933. Perkins, *Agricultural development in China,* pp. 29-32 and app. D.

8. This summary discussion follows Dwight H. Perkins, "Growth and changing structure of China's twentieth-century economy," in Perkins, ed., *China's modern economy in historical perspective,* 116-25.

9. Ou Pao-San (WuPao-san), "Chung-kuo-kuo-min so-te, 1933, 1936, chi 1946" (China's national income, 1933, 1936, and 1946), *She-hui k'o-hsueh tsa-chih,* 9.2 (December 1947), pp. 12-30, estimates national income in 1946 as 6% lower than 1933 (in 1933 prices). On Shanghai workers, see A. Doak Barnett, *China on the eve of communist takeover,* pp. 78-80; on the North China rural economy during 1937-49, Ramon H. Myers, *The Chinese peasant economy: agricultural development in Hopei and Shantung, 1890-1949,* pp. 278-87; on wartime unoccupied China and post-war inflation, Chang Kia-ngau, *The inflationary spiral: the experience of China, 1939-1950,* pp. 59-103.

10. Perkins, "Growth and changing structure of China's twentieth-century economy," p. 124, who cites Myers, *The Chinese peasant economy,* pp. 234-40, and Perkins, *Agricultural development in China,* ch. 5.

11. A. Feuerwerker, "Economic trends in the late Ch'ing empire, 1870-1911," *CHOC,* vol. 11, ch. 1.

12. Ch'en Chen, *et al.,* comps. *Chung-kuo chin-tai kung-yeh shih tzu-liao* (Source materials on the history of modern industry in China; hereafter *CKCT*), 1.55-56.

13. Nankai Institute of Economics, *Nankai weekly statistical service,* 4.33 (17 August 1931), pp. 157-58.

14. Liu Ta-chün (D. K. Lieu), *Chung-kuo kung-yeh tiao-ch'a pao-kao* (Report on a survey of China's industry). "Factory" was defined according to the 1929 Factory Law as an enterprise using mechanical power and employing 30 or more workers.

15. Ou Pao-san (Wu Pao-san), *Chung-kuo kuo-min so-te i-chiu-san-san-nien* (China's national income, 1933), vol. 1. Tables 1-2 following p. 64; table 5, pp.

70-11; additional data in Ou, "Chung-kuo kuo-min so-te i-chiu-san-san hsiu-cheng" (Corrections to China's national income, 1935), *She-hui k'o-hsueh tsa-chih,* 9.2. (December 1947), pp. 130-36, 144-47, which incorporated the estimates of Wang Fu-sun, "Chan-ch'ien Chung-kuo kung-yeh sheng-ch'an-chung wai-ch'ang sheng-ch'an ti pi-chung wen-t'i" (The proportion of industrial production by foreign-owned factories in total industrial production in pre-war China), *Chung-yang yin-hang yueh-pao,* 2.3 (March 1947), pp. 1-19.

16. *CKCT,* 4.92.

17. *Ibid.,* 1.89-97; 4.93-96, excerpts from Directorate of Economic Statistics, "Hou-fang kung-yeh kai-k'uang t'ung-chi" (Statistics on industry in the interior), May 1943.

18. Yen Chung-p'ing, comp., *Chung-kuo chin-tai ching-chi-shih t'ung-chi tzu-liao hsuan-chi* (Selected statistics on modern Chinese economic history; hereafter *CKCTC*), pp. 147-50; Wang Fu-sun, "Chan-shih Hua-pei kung-yeh tzu-pen chiu-yeh yü sheng-ch'an" (Wartime industrial capital, employment, and production, in North China), *She-hui k'o-hsueh tsa-chih,* 9. 2. (December 1947), p. 48.

19. Wang Chi-shen, *Chan-shih Shang-hai ching-chi* (The economy of wartime Shanghai), pp. 192, 194. I am grateful to Professor Thomas Rawski for this reference.

20. Alexander Eckstein, Kang Chao, and John Chang, "The economic development of Manchuria: the rise of a frontier economy," *Journal of Economic History,* 34.1 (March 1974): 251-60.

21. Substantial data on the relative positions of state-owned and private mining and producers' goods enterprises 1938-48 may be found in *CKCT,* 3. 1439-45, 873-79, 882-87.

22. State Statistical Bureau, Industrial Statistics Department, *Wo-kuo kang-t'ieh, tien-li, mei-tan, chi-hsieh, fang-chih, tsao-chih kung-yeh ti chin-hsi* (Past and present of China's iron and steel, electric power, coal, machinery, textile, and paper industries), pp. 148-9; *CKCT,* 3. 1051-74.

23. John K. Chang, *Industrial development in Communist China: a quantitative analysis,* pp. 70-74.

24. Ou, "Chung-kuo kuo-min so-te i-chiu-san-san hsiu-cheng," pp. 137-42, shows the net value added by handicrafts as 72% for all industries, based however on a definition of "factory" which includes only firms employing 30 or more workers and using mechanical power.

25. This theme is implied in the arrangement of the materials in P'eng Tse-i, comp., *Chung-kuo chin-tai shou-kung-yeh shih tzu-liao, 1840-1949* (Source materials on the history of the handicraft industry in modern China, 1840-1949), valuable documentation that has not yet been adequately exploited.

26. See Feuerwerker, "Economic trends, 1870-1911," *CHOC,* vol. 11, ch. 1.

27. See P'eng Tse-i, *Chung-kuo chin-tai shou-kung-yeh shih tzu-liao, 1840-1949*, 2. 331-449.

28. See Lillian Ming-tse Li, "Kiangnan and the silk export trade, 1842-1937," (Ph.D. diss., Harvard University, 1975), pp. 234-73.

29. Reynolds' results for 1875 and 1905, arrived at by a much different route, are very close to my estimates in "Handicraft and manufactured cotton textiles in China, 1871-1910," *Studies in the Economic History of Late Imperial China* (Ann Arbor: Center for Chinese Studies, The University of Michigan, 1995). I use his figures here rather than my own because they are part of a methodologically consistent estimate for the whole period 1875-1931.

30. See Kang Chao, "The growth of a modern cotton textile industry and the competition with handicrafts," in Perkins, ed., *China's modern economy*, pp. 167-201.

31. Chao, *ibid.*, pp. 173-75, offers examples.

32. Ta-chung Liu and Kung-chia Yeh, *The economy of the Chinese mainland: national income and economic development, 1933-1959*, pp. 142-43, 512-13; Hsiao Liang-lin, *China's foreign trade statistics, 1864-1949*, pp. 32-3.

33. Chi-ming Hou, *Foreign investment and economic development in China, 1840-1937*, pp. 169-70.

34. Li, "Kiangnan and the silk export trade, 1842-1957," pp. 266-73

35. Perkins, *Agricultural development in China*, pp. 29-30.

36. Perkins, "Growth and changing structure of China's twentieth-century economy," pp. 122-23.

37. Ku Ch'un-fan (Koh Tso-fan), *Chung-kuo kung-yeh-hua t'ung-lun* (A general discussion of China's industrialization), p. 170.

38. On the origins, recruitment, wages and working conditions of labor in the 1920s, See Jean Chesneaux, *The Chinese labor movement, 1919-1927*, pp. 48-112. The structure of industrial wages before 1949 is analyzed in Christopher Howe, *Wage patterns and wage policy in modern China, 1919-1972*, pp. 16-27. For an example of Japanese-style "permanent" employment for skilled male workers, see *Andersen, Meyer and Company Limited of China*, p. 114. I am indebted to Professor Thomas Rawski for this last reference.

39. Kang Chao, "Policies and performance. in industry," in Alexander Eckstein, Walter Galenson, and Ta-chung Liu, eds., *Economic trends in communist China*, table 3, p. 579.

40. Feng-hwa Mah, *The foreign trade of mainland China*, app. C, pp. 194-200.

41. Thomas G. Rawski, "The growth of producer industries, 1900-1971," in Perkins, ed. *China's modern economy*, pp. 228-32.

42. Perkins, "Growth and changing structure of China's twentieth-century economy," p. 125.

43. Perkins, *Agricultural development in China*, pp. 233-40.

44. These are data for China as a whole, including Manchuria. For North China, see Myers, *The Chinese peasant economy*, pp. 177-206; many local studies are summarized in Amano Motonosuke, *Chūoku nōgyō no shomondai* (Problems of Chinese agriculture), 1.3-148.

45. For rice, wheat, and wheat flour imports, see Hsiao, *China's foreign trade statistics, 1864-1949*, pp. 32-34. Wu Pao-san, *Chung-kuo liang-shih tui-wai mao-i ch'i ti-wei ch'ü-shih chi pien-ch'ien chih yuan-yin, 1912-1931* (Causes of trends and fluctuations in China's foreign trade in food grains, 1912-1931).

46. Hsiao, *China's foreign trade statistics, 1864-1949*, pp. 274-75.

47. Amano Motonosuke, *Shina nōgyō keizai ron* (On the Chinese agricultural economy; hereafter *Agricultural economy)*, 2.696-98 provides a listing of civil wars, floods, droughts, pestilence, and the provinces affected, 1912-31. See also Buck, *Land utilization in China. Statistics*, pp. 13-20, for "calamities" by locality during 1904-29.

48. Amano Motonosuke, *Chūgoku nōgyō shi kenkyū* (A study of the history of Chinese agriculture) 389-423, for example, on rice technology. F. H. King, *Farmers of forty centuries*, provides a vivid description of the "permanent agriculture in China, Korea and Japan" in the early twentieth century.

49 Li Wen-chih and Chang Yu-i, comps., *Chung-kuo chin-tai nung-yeh shih tzu-liao* (Source materials on China's modern agricultural history; hereafter *Agricultural history*), 2.182. The first volume in this collection, edited by Li, covers 1840-1911; the second and third, edited by Chang, cover 1912-27 and 1927-37 respectively.

50. Ramon H. Myers, "Agrarian policy and agricultural transformation: mainland China and Taiwan, 1895-1954," *Hsiang-kang Chung-kuo wen-hua yen-chiu-so hsueh-pao* (Journal of the Institute of Chinese Studies of the Chinese University of Hong Kong), 3.2 (1970): 532-35.

51. Eckstein, Chao and Chang, "The economic development of Manchuria," pp. 240-51.

52. Li Wen-chih and Chang Yu-i, comps., *Agricultural history*, 3. 476-80, 622-41.

53. *Ibid.* 3. 480-85.

54. *Nung-ch'ing pao-kao*, 7.4 (April 1939): 49-50, in Li Wen-chih and Chang Yu-i, comps., *Agricultural history*, 5. 709-10.

55. Perkins, Agricultural *development in China*, p. 136; Li Wen-chih and Chang Yu-i, comps., *Agricultural history*, 2. 131-300; Chang Jen-chia, *Konan no beikoku* (Rice in Hunan; trans. of 1936 report by Hunan provincial economic research institute), pp. 87-113.

56. Liu Ta-chung and Yeh Kung-chia, *The economy of the Chinese mainland*, p. 68, table 10.

57. Perkins, *Agricultural Development in China*, pp. 31-36; Li Wen-chih and Chang Yu-i, comps., *Agricultural history*, 2. 406-07; Buck, *Land Utilization in China*, pp. 281-82.

58. See Myers, *The Chinese peasant economy, passim.*

59. Robert Ash, *Land tenure in pre-revolutionary China: Kiangsu province in the 1920s and 1930s*, p. 50. Ash himself also gives some weight to the more "purely economic factors." His study, however, appears unconvincing in its evaluation of the degree and sources of agricultural investment in twentieth-century Kiangsu.

60. Carl Riskin, "Surplus and Stagnation in Modern China," in Perkins, ed., *China's modern economy*, p. 57.

61. *Ibid.*, pp. 68, 74, 77-81; Victor D. Lippit, *Land reform and economic development in China*, pp. 36-94.

62. Buck, *Land utilization in China*, pp. 269-70.

63. *Ibid.*, pp. 181-85, 294, 297.

64. *Ibid.*, pp. 193-96.

65. Perkins, *Agricultural development in China*, pp. 87, 89; Lippit, *Land reform and economic development in China*, p. 95; Kenneth R. Walker, *Planning in Chinese agriculture: socialisation and the private sector, 1956-1962*, p. 5.

66. See Muramatsu Yūji, *Kindai Kōnan no kenkyū—Chūgoku jinushi seido no kenkyū* (Bursaries in modern Kiangnan—a study of the Chinese landlord system), pp. 47-237, 391-636; and "A documentary study of Chinese landlordism in late Ch'ing and early republican Kiangnan," *Bulletin of the School of Oriental and African Studies*, 29.3 (1966): 566-99.

67. Perkins, *Agricultural development in China*, pp. 92-98.

68. Ch'en Cheng-mo, *Chung-kuo ko-sheng ti ti-tsu* (Land rents in China by Province), p. 43, found the incidence of labor rents to be highest in Honan, Szechwan, Kweichow, and Yunnan based on reports from 1,520 localities in 22 provinces excluding Manchuria.

69. National government, Directorate of Statistics, *Chung-hua min-kuo t'ung-chi t'i-yao, 1935* (Statistical abstract of the Republic of China, 1935), pp. 462-63, shows land values in Shantung in 1933 as roughly the same as those in Chekiang; the NARB 1934 Shantung value, however, is one-third lower than Chekiang.

70. In table 38(1) I have used Buck's alternative estimate derived from his "agricultural survey" rather than his "farm survey" percentages which are usually cited. The latter are obviously too low both because his sample gives inadequate weight to the southern provinces, and because the nature of the survey dictated that relatively accessible localities dominated the data.

71. For regional variations in Kiangsu, see Ash, *Land tenure in pre-revolutionary China*, pp. 11-22; for Shantung and Hopei, Myers, *The Chinese economy*, pp. 234-40.

72. George Jamieson, "Tenure of land in China and the condition of the rural population," *Journal of the North China Branch of the Royal Asiatic Society*, 23 (1889): 59-117.

73. *Nung-ch'ing pao-kao*, 5.12 (December 1937): 330, in Li Wen-chih and Chang Yu-i, comps., *Agricultural history*, 3. 728-30.

74. Myers, *The Chinese peasant economy*, p. 223.

75. Amano Motonosuke, *Agricultural economy*, 1. 299.

76. Buck, *Land utilization in China*, p. 533.

77. National government, Directorate of Statistics, *Chung-kuo tsu-tien chih-tu chih t'ung-chi fen-hsi* (Statistical analysis of China's land rent system), p. 19.

78. National Land Commission, *Ch'üan-kuo t'u-ti tiao-ch'a pao-kao kang-yao* (Preliminary report of the national land survey), p. 46.

79. Ministry of the Interior, *Nei-cheng nien-chien* (Yearbook of the Interior Ministry), 3. *T'u-ti*, ch. 12, (D) pp. 993-94. Ch'en Cheng-mo found *ya-tsu* widespread in 30% of reporting localities in 1933-34, and present in 6% more. Ch'en Cheng-mo, *Chung-kuo ko-sheng ti ti-tsu*, p. 61.

80. National Land Commission, *Ch'üan-kuo t'u-ti tiao-ch'a pao-kao kang-yao*, p. 44.

81. National government, Directorate of Statistics, *Chung-kuo tsu-tien chih-tu chih t'ung-chi fen-hsi*, p. 43. The data, comparing 1924 and 1934, show such small changes that they may not be significant at all.

82. Buck, *Land utilization in China*, p. 462; *Nung-ch'ing pao-kao*, 2.4 (April 1934): 30, in *CKCTC*, p. 342; National Land Commission, *Ch'üan-kuo t'u-ti tiao-ch'a pao-kao kang-yao*, p. 51.

83. Buck, *Land utilization in China*, p. 462: 76% of farm credit was for "non-productive purposes"; Amano Motonosuke, *Agricultural economy*, 2. 219-20, citing seven national and local studies.

84. *Nung-ch'ing pao-kao*, 2.11 (November 1934): 108-09, in *The Chinese Economic and Statistical Review*, 1.11 (November 1934): 7.

85. *The Chinese Economic and Statistical Review*, 1.11 (November 1954): 2.

86. See Li Wen-chih and Chang Yu-i, comps., *Agricultural history*, 3. 206-14; Amano Motonosuke, *Agricultural economy*, 2. 308-49.

87. Buck, *Land utilization in China*, p. 233.

88. See Li Wen-chih and Chang Yu-i, comps., *Agricultural history*, 2. 559-80; 3. 9-65. Amano Motonosuke, *Agricultural economy*, 2. 1-158.

89. Myers, *The Chinese peasant economy*, 278-87, briefly describes the damage and dislocations suffered by the North China rural economy during 1957-48.

90. Central Ministry of Agriculture, Planning Office, *Liang-nien-lai ti Chung-kuo nung-ts'un ching-chi tiao-ch'a hui-pien* (Collection of surveys of the rural economy of China during the past two years), pp. 141-44, 149-51, 160, 162, 226-36.

91. D. K. Lieu, *China's industries and finance*, pp. 197-219; Ku Lang, *Chung-kuo shih ta-k'uang tiao-ch'a chi* (Report of an investigation of the 10 largest mines in China), pp. 3-49.

92. American Bankers Association. Commission on Commerce and Marine, *China, an economic survey, 1923*, p. 16.

93. National Economic Council. Bureau of Public Roads, *Highways in China.*

94. *CKCTC*, pp. 172-80. Mileage estimates in other sources differ slightly.

95. Chang Kia-ngau, *China's struggle for railroad development*, pp. 170-1, table III.

96. Hou, *Foreign investment and economic development in China*, pp. 32, 39-42.

97. *CKCTC*, p. 210.

98. Chinese Ministry of Information, *China handbook, 1937-1945*, p. 217.

99. Mantetsu Chōsabu, *Chū-shi no minsengyō* (The junk trade of central China), pp. 134-35.

100. Yang Tuan-liu, *et al.*, *Liu-shih-wu-nien-lai Chung-kuo kuo-chi mao-i t'ung-chi* (Statistics of China's foreign trade during the last 65 years), p. 140.

101. *CKCTC*, pp. 228-29, 235-36.

102. Chia Shih-i, *Min-kuo ts'ai-cheng shih* (Fiscal history of the republic), 1.45-77.

103. Stanley F. Wright, *China's customs revenue since the Revolution of 1911* (3rd ed., 1935), pp. 440-41.

104. P. T. Chen, "Public finance," *The Chinese year book, 1935-36*, pp. 1298-99.

105. Ch'ien Chia-chü, *Chiu Chung-kuo kung-chai shih tzu-liao, 1894-1949* (Source materials on government bond issues in old China, 1894-1949), pp. 366-69.

106. Chia Te-huai, *Min-kuo ts'ai-cheng chien shih* (A short fiscal history of the republic), pp. 697-98; Kashiwai Kisao, *Kindai Shina zaisei shi* (History of modern Chinese finance), pp. 63-4.

107. C. M. Chang, "Local government expenditure in China," *Monthly Bulletin of Economic China*, 7.6 (June 1934): 233-47.

108. C. F. Remer, *Foreign investments in China*, pp. 123-47; Hsu I-sheng, *Chung-kuo chin-tai wai-chai shih t'ung-chi tzu-liao, 1853-1927* (Statistical materials on foreign loans in modern China, 1853-1927), pp. 240-45.

109. Remer, *Foreign investments in China*, p. 160.

110. Arthur N. *Young, China's nation-building effort, 1927-1937: the financial and economic record* provides a comprehensive account. Douglas S. Paauw, "Chinese public finance during the Nanking government period" (Ph.D. diss., Harvard University, 1950); "Chinese national expenditure during the Nanking period," *FEQ*,

12.1 (November 1952): 3-26; and "The Kuomintang and economic stagnation," *JAS*, 16.2. (February 1957): 213-20, are less sanguine than Young.

111. U. S. Bureau of the Census, *Historical statistics of the United States, 1789-1945*, p. 12.

112. Shun-hsin Chou, *The Chinese inflation, 1937-1949*; pp. 64-65; Chang, *The inflationary spiral*, pp. 140-41.

113. Arthur N. Young, *China and the helping hand, 1937-1941*, pp. 440-42.

114. Ch'ien Chia-chü, *Chiu Chung-kuo kung-chai shih tzu-liao*, pp. 370-75; Young, *China's nation-building effort*, pp. 459-68.

115. Young, *China's nation-building effort*, pp. 98, 509-10. Young, financial adviser to the Ministry of Finance, 1929-47, disagrees strongly with the lower estimate of a 50 to 60% net return which appears in Leonard G. Ting, "Chinese modern banks and the finance of government and industry," *Nankai social and economic quarterly*, 8.3 (October 1935): 591, and which originated with Chu Hsieh, *Chung-kuo ts'ai-cheng wen-t'i* (Problems of China's public finance), pp. 231-32.

116. Young, *China's nation-building effort*, pp. 98-99.

117. Frank M. Tamagna, *Banking and finance in China*, pp. 121-96; Miyashita Tadao, *Shina ginkō seido ron* (A treatise on the Chinese banking system), pp. 103-221; Tokunaga Kiyoyuki, *Shina chūō ginkō seido ron* (A treatise on central banking in China), pp. 255-350; Andrea Lee McElderry, *Shanghai old-style banks (ch'ien-chuang), 1800-1935*, pp. 131-85. Through 1934 only the Central Bank of China and the Farmers Bank of China were completely controlled by the government. Twenty per cent of the shares of the Bank of China and the Bank of Communications were owned by Nanking, which also had some influence on the appointment of key personnel; but the two banks exercised considerable independence and at times opposed government fiscal and monetary policies. In March 1935 the Bank of China and the Bank of Communications were "nationalized" in a carefully planned coup executed by the minister of finance, H. H. Kung.

118. On wartime and post-war public finance and the inflation, see Chou, *The Chinese inflation*; Chang, *The inflationary spiral*; and Arthur N. Young, *China's wartime finance and inflation, 1937-1945*.

119. Robert F. Dernberger, "The role of the foreigner in China's economic development," in Perkins, ed., *China's modern economy*, pp. 28-30.

120. C. F. Remer, *Foreign investments in China*, pp. 170-71.

121. Hou, *Foreign investment and economic development in China*, pp. 17-22.

122. *Ibid.*, pp. 138-41.

123. Dernberger, "The role of the foreigner in China's economic development," pp. 39-40.

124. Hou, *Foreign investment and economic development in China*, p. 29.

125. See Albert Feuerwerker, "The foreign presence in China," in John K. Fairbank, ed., *The Cambridge History of China*, vol. 12, ch. 3.

# Bibliographical Essay

## 1. Economic Trends, 1870–1911

No satisfactory synthetic treatment of China's modern economic history has been published in any language. A two-volume Hong Kong collection of photolithographed reprints of forty-six articles on modern economic and social history published in the People's Republic and Taiwan during 1953–67 gives some indication of the state of the field: *Chung-kuo chin san-pai-nien she-hui ching-chi shih lun-chi* (Collected articles on China's social and economic history in the last 300 years). Twenty-one important older articles originally published in the journal *Chung-kuo she-hui ching-chi shih chi-k'an* (Chinese Social and Economic History Review) between 1932 and 1949 have also been conveniently reprinted: *Chung-kuo chin-tai she-hui ching-chi shih lun-chi* (Collected articles on China's modern social and economic history).

Published sources for the economy in the late Ch'ing period include two large collections of documents photographically reproduced from the archives of the Tsungli Yamen and the Ministry of Foreign Affairs: Chung-yang yen-chiu-yuan chin-tai-shih yen-chiu-so (Academia Sinica, Institute of Modern History), *Hai-fang tang* (Archives on coastal defense), which cover the purchase of foreign weapons and the establishment of arsenals and machine shops, telegraphs and railways in the period 1861–1911; and *idem, K'uang-wu tang* (Archives on mining affairs) for the years 1865–1911.

Substantial quantities of raw data—more often consisting of excerpts from relatively inaccessible printed sources than of previously unpublished documents, and sometimes arranged under tendentious headings—were assembled and published in the first decade of the People's Republic. Li Wen-chih, comp. *Chung-kuo chin-tai nung-yeh shih tzu-liao ti-i chi, 1840–1911* (Source materials on the history of agriculture in modern China, first collection, 1840–1911) includes an extensive bibliography. The first two volumes of P'eng Tse-i, comp. *Chung-kuo chin-tai shou-kung-yeh shih tzu-liao, 1840–1949* (Source materials on the history of handicraft industry in modern China, 1840–1949) cover the late Ch'ing. On factory industry before World War I, see Sun Yü-t'ang, comp. *Chung-kuo chin-tai kung-yeh shih tzu-liao, ti-i chi, 1840–1895 nien* (Source materials on the history of industry in China, 1st collection, 1840–1895); and Wang Ching-yü, comp., *Chung-kuo chin-tai kung-yeh shih tzu-liao, ti-erh chi, 1895–1914 nien* (Source materials on the history of modern industry in China, 2nd collection, 1895–1914). Documents on the history of railways are collected in Mi Ju-ch'eng, comp., *Chung-kuo chin-tai t'ieh-lu shih tzu-liao, 1863–1911* (Source materials on the history of railways in modern China, 1863–1911). But the most important single source on transportation and communications is National Government, Ministries of Communications and Railroads (Chiao-t'ung t'ieh-tao pu chiao-t'ung shih pien-tsuan wei-yuan hui), *Chiao-t'ung shih* (History of transport and communications). Microfilm and 'a grand table of contents' published in 1970 and available at Center for Chinese Research Materials, Washington, D.C., provide access to the 23,776 pages of documents in this collection. Very detailed data on foreign loans appear in Hsu I-sheng, *Chung-kuo chin-tai wai-chai shih t'ung-chi tzu-liao, 1853–1927* (Statistical materials on the history of China's foreign loans, 1853–1927). Yen Chung-p'ing *et al.*, comps., *Chung-kuo chin-tai ching-chi shih t'ung-chi tzu-liao hsuan-chi* (Selected statistics on China's modern economic history) draws on a wide range of sources which are carefully noted, but the compiler sometimes ignores the index number problem.

For foreign trade and much else the voluminous publications of the Chinese Maritime Customs are indispensable. These have now been made available on microfilm by the Center for Chinese Research Materials, Washington, D.C. The trade statistics are usefully collated, with full reference to the original sources, in Hsiao Liang-lin, *China's foreign trade statistics, 1864–1949.*

The monographic literature is scanty. Probably the best place to begin is with the relevant sections of G. William Skinner *et al.*, eds., *Modern Chinese society: an analytical bibliography*, which covers publications in Western, Chinese, and Japanese languages, dealing with the period 1644–1972.

Among many monographs on particular subjects, the following may be noted. On agriculture, in addition to the work of John Lossing

Buck, see Dwight H. Perkins, *Agricultural development in China, 1368–1968,* a brilliant study showing how expansion of cultivated acreage and increased yields per acre enabled China's farmers to feed a growing population; and Amano Motonosuke, *Shina nōgyō keizai ron* (On the Chinese agricultural economy), a massive summary of the available data on the twentieth-century economy until 1949, but valuable for the previous century as well. A fair amount of scholarly attention has been given to modern manufacturing and mining, but little to handicrafts. Albert Feuerwerker, *China's early industrialization: Sheng Hsuan-huai (1844–1916) and mandarin enterprise* defines the nature of late-Ch'ing industrialization. On military industries, see Wang Erh-min, *Ch'ing chi ping-kung-yeh ti hsing-ch'i* (The rise of the armaments industry in the late Ch'ing period). On railways, Li Kuo-ch'i, *Chung-kuo tsao-ch'i ti t'ieh-lu ching-ying* (China's early railway enterprises). On steamships, Kwang-Ching Liu, *Anglo-American steamship rivalry in China, 1862–1874.* On mining, Ellsworth C. Carlson, *The Kaiping mines, 1877–1912: a case study of early Chinese industrialization.* Yen Chung-p'ing, *Chung-kuo mien-fang-chih shih-kao* (Draft history of the Chinese cotton industry) is the best available study of a single industry. The impact of foreign industrial investment is well-handled in Chi-ming Hou, *Foreign investment and economic development in China, 1849–1937.* On population, see Ping-ti Ho, *Studies on the Population of China, 1368–1953.* The administration and size of the land tax are treated in Yeh-chien Wang, *Land taxation in imperial China, 1750–1911,* and the fiscally important salt monopoly in Saeki Tomi, *Shindai ensei no kenkyū* (A study of the Ch'ing salt administration). On the monetary system, see Yang Tuan-liu, *Ch'ing-tai huo-pi chin-jung shih kao* (Draft history of money and money markets in the Ch'ing period), and Frank H. H. King, *Money and monetary policy in China, 1845–1895.*

The several essays in three recent volumes of conference papers touch on many aspects of the late-Ch'ing economy: W. E. Willmott, ed., *Economic organization in Chinese society*; Mark Elvin and G. William Skinner, eds., *The Chinese city between two worlds*; Dwight H. Perkins, ed., *China's modern economy in historical perspective.*

## 2. Economic Trends, 1912–49

National economic statistics that are either comprehensive or reliable are a regrettable lacuna even for twentieth-century China. The Ministry of Agriculture and Commerce of the Peking government did publish a series of annual statistical tables (Ministry of Agriculture and Commerce, *Nung-shang t'ung-chi piao* [Tables of agricultural and commercial statistics; Shanghai, 1914–19; Peking, 1920–24]). The volumes for 1914 and 1918 are relatively better than the others; as a whole the data are estimates rather than the products of controlled surveys. Statistical reports were issued, for example, by the national railways (Ministry of Communications [from 1925 issue, Ministry of Railways, Bureau of Railway Statistics], *Statistics of government railways, 1915–36* [from 1922 issue, *Statistics of railways*] (Peking, 1916–28; Nanking, 1931–36]). And of course the generally excellent foreign trade statistics of the foreign-administered Chinese Maritime Customs appeared annually. The customs statistics are usefully collated, with full references to the original sources, in Hsiao Liang-lin *China's foreign trade statistics, 1864–1949.* For the most part, however, before 1928 the central government was so weak and ineffectual that no systematic national effort was made to collect economic data.

With the establishment of the Kuomintang Nationalist government, the statistical situation improved somewhat. The *Annual reports* of the Ministry of Finance for the years 1928–34 are the only genuine reports on Chinese national finance ever issued (Ministry of Finance, *Annual reports for the 17th, 18th, 19th, 21st, 22nd, and 23rd fiscal years* [Nanking, 1930–36]). For the 1930s agricultural statistics, including acreage and crop production, were compiled by the National Agricultural Research Bureau of the Ministry of Industries and made available in its monthly publication *Nung-ch'ing pao-kao* (Crop reports 1933–39). These estimates, together with the privately sponsored work of J. L Buck covering the late 1920s and early 1930s at the College of Agriculture, University of Nanking, are about the best data available on Chinese agriculture (John Lossing Buck, *Land utilization in China: a study of 16,786 farms in 168 localities, and 38,256 farm families in twenty-two provinces in China, 1929–33.* Vol. 2 presents Buck's statistics in 475 folio pages). The only year for which we have detailed industrial statistics is 1933. These are the product of a large-scale survey made by D. K. Lieu for the National Resources Commission of the National Military Council (Liu Ta-chün [D. K. Lieu], *Chung-kuo kung-yeh tiao-ch'a pao-ko* [Report on a survey of China's industry; 3 vols.]). Lieu's data exclude both Manchuria and foreign-owned factories in China outside of Manchuria. Japanese studies of Manchurian industry are, however, available (see John Young, *The research activities of the South Manchurian Railway Company, 1907–45: a history and bibliography*). There are also a number of estimates of foreign-owned industry in China, but none of them is comparable to Lieu's survey. In addition to government-sponsored collections of statistics, good but fragmentary private collections of data were carried out by the Nankai Institute of Economics in Tientsin (mainly price data: see *1913 nien-1952 nien Nan-k'ai chih-shu tzu-liao hui-pien* [Nankai price indexes, 1913–52]), and in Shanghai by the China Institute of Economic and Statistical Research (published in its bilingual monthly journal, *Ching-chi t'ung-chi yueh-chih* [The Chinese economic and statistical review, 1934–41]). Shanghai price indices are collected in Academy of Sciences, Shanghai Institute of Economic Research, *Shang-hai chieh-fang ch'ien-hou wu-chia tzu-liao hui-pien (1921 nien-1957 nien)* (Collected materials on Shanghai prices before and after Liberation, 1921–57).

Although in quantity and quality they were much superior to pre-1928 data, the economic statistics of the Kuomintang period still leave much to be desired, in part because China was still far from being politically unified; in part because a large proportion of economic activity continued to be carried on outside of any market transactions and thus could not easily be measured; and finally because of the continued technical backwardness of the statistical services. But even the relatively deficient data of 1928–37 are a godsend when compared to what is available thereafter. War and civil war did not spare statistical collection any more than other parts of the administrative organization. For 1937–49, macrodata of any kind, apart from fiscal and monetary statistics, are scarce and unreliable. Chang Kia-ngau, *The inflationary spiral: the experience of China, 1939–50* includes data available only to the author, who was governor of the Central Bank of China.

The statistical publications that I have noted are, of course, only examples. There was more—the publications of the Ministry of Industry and the Bureau of Foreign Trade of the Nanking government, for instance, or the rural surveys prepared for the Executive Yuan's Rural Recovery Commission and the comprehensive mineral output data for China proper and Manchuria published by the Geological Survey of China. In addition to these official reports, Chinese and Japanese researchers (the latter mainly on behalf of the South Manchurian Railway Company) produced hundreds of fragmentary local studies. But none of these individually—nor all of them collectively—supply or easily permit the derivation of the comprehensive data on population, employment, capital stock, national product and expenditure, prices, taxation, monetary flows and the like, which the economic historian might use for a definitive analysis of China's economy in the first half of the twentieth century. The introductory matter to each of the 36 sections of National government, Directorate of Statistics, *Chung-hua min-kuo t'ung-chi t'i-yao, 1935* (Statistical abstract of the Republic of China, 1935) includes useful descriptions of most of the statistical publications of republican China. Yen Chung-p'ing, comp., *Chung-kuo chin-tai ching-chi t'ung-chi tzu-liao hsuan-chi* (Statistical materials on modern Chinese economic history) draws on a wide range of sources which are carefully noted and—in spite of its tendentious arrangement and commentaries, not to speak of the compiler's apparent innocence about "the index number problem"—is of substantial value. Other collections of source materials and monographic works are cited in the footnotes.

It is under these handicaps that the Chinese economy in the period of the republic must be surveyed. That so much of the macroeconomic description included in this chapter hangs on what are, after all, only intelligent guesses for 1933 makes it admittedly a hostage to fortune. Chinese domestic materials, inadequate as they are, have not yet been fully exploited, and careful use of studies of the twentieth-century Chinese economy by such Japanese agencies as the South Manchurian Railway will probably show them to contribute more than we have seemed to credit them with. *Caveat lector.*

# Bibliography of Works Cited

Allen, G. C. and Donnithorne, Audrey G. *Western enterprise in Far Eastern economic development: China and Japan.* London: George Allen & Unwin, 1954.

Amano Motonosuke 天野元之助. *Shina nōgyō keizai ron* 支那農業經濟論 (On the Chinese agricultural economy). 2 vols. Tokyo: Kaizōsha, 1940-42.

Amano Motonosuke. *Chūgoku nōgyō no shomondai* 中國農業の諸問題 (Problems of Chinese agriculture). 2 vols. Tokyo: Gihōdō, 1952-53.

Amano Motonosuke. *Chūgoku nōgyō shi kenkyū* 中國農業史研究 (A study of the history of Chinese agriculture). Tokyo: Ochanomizu, 1962.

American Bankers Association, Commission on Commerce and Marine. *China, an economic survey, 1923.* New York, 1928.

*Andersen, Meyer and Company Limited of China.* Shanghai: Kelley and Walsh, 1931.

Ash, Robert. *Land tenure in pre-revolutionary China: Kiangsu province in the 1920s and 1930s.* London: Contemporary China Institute, School of Oriental and African Studies, University of London, 1976.

Barnett, A. Doak. *China on the eve of Communist takeover.* New York: Praeger, 1963.

Blackburn Chamber of Commerce. *Report of the mission to China of the Blackburn Chamber of Commerce, 1896-7.* Blackburn: North East Lancashire Press, 1898.

Buck, John Lossing. *Land utilization in China: a study of 16,786 farms in 168 localities, and 38,2256 farm families in twenty-two provinces in China, 1929-1933.* 3 vols. Nanking: University of Nanking, 1937.

Carlson, Ellsworth C. *The Kaiping mines, 1877-1912: a case study of early Chinese industrialization.* 2d ed. Cambridge MA: Harvard University Press, 1971.

Chang, Chung-li. *The income of the Chinese gentry.* Seattle: University of Washington Press, 1962.

Central Ministry of Agriculture, Planning Office 中央農業部計劃司. *Liang-nien-lai ti Chung-kuo nung-ts'un ching-chi tiao-ch'a hui-pien* 兩年來的中國農村經濟調查彙編 (Collection of surveys of the rural economy of China during the past two years). Shanghai: Chung-hua, 1952.

Chang, C. M. "Local government expenditure in China." *Monthly Bulletin of Economic China* (formerly *Nankai Weekly Statistical Service*), 7.6 (June 1934): 233-47.

Chang Jen-chia 張人价. *Konan no kokumai* 湖南M穀米 (Rice in Hunan). Trans. of 1936 report by Hunan provincial economic research institute. Tokyo: Seikatsusha, 1940.

Chang, John K. *Industrial development in pre-communist China: a quantitative analysis.* Chicago: Aldine, 1969.

Chang Kia-ngau 張嘉璈. *China's struggle for railway development.* New York: John Day, 1943.

Chang Kia-ngau. *The inflationary spiral: the experience of China, 1939-1950.* New York: M.I.T. Press and Wiley, 1958.

Chao Kang. "Policies and performance in industry," in Alexander Eckstein, Walter Galenson, and Ta-chung Liu, eds. *Economic trends in communist China,* pp. 549-95. Chicago: Aldine, 1968.

Chao Kang. "The growth of a modern cotton textile industry and the competition with handicrafts," in Dwight H. Perkins, ed., *China's modern economy in historical perspective*, pp. 167-201. Stanford: Stanford University Press, 1975.

Chao Kang. *The development of cotton textile production in China.* Cambridge MA: East Asian Research Center, Harvard University. Distributed by Harvard University Press, 1977.

Chen, P T. "Public finance." *The Chinese year book, 1935-1936*, pp. 1163-428. Shanghai: Commercial Press, 1935.

Ch'en Chen 陳眞 *et al.*, comps. *Chung-kuo chin-tai kung-yeh shih tzu-liao* 中國近代工業史資料 (Source materials on the history of modern industry in China). 6 vols. Peking: San-lien, 1957-61.

Ch'en Cheng-mo 陳正謨. *Chung-kuo ko-sheng ti ti-tsu* 中國各省的地租 (Land rents in China by province). Shanghai: Commercial Press, 1936.

Cheng Kuan-ying. *Sheng-shih wei-yen tseng-ting hsin-pien* 盛世危言增訂新編 (Warnings to a prosperous age), rev. ed., 1892. Rpt. of 1910 ed. Taipei: Hsueh-sheng, 1965.

Cheng, Yu-Kwei. *Foreign trade and industrial development of China.* Washington DC: University Press of Washington, D.C., 1956.

Chesneaux, Jean. *The Chinese labor movement, 1919-1927.* Trans. from the French by H. M. Wright. Stanford: Stanford University Press, 1968.

Chia Shih-i 賈士毅. *Min-kuo ts'ai-cheng shih* 民國財政史 (Fiscal history of the republic). 2. vols. Shanghai: Commercial Press, 1917.

Chia Shih-i. *Min-kuo hsü ts'ai-cheng shih* 民國續財政史 (A history of public finance under the republic, supplement). 7 vols. Shanghai: Commercial Press, 1932-34.

Chia Shih-i. *Min-kuo ts'ai-cheng shih san-pien* 民國財政史三編 (A history of public finance under the republic, second supplement). 2 vols. Taipei: Commercial Press, 1962.

Chia Te-huai 賈德懷. *Min-kuo ts'ai-cheng chien-shih* 民國財政簡史 (A short fiscal history of the republic). Shanghai: Commercial Press, 1946.

Ch'ien Chia-chü 千家駒. *Chiu Chung-kuo kung-chai shih tzu-liao, 1894-1949* 舊中國公債史資料, 1894-1949 (Source materials on government bond issues in old China, 1894-1949). Peking: Ts'ai-cheng ching-chi, 1955.

*The China year book*. H. G. W. Woodhead, ed. London: George Routledge & Sons, Ltd., 1912-21; Tientsin: The Tientsin Press, 1921-30; Shanghai: The North China Daily News & Herald, Ltd., 1931-39.

Chinese Ministry of Information. *China handbook, 1937-1945*. New York: Macmillan, 1947.

*Ching-chi t'ung-chi yueh-chih* 經濟統計月誌 (The Chinese economic and statistical review). Monthly. Shanghai: 1934-41.

Chou, Shun-hsin. *The Chinese inflation, 1937-1949*. New York: Columbia University Press, 1963.

Chu Hsieh 朱偰. *Chung-kuo ts'ai-cheng wen-ti* 中國財政問題 (Problems of China's public finance). Shanghai: Commercial Press, 1934.

Chung-kuo k'o-hsueh-yuan Shang-hai ching-chi yen-chiu-so 中國科學院上海經濟研究所 (Academy of Sciences, Shanghai Institute of Economic Research). *Shang-hai chieh-fang ch'ien-hou wu-chia tzu-liao hui-pien (1921 nien-1957 nien)* 上海解放前後物價資料匯編 (1921¦- -1957¦- ) (Collected materials on Shanghai prices before and after Liberation, 1921-57). Shanghai: Jen-min, 1958.

Chiao, C. M., and Buck, J. L. "The composition and growth of rural population groups in China." *Chinese Economic Journal*, 2.2 (March 1928): 219-35.

Chiao-t'ung t'ieh-tao pu chiao-t'ung shih pien-tsuan wei-yuan hui 交通鐵道部
交通史編纂委員會, comp. *Chiao-t'ung shih* 交通史 (History of transport and communications) 37 vols. Nanking: Ministry of Communications, 1930-37. Microfilm copy and a "grand table of contents" were published in 1970 by the Center for Chinese Research Materials, Association of Research Libraries, Washington, D.C.

China. Inspectorate-General of Customs. *Decennial reports on the trade, navigation, industries, etc. of the ports open to commerce ..., 1882-1891*. Shanghai: Imperial Maritime Customs, 1893.

China. Inspectorate-General of Customs. *Decennial reports on the trade, navigation, industries, etc. of the ports open to commerce ..., 1902-1911*. 2 vols. Shanghai: Imperial Maritime Customs, 1913.

China. Inspectorate-General of Customs. *Decennial reports on the trade, navigation, industries, etc. of the ports open to commerce ..., 1922-1931*. Shanghai: Inspectorate General of Customs, 1933.

China. Inspectorate-General of Customs. *Returns of trade and trade reports, 1906*. Shanghai: Imperial Maritime Customs, 1907.

Chung-yang yen-chiu-yuan chin-tai-shih yen-chiu-so, 中央研究院近代史研究所, comp. *Hai-fang tang* 海防檔 (Archives on coastal defence). Hardback, 9 vols.; paperback, 17 vols. Taipei: IMH, Academia Sinica, 1957.

Chung-yang yen-chiu-yuan chin-tai-shih yen-chiu-so. *K'uang-wu tang* 礦務檔 (Archives on mining affairs). 8 vols. Taipei: IMH, Academia Sinica, 1960.

Dernberger, Robert F. "The role of the foreigner in China's economic development, 1840-1949," in Dwight H. Perkins, ed., *China's modern economy in historical perspective*, pp. 19-47. Stanford: Stanford University Press, 1975.

Eckstein, Alexander, Galenson, Walter and Liu Ta-chung, eds. *Economic trends in communist China.* Chicago: Aldine, 1968.

Eckstein, Alexander, Chao Kang, and Chang, John. "The economic development of Manchuria: the rise of a frontier economy." *The Journal of Economic History*, 34.1 (March 1974): 239-64.

Elvin, Mark, and Skinner, G. William, eds. *The Chinese city between two worlds.* Stanford: Stanford University Press, 1974.

Fan Pai-ch'uan 樊百川. "Chung-kuo shou-kung-yeh tsai wai-kuo tzu-pen-chu-i ch'in-ju hou ti tsao-yü ho ming-yun" 中國手工業在外國資本主義侵入後的遭遇和命運 (The fate of Chinese handicraft industry after the incursion of foreign capitalism). *Li-shih yen-chiu* 歷史研究, 1962.3, pp. 88-115.

Feuerwerker, Albert. *China's early industrialization: Sheng Hsuan-huai (1844-1916) and mandarin enterprise.* Cambridge MA: Harvard University Press, 1958.

Feuerwerker, Albert. "Handicraft and manufactured cotton textiles in China, 1871-1910." *Journal of Economic History*, 30.2 (June 1970): 338-78.

Feuerwerker, Albert. "Economic trends in the late Ch'ing empire, 1870-1911," in J. K. Fairbank and Kwang-Ching Liu, eds. *Cambridge history of China*, vol. 11, *Late Ch'ing, 1800-1911*, Part 2. Cambridge: Cambridge University Press, 1980.

Feuerwerker, Albert. *The foreign establishment in China in the early twentieth century.* Ann Arbor: Center for Chinese Studies, University of Michigan, 1976.

Gerschenkron, Alexander. *Economic backwardness in historical perspective.* Cambridge MA: Harvard University Press, 1962.

Ho, Ping-ti 何炳棣. *Studies on the population of China, 1368-1953.* Cambridge MA: Harvard University Press, 1959.

Hou, Chi-ming 侯繼明. *Foreign investment and economic development in China, 1849-1937.* Cambridge MA: Harvard University Press, 1965.

Howe, Christopher. *Wage patterns and wage policy in modern China, 1919-1972.* Cambridge: Cambridge University Press, 1972.

Hsiao Liang-lin. *China's foreign trade statistics, 1864-1949.* Cambridge MA: Harvard University Press, 1974.

Hsien K'o 獻可. *Chin pai-nien-lai ti-kuo chu-i tsai-Hua yin-hang fa-hsing chih-pi kai-k'uang* 近百年來帝國主義在華銀行發行紙幣概況 (The issue of bank notes in China by imperialist banks in the past 100 years). Shanghai: Jen-min, 1958.

Hsu I-sheng 徐義生. *Chung-kuo chin-tai wai-chai shih t'ung-chi tzu-liao, 1853-1927* 中國近代外債史統計資料, 1853-1927 (Statistical materials on foreign loans in modern China, 1853-1927). Peking: Chung-hua, 1962.

Ishikawa, Shigeru. *Economic development in Asian perspective.* Tokyo: Kinokuniya, 1967

Jamieson, George. *Report on the revenue and expenditure of the Chinese Empire.* Foreign Office, Miscellaneous series, no. 415. London: HM Stationery Office, 1897.

Jamieson, George. "Tenure of land in China and the condition of the rural population." *Journal of the North China Branch of the Royal Asiatic Society,* new series 23.2 (1888-89): 59-118.

Kashiwai Kisao 柏井象雄. *Kindai Shina zaisei shi* 近代支那財政史 (History of modern Chinese finance). Kyoto: Kyōiku Tosho, 1942.

King, F. H. *Farmers of forty centuries.* Madison WI, 1911; 2nd ed., London: J. Cape, 1927.

King, Frank H. H. *Money and monetary policy in China, 1845-1895.* Cambridge MA: Harvard University Press, 1965.

Kōno Michihiro 河野通博. "Shindai Santōshō no kansei rikujō kōtsūro" 清代山東省ÇU官制陸上交通路 (Official overland communication routes in Shantung in the Ch'ing dynasty). *Shirin* MM, 33.3 (May 1950): 317-36.

Ku Ch'un-fan (Koh Tso-fan). 谷春帆. *Chung-kuo kung-yeh-hua t'ung-lun* 中國工業化通論 (A general discussion of China's industrialization). Shanghai: Commercial Press, 1947.

Ku Lang 顧琅. *Chung-kuo shih ta k'uang-ch'ang tiao-ch'a chi* 中國十大礦廠調查記 (Report of an investigation of the 10 largest mines in China). Shanghai, 1916.

Kung, H. O. "The growth of population in six large Chinese cities." *Chinese Eronomic Journal,* 20.3 (March 1937): 301-14.

Kuznets, Simon. *Modern economic growth: rate, structure, spread.* New Haven: Yale University Press, 1966.

Li Kuo-ch'i 李國祁. *Chung-kuo tsao-ch'i ti t'ieh-lu ching-ying* 中國早期的鐵路經營 (China's early railway enterprises). Taipei: IMH, Academia Sinica, 1961.

Li, Lillian Ming-tse. "Kiangnan and the silk export trade, 1842-1957." Ph.D. diss., Harvard University, 1975.

Li Wen-chih 李文治, comp. *Chung-kuo chin-tai nung-yeh shih tzu-liao ti-i chi, 1840-1911* 中國近代農業史資料第一輯 1840-1911 (Source materials on the history of agriculture in modern China, 1st collection, 1840-1911). Peking: San-lien, 1957.

Li Wen-chih 李文治 and Chang Yu-i 章有義, comps. *Chung-kuo chin-tai nung-yeh shih tzu-liao* 中國近代史資料 (Source materials on China's modern agricultural history). 3 vols. Peking: San-lien, 1957.

Lieu, D. K. *China's industries and finance.* Peking: Chinese Government Bureau of Economic Information, 1927.

Lippit, Victor D. *Land reform and economic development in China.* White Plains NY: International Arts and Sciences Press, 1974.

Liu, Kwang-ching. *Anglo-American steamship rivalry in China, 1862-1874.* Cambridge MA: Harvard University Press, 1962.

Liu Ta-chün (D. K. Lieu) 劉大鈞. *Chung-kuo kung-yeh tiao-ch'a pao-kao* 中國工業調查報告 (Report on a survey of China's industry). 3 vols. Nanking, 1937.

Liu, Ta-chung, and Yeh, Kung-chia. *The economy of the Chinese Mainland: national income and economic development, 1933-1959.* Princeton: Princeton University Press, 1965.

Mah Feng-hwa. *The foreign trade of mainland China.* Chicago: Aldine, 1971.

Mantetsu Chōsabu 滿鐵調查部 (South Manchurian Railway Research Department). *Chū-shi no minsengyō* 中支ÇU民船業 (The junk trade of central China). Tokyo: Hakubunkan, 1943.

McElderry, Andrea Lee. *Shanghai old-style banks (ch'ien-chuang), 1800-1935.* Ann Arbor: Center for Chinese Studies, University of Michigan, 1976.

Mi Ju-ch'eng 宓汝成, comp. *Chung-kuo chin-tai t'ieh-lu shih tzu-liao, 1863-1911* 中國近代鐵路史資料 1863-1911. (Source materials on thc history of railways in modern China, 1863-1911). 3 vols. Peking: Chung-hua, 1963.

Ministry of Agriculture and Commerce. *Nung-shang t'ung-chi piao* 農商統計表 (Tables of agricultural and commercial statistics). Shanghai, 1914-19; Peking, 1920-24.

Ministry of Communications (Ministry of Railways, Bureau of Railway Statistics, from 1925 issue). *Statistics of government railways, 1915-1936.* Peking, 1916-28; Nanking, 1931-36.

Ministry of Finance. *Annual reports for the 17th, 18th, 19th, 21st, 22nd, and 23rd fiscal years.* Nanking, 1930-36.

Ministry of Industries, National Agricultural Research Bureau, *Nung-ch'ing pao-kao* 農情報告 (Crop reports). Nanking, 1933-39.

Ministry of Industries, National Agricultural Research Bureau, Department of Agricultural Economics. *Crop reporting in China, 1934.* Nanking: Ministry of Industries, August 1936.

Ministry of the Interior. *Nei-cheng nien-chien* 内政年鑑 (Yearbook of the Interior Ministry). 4 vols. Shanghai: Commercial Press, 1936.

Miyashita Tadao 宫下忠雄. *Shina ginkō seido ron* 支那銀行制度論 (A treatise on the Chinese banking system). Tokyo: Ganshōdō, 1941.

Muramatsu Yūji. "A documentary study of Chinese landlordism in late Ch'ing and early republican Kiangnan." *Bulletin of the School of Oriental and Studies,* 29.3 (1966): 566-99.

Muramatsu Yūji 村松祐次. *Kindai Kōnan no sosan—Chūgoku jinushi seido no kenkyū* 近代江南ÇU租棧—中國地主ÇU研究 (Bursaries in modern

Kiangnan—a study of the Chinese landlord system). Tokyo: Tokyo University Press, 1970.

Murphey, Rhoads. *The outsiders: the Western experience in India and China.* Ann Arbor: The University of Michigan Press, 1977.

Myers, Ramon H. *The Chinese peasant economy: agricultural development in Hopei and Shantung, 1890-1949.* Cambridge MA: Harvard University Press, 1970.

Myers, Ramon H. "Agrarian policy and agricultural transformation: mainland China and Taiwan, 1895-1954." *Hsiang-kang Chung-wen ta-hsueh Chung-kuo wen-hua yen-chiu-so hsueh-pao* 香港中文大學中國文化研究所學報 (Journal of the Institute of Chinese Studies of the Chinese University of Hong Kong), 3.2 (1970): 521-44.

Nankai Institute of Economics. *Nankai index numbers, 1935.* Tientsin: Nankai University, 1936.

Nankai Institute of Economics, *Nankai Weekly Statistical Service.* Tientsin, 1928-.

Nan-k'ai ta-hsueh ching-chi yen-chiu so 南開大學經濟研究所 (Nankai Institute of Economics), comp. *1913 nien-1952 nien Nan-k'ai chih-shu tzu-liao hui-pien* 1913年-1952年 南開指數資料彙編 (Nankai price indexes 1913-52). Peking: T'ung-chi ch'u-pan-she, 1958.

National Economic Council. Bureau of Public Roads. *Highways in China.* Nanking, 1935.

National Government. Directorate of Statistics. *Chung-hua min-kuo t'ung-chi t'i-yao, 1935* 中華民國統計提要 (Statistical abstract of the Republic of China, 1935). Nanking, 1936.

National Government. Directorate of Statistics. *Chung-kuo tsu-tien chih t'ung-chi fen-hsi* 中國租佃制度之統計分析(Statistical analysis of China's land rent system). Shanghai: Cheng-chung, 1946.

National Land Commission. *Ch'üan-kuo t'u-ti tiao-ch'a pao-kao kang-yao* 全國土地調查報告綱要 (Preliminary report of the national land survey). Nanking, 1937.

Paauw, Douglas S. "Chinese national expenditure during the Nanking period." *FEQ*, 12.1 (November 1952): 3-26.

Paauw, Douglas S. "Chinese public finance during the Nanking government period." Ph.D. diss., Harvard University, 1950.

Paauw, Douglas S. "The Kuomintang and economic stagnation 1928-1937." *JAS*, 16.2 (February 1957): 213-20.

P'eng Tse-i 彭澤益, comp. *Chung-kuo chin-tai shou-kung-yeh shih tzu-liao, 1840-1949* 中國近代手工業史資料, 1840-1949 (Source materials on the history of handicraft industry in modern China, 1840-1949). 4 vols. Peking: San-lien, 1957.

Perkins, Dwight H. *Agricultural development in China, 1368-1968.* Chicago: Aldine, 1969.

Perkins, Dwight H., ed. *China's modern economy in historical perspective.* Stanford: Stanford University Press, 1975.

Perkins, Dwight H. "Growth and changing structure of China's twentieth-century economy," in Dwight H. Perkins, ed., *China's modern economy in historical perspective*, pp. 115-61. Stanford: Stanford University Press, 1975.

Rawski, Thomas G. "The growth of producer industries, 1900-1971," in Dwight H. Perkins, ed., *China's modern economy in historical perspective,* pp. 203-34. Stanford: Stanford University Press, 1975.

Remer, Carl F. *Foreign trade of China.* Shanghai: Commercial Press, 1926.

Remer, C. F. *Foreign investments in China.* New York: Macmillan, 1933.

*Report on the native cloth in use in the Amoy consular district.* Foreign Office, miscellaneous series, no. 19. London: 1886.

Reynolds, Bruce Lloyd. "The impact of trade and foreign investment on industrialization: Chinese textiles, 1875-1931, Ph.D. diss., University of Michigan, 1974.

Riskin, Carl. "Surplus and stagnation in modern China," in Dwight H. Perkins, ed., *China's modern economy in historical perspective,* pp. 49-84. Stanford: Stanford University Press, 1975.

Rozman, Gilbert. *Urban networks in Ch'ing China and Tokugawa Japan.* Princeton: Princeton University Press, 1973.

Saeki Tomi 佐伯富. *Shindai ensei no kenkyū* 清代鹽政の 研究 (A study of the Ch'ing salt administration). Kyoto: Tōyōshi Kenkyūkai, 1956.

Schran, Peter. *Guerrilla economy: the development of the Shensi-Kansu-Ninghsia border region, 1937-1945.* Albany: State University of New York Press, 1976.

Skinner, G. William. "Marketing and social structure in rural China," part 1, *JAS,* 26.1 (November 1964): 3-44.

Skinner, G. William. "Marketing and social structure in rural China," part 2. *JAS,* 24.2 (February 1965): 195-228.

Skinner, G. William, et al., eds. *Modern Chinese society: an analytical bibliography.* 3 vols. Stanford University Press, 1973.

State Statistical Bureau. Industrial Statistics Department. *Wo-kuo kang-t'ieh, tien-li, mei-t'an, chi-hsieh, fang-chih, tsao-chih kung-yeh ti chin-hsi* 我國鋼鐵, 電力, 煤炭, 機械, 紡織, 造紙工業的今昔 (Past and present of China's iron and steel, electric power, coal, machinery, textile and paper industries). Peking: T'ung-chi ch'u-pan-she, 1958.

Sun Yü-t'ang 孫毓堂, comp. *Chung-kuo chin-tai kung-yeh shih tzu-liao, ti-i chi, 1840-1895 nien* 中國近代工業史資料第一輯 1840-1895 年 (Source materials on the history of modern industry in China, 1st collection, 1840-1895). 2 vols. Peking: K'o-hsueh, 1957.

*Ta-Ch'ing Kao-tsung shun-huang-ti shih-lu* 大清高宗純皇帝實錄 (Veritable records of the Ch'ien-lung Emperor of the Ch'ing dynasty). 1,500 *chüan.* See *Ta-Ch'ing* li-ch'ao shih-lu.

*Ta-Ch'ing li-ch'ao shih-lu* 大清歷朝實錄 (Veritable records of successive reigns of the Ch'ing dynasty). Totalling 4,485 *chüan,* but with new *chüan* sequence under each reign. Mukden: Man-chou-kuo kuo-wu-yuan 滿國國務院, 1937-8; Rpt. in 94 vols. Taipei: Hua-lien and Hua-wen, 1964.

Tamagna, Frank M. *Banking and finance in China.* New York: Institute of Pacific Relations, 1942.

Ting, Leonard G. "Chinese modern banks and the finance of government and industry." *Nankai Social and Economic Quarterly,* 8.3 (October 1935): 578-616.

Tokunaga Kiyoyuki 德永清行. *Shina chūō ginkō ron* 支那中央銀行論 (A treatise on central banking in China). Tokyo: Yūhikaku, 1942.

Ts'un-ts'ui hsueh-she 存粹學社, comp. *Chung-kuo chin-tai she-hui ching-chi shih lun-chi* 中國近代經濟史論集 (Collected articles on China's modern social and economic history). 2¡¡vols. Hong Kong: Ch'ung-wen, 1971.

Ts'un-ts'ui hsueh-she, comp. *Chung-kuo chin san-pai-nien she-hui ching-chi shih lun-chi* 中國近三百年經濟史論集 (Collected articles on China's social and economic history in the last 300 years). 2 vols. Hong Kong: Ch'ung-wen, 1972.

U. S. Bureau of the Census. *Historical statistics of the United States, 1789-1945.* Washington, D.C., 1949.

Walker, Kenneth R. *Planning in Chinese agriculture: socialisation and the private sector, 1956-1962.* Chicago: Aldine, 1965.

Wang Chi-shen 王季深. *Chan-shih Shang-hai ching-chi* 戰時上海經濟 (The economy of wartime Shanghai). Shanghai: Shang-hai ching-chi yen-chiu-so, 1945.

Wang Ching-yü 汪敬虞, comp. *Chung-kuo chin-tai kung-yeh shih tzu-liao, ti-erh chi, 1895-1914 nien* 中國近代工業史資料第二輯 1895-1914年 (Source materials on the history of modern industry in China, 2nd collection 1895-1914). 2 vols. Peking: K'o-hsueh, 1957.

Wang Ching-yü. "Shih-chiu shih-chi wai-kuo ch'in Hua ch'i-yeh chung ti Hua-shang fu-ku huo-tung" 十九世紀外國侵華企業中的華商附服活動 (Investment by Chinese merchants in the foreign firms which invaded China in the nineteenth century). *Li-shih yen-chiu* 歷史研究 1965.4, pp. 39-74.

Wang Fu-sun 汪馥蓀. "Chan-ch'ien Chung-kuo kung-yeh sheng-ch'an-chung wai-ch'ang sheng-ch'an ti pi-chung wen-t'i" 戰前中國工業生產中外幣生產的比重問題 (The proportion of industrial production by foreign-owned factories in total industrial production in pre-war China). *Chung-yang yin-hang yueh-pao* 中央銀行月報, 2.3 (March 1947): 1-19.

Wang Fu-sun. "Chan-shih Hua-pei kung-yeh tzu-pen chiu-yeh yü sheng-ch'an 戰時華北工業資本就業與生產 (Wartime industrial capital, employment and production in North China). *She-hui k'o-hsueh tsa-chih* 社會科學雜志 9.2 (December 1947): 31-70.

Wang Erh-min 王爾敏. *Ch'ing-chi ping-kung-yeh ti hsing-ch'i* 清季兵工業的興起 (The rise of the armaments industry in the late Ch'ing period). Taipei: IMH, Academia Sinica, 1963.

Wang, Yeh-chien. *Land taxation in imperial China, 1750-1911.* Cambridge MA: Harvard University Press, 1973.

Willmott, W. E., ed. *Economic organization in Chinese society.* Stanford: Stanford University Press, 1972.

Wright, Stanley F. *China's customs revenue since the Revolution of 1911.* Shanghai: Shanghai : Inspectorate General of Customs, 3rd ed., 1935.

Wu Pao-san (Ou Pao-san) 巫寶三. *Chung-kuo liang-shih tui-wai mao-i ch'i ti-wei, ch'ü-shih chi pien-ch'ien chih yuan-yin, 1912-1931* 中國糧食對外貿易其地位趨勢及變遷之原因, 1912-1931 (Causes of trends and fluctuations in China's foreign trade in food grains, 1912-1931). Nanking, 1934.

Wu Pao-san (Ou Pao-san). *Chung-kuo kuo-min so-te, i-chiu-san-san-nien* 中國國民所得, 1933年 (China's national income, 1933). 2 vols. Shanghai: Chunghua, 1947.

Wu Pao-san (Ou Pao-san). "Chung-kuo kuo-min so-te i-chiu-san-san hsiu-cheng" 中國國民所得, 一九三三年修正 (Correction to China's national income, 1933). *She-hui k'o-hsueh tsa-chih,* 9. 2 (December 1947): 92-153.

Wu Pao-san (Ou Pao-san). "Chung-kuo kuo-min so-te, 1933, 1936, chi 1946" 中國國民所得, 1933, 1936, 及 1946 (China's national income, 1933, 1936, and 1946). *She-hui k'o-hsueh tsa-chih,* 9.2 (December 1947): 12-30.

Yang Tuan-liu 楊端六 and Hou Hou-pei 侯厚培. *Liu-shih-wu-nien-lai Chung-kuo kuo-chi mao-i t'ung-chi* 六十五年來中國國際貿易統計 (Statistics of China's foreign trade during the last sixty-five years). National Research Institute of Social Sciences, Academia Sinica, 1931.

Yang Tuan-liu. *Ch'ing-tai huo-pi chin-jung shih kao* 清代貨幣金融史稿 (Draft history of money and money markets in the Ch'ing period). Peking: San-lien, 1962.

Yen Chung-p'ing 嚴中平. *Chung-kuo mien-fang-chih shih-kao, 1289-1937* 中國棉紡織史稿, 1289-1937 (Draft history of the Chinese cotton industry, 1289-1937). Rev. ed. Peking: K'o-hsueh, 1955; 3rd printing, 1963.

Yen Chung-p'ing, et al., comps. *Chung-kuo chin-tai ching-chi-shih t'ung-chi tzu-liao hsuan-chi* 中國近代經濟史統計資料選輯 (Selected statistical materials on modern Chinese economic history). Peking: K'o-hsueh, 1955.

Young, Arthur N. *China and the helping hand, 1937-1945.* Cambridge MA: Harvard University Press, 1963.

Young, Arthur N. *China's wartime finance and inflation, 1937-1945.* Cambridge MA: Harvard University Press, 1965.

Young, Arthur N. *China's nation-building effort, 1927-1937: the financial and economic record.* Stanford: Hoover Institution Press, 1971.

Young, John. *The research activities of the South Manchurian Railway Company, 1907-1945: a history and bibliography.* New York: East Asian Institute, Columbia University, 1966.

# Index